THE DESIGNER'S SOURCEBOOK 12

# ART FOR THE WALL
# FURNITURE & ACCESSORIES

::: THE GUILD®

Madison, Wisconsin
USA

*Published by*
THE GUILD
931 E. Main Street #106
Madison, WI 53703-2955
USA
FAX 608-256-1938
TEL 608-256-1990
TEL 800-969-1556
E-Mail: guild@guild.com
http://www.guild.com

*Administration*
Toni Fountain Sikes, President
James F. Black, Jr., Vice President
Susan K. Evans, Vice President
Raymond Goydon, Consultant
Theresa Ace, Business Manager
Marcia M. Kraus, Operations Manager
Jennifer Thelen, Systems Coordinator

*Production, Design, Editorial*
John Driscoll, Production Manager
Amy Muelver, Production Assistant

Katie Kazan, Editorial Manager
Sarah Mollet, Editorial Assistant
David Becker, Writer
Susan Cosgrove, Writer

Printed by DNP America, Inc.

*Publisher's Representatives*
Susan K. Evans
Karen O. Brown • Martha Johnson
Reed J. McMillan • Sarah Mollet

*Worldwide Distribution*
Hearst Books International
1350 Avenue of the Americas
New York, NY 10019



ISBN (softback) 1-880140-27-6 ISBN (hardback) 1-880140-26-8
Printed in Hong Kong

*Special thanks to our 1997 Review Committee*
Cindy Beard, ASID • American Family Insurance
Kim Donovan • A&D Interior Design, Inc.

*Cover art*
*Fall Leaves,* by Laura Militzer Bryant, 1996, weaving on copper, 20" x 20", photo: Thomas Bruce. Details from this artwork also appear throughout the book. See page 185.

*Title page art*
*Pear,* by L. Kristin Dahlgren, oil on canvas, 8" x 8", photo: Frank Cordelle. See page 71.

# ONLY CONNECT

"Only connect!  Always connect!"  reads the inscription on the title page of E.M. Forster's brilliant novel, *Howard's End.*

I toyed briefly with the idea of stealing this inscription for **THE GUILD.**  It seems so appropriate.  After all, those of us in this field do what we do because we are so extraordinarily *connected* to the objects in our environment.  We value these things, invest them with a power, forge relationships with them.

We psychically connect to them, and often we physically connect to them.  I know I can't help it — this desire to touch, to hold, to have things around that speak to me.

(Do you think it's just coincidence that the word *connect* is so similar to the word *collect?*)

**THE GUILD**'s mission is to connect you, the design professional or individual connoisseur, with access to outstanding artists.  These men and women are available to help you find beautiful, functional solutions to your design problems, to work with you in making the kinds of things people connect with.

We are accomplishing our mission every time you use this book in a client presentation, or call an artist for more information. Interspersed throughout the following pages are stories about projects that happened through **THE GUILD** connection, with marvelous results.  The fruits of our labors, so to speak.

Enjoy!

**Toni Fountain Sikes**
**Publisher**

# TABLE OF CONTENTS

## FEATURES

*The Commissioning Process* 9

The path to site-specific installations can be full of twists and turns. Our roadmap will keep you headed in the right direction and enjoying the scenic view.

*Project Profiles*

What happens after a design professional lifts the phone to call a GUILD artist? Nine project profiles offer an inside look — and a glimpse of finished products by these outstanding artists.

## RESOURCES

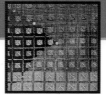

# TABLE OF CONTENTS

## ARTISTS

*Artists by Section*
Turn the page for a listing of featured artists.

# ARTISTS BY SECTION

# ARTISTS BY SECTION

# 10 Great Ways
## to use *The Designer's Sourcebook 12*

**1** QUALITY CONTROL.  This book begins with an assurance: These artists are reliable and professional. Featured artists in GUILD sourcebooks have been juried in on the basis of experience, quality of work, and a solid reputation for working with architects and designers.

**2** MOTIVATION.  *The Designer's Sourcebook* is a great resource for client meetings. Clients have been known to reach levels of extreme excitement upon viewing the artistic possibilities showcased here.

**3** GO AHEAD AND CALL.  If something intrigues you while perusing *The Designer's Sourcebook* — a shape, a form, an exotic use of the commonplace — please give the artist a call. Serendipity often leads to a wonderful creation.

**4** FIRE UP THE COMPUTER.  THE GUILD's site on the World Wide Web (http://www.guild.com) includes a uniquely useful resource. The Commissions Clearinghouse lists notices from individuals and design professionals seeking artists for their projects. Artists respond directly, and there is no fee. So, list a project, find an artist. Only GUILD artists have access, so you can be assured of quality responses.

**5** MORE ARTISTS ... AND MORE.  The right artist, the right medium, the right region, and the right price. That's a lot of information, and we've got it. Each GUILD REGISTER lists contact, product and pricing information for hundreds of artists working in glass, fiber, and ceramic art for the wall.

**6** DESKTOP DIRECTORY.  *The Designer's Sourcebook 12* is designed for quick reference, as well as leisurely browsing. The "Index of Artists and Companies" includes artists listed in THE GUILD REGISTERs, as well as those featured in the full-color pages, so finding a current phone number or checking product information is easily done. The information in your rolodex may grow stale; *The Designer's Sourcebook* is fresh each year.

**7** ARTISTS NEAR AND FAR.  Our "Index of Advertisers by State" begins on page 238. Check it out. You just never know . . . you could discover a wellspring of inspiration in your own backyard.

**8** ARTISTS THEN AND NOW.  Many of the artists whose work you see here are also represented in earlier GUILD publications; look for references on artists' pages. You can order most of these early volumes through our main office. Call 1-800-969-1556 for order information.

**9** HOW IT'S DONE.  A wise guide is a great gift. Look throughout this volume for short features about artists who have created beautiful commissioned artwork with the help of THE GUILD. Their thoughts are insightful; their art inspiring.

**10** LET US HEAR FROM YOU.  We love hearing stories about GUILD-inspired projects, and we love passing them on through the pages of our sourcebooks. Let us know about *your* project ... perhaps we'll feature it in next year's edition.

# THE COMMISSIONING PROCESS

Because THE GUILD operates as a kind of matchmaker between artists and design professionals, we have considerable interest in how the matches that begin with our sourcebooks turn out. We want to help these relationships work by doing everything we can to make the contact between designer and artist satisfying and profitable.

Successful projects result when designers and artists form good relationships with each other, relationships founded on mutual understanding of expectations, clear communication and a willingness of both parties to accept their responsibilities for making a good project.

This article is a how-to guide of the commissioning process ... how it comes about, the steps to take and when to take them, what to prepare for, and how to avoid problems. We hope it answers some questions and offers encouragement to those who work directly with artists in commissioning artwork.

By far the most important step in getting great work is choosing a great artist — or at least the right artist for your particular project and pocketbook. This choice is the decision from which all others will flow, so it's worth investing time and energy in the selection process and seasoning the process with both wild artistic hopes and hard-nosed realism. The right choices at this early stage will make things go easier later on.

Some clients will be very interested in helping select the artist, and working closely with him or her once the choice is made. Others will want only minimal involvement, leaving most of the decision-making to the design team.

## FINDING YOUR ARTIST

Whoever is making the decision, there are several ways to find the right artist. Obviously, we recommend browsing through GUILD sourcebooks. Not only do they show a wide range of top art-

work, they also have the advantage of weeding out people who may not really want to work with designers and architects on a commission basis. Every GUILD artist is looking for collaborative work — that's why they're here. Many already have a strong track record of working with designers, architects and their clients. You will gain from their professionalism and experience.

Your first contact with an artist sets the tone for the relationship to follow. With that contact, via telephone or letter, be prepared to provide information about the size and scope of your project, the budget, the deadlines, and any relevant details about the building site. This will help the artist tailor his or her response more specifically, giving you a better sense of whether this is the right person for your project.

Make your initial selection on the basis of what you like about an artist's past work. Most experienced artists will be pleased

to provide a portfolio — usually on slides, but sometimes printed. Don't, however, expect to see the exact piece you're looking for in a portfolio. Remember, you're choosing an artist at this point, not a piece of art. Look for creativity, command of the materials or technology, and how the artist's style fits the specific environment.

## EXPECT PROFESSIONALISM

Once you've made a tentative selection based on a portfolio and the artist's past experience and reputation, it's time to get serious. Meet with the artist, either face-to-face or by phone, to begin discussion about building codes, lighting specifications, deadlines and budgets. Most designers find that the artist's professionalism and knowledge of subject, materials, and details of code, safety and engineering is both complete and reassuring.

If all goes well and you decide to move ahead with the artist, your next communication will be to agree on a budget and timetable. These will become part of the contract.

With this and subsequent discussions, be resolved that silence is not golden and ignorance not bliss! Be frank. Tell the artist what you expect. Now is the time for any possible misunderstandings to be brought up and resolved, not later, after the work is half done and deadlines loom.

## STARTING RIGHT

Bring the artist into the process at the earliest possible stage — at about the same time you hire the general contractor — and include the artist in discussions with other members of the design team. With this approach there should be no unpleasant surprises about size or suitability of the artwork to the space. Furthermore, when art is planned early on, it's far less likely to be cut at the end of the project, when money may be running low.

Early inclusion of the artist also helps ensure that the collaborative effort will go smoothly throughout all phases of the project. If the artist is respected as part of the team, his work can benefit the project's overall design.

Naturally, the scope of the project will determine the number of players to be involved with the artist. Think ahead about how decisions will be made. Will a single person sign off on recommendations? Are committees necessary? Depending on the complexity of the project, it may be a good idea to designate one person to serve as liaison with the artist to avoid mixed signals.

## SOME SIMPLE RULES

By following these rules, you'll avoid the most common problems in a collaborative relationship, problems that can create conflict and sabotage the effort.

EARLY PLANNING
- Bring the artist into the project as early as possible. This helps insure that the space is designed with art in mind, and that the art is created to enhance the space.

COMMUNICATION
- Be as organized and specific as possible about the scope and range of the project, even in initial meetings with artist candidates.

- When you have questions, ask them. All questions should be cleared up before the work begins. Silence is not golden.

SELECTING THE RIGHT ARTIST
- Chose an artist based on a solid portfolio of previous work. And remember: it's less risky to use an artist who has worked on projects that are similar in size and scope, who can handle the demands of your kind of job.

- Trust your instincts when you're choosing an artist. Like selecting an advertising agency or an architect, choosing an artist is based partly on chemistry. You need to like the work and respect the artist — and you also have to be able to work with him or her.

THE CONTRACT
- For larger projects, use specific milestones to assure a continuing consensus on project scope and budget. It may also be necessary to make adjustments at these points.

- Be honest and realistic, and expect the same from the artist. When you're getting down to details regarding deadlines, responsibilities and specific project requirements, pay extra attention to any areas where there seem to be lingering questions.

GETTING HELP
- Consider hiring an art consultant or additional trouble shooter if the commission is particularly large or complex. The consultant should help with complicated contract arrangements and details, and should make certain that communication between artists and support staff (including subcontractors and engineers) is thoroughly understood.

THE GOAL
- Successful projects result from designers and artists forming good professional, and often personal, relationships. When the mix is right and the collaboration process works well, it not only benefits the project, but is a pleasure for all the people connected with it. This should be the goal for every collaborative effort.

Be sure the artist understands the technical requirements of the job, including traffic flow in the space, the intended use of the space, the building structure, maintenance, lighting and environmental concerns. By doing this, you ensure that the artist's knowledge, experience and skill become part of the project.

## BUILD UNDERSTANDING

Keep the artist appraised of any changes you make that will affect the work in progress. Did you find a certain material you specified unavailable and replace it with something else? Did the available space become bigger or smaller? These may seem like small changes to you, but they could have a profound impact on an artist's planning and work.

At the same time, the artist should let you know of any special requirements his or her work will place on the space. Is it especially heavy? Does it need to be mounted in a specific way? Must it be protected from theft or vandalism? What kind of lighting is best? You may want to set aside a contingency budget to fund design changes or omissions once the project begins.

## DESIGN DIALOG

Most artists experienced with commissioned work factor the notion of a continuing design dialog into their fee. There is an unfortunate belief — harbored by some architects, designers and, yes, artists too — that a willingness to change and compromise somehow indicates a lack of commitment or creativity. On the contrary. The ability to compromise on execution, without compromising on artistic quality, is a mark of professionalism. We recommend that you look for this quality in the artist you choose, and respect it by treating the artist as a partner in decisions made affecting his or her work.

## PUT IT IN WRITING

It is a truism in any kind of business that it is much cheaper to get the lawyers involved at the beginning of a process than after something goes wrong. A contract or letter of agreement will assure you and the client that the artist will complete his or her work on time and to specifications. It will also assure the artist that he or she will get paid the right amount at the right time. That just about eliminates the biggest conflicts that can arise.

Contracts should be specific to the job. Customarily, artists are responsible for design, production, shipping and installation. If someone else is to be responsible for installation, be sure you specify who will coordinate it and who will pay for it — if it is not the artist, it is usually the client. With a large project, it is helpful to identify the tasks that, if held up for any reason, would delay completion of the project. They should be discussed up front to assure that both parties agree on requirements and expectations.

## PAYMENT SCHEDULE

Payments are usually tied to specific points in the process. These serve as check points to make sure the work is progressing in a satisfactory manner, on time and on budget. Payment is customarily made in three stages, although this certainly depends on the circumstances, scope and complexity of the project.

The first payment is usually made when the contract is signed. It covers the artist's time and creativity in developing a design specific to your needs. You can expect to go through several rounds of trial and error in the design process, but at the end of this stage you will have detailed drawings and, for three-dimensional work, a maquette (model) that everyone agrees upon. The artist usually charges a fee to cover the costs of the maquette and design time.

The second payment is generally set for a mid-way point in the project and is for work done to date. If the materials are expensive, the client may be asked to advance money at this stage to cover their costs. If the commission is cancelled during this period, the artist keeps the money already paid for work performed.

Final payment is usually due when the work is installed. If the piece is finished on time but the building or project is delayed, the artist is customarily paid on delivery, but still has the obligation to oversee installation.

## FORGING A PARTNERSHIP

You will find that most artists keep tabs on the project budget. Be sure that the project scope does not deviate from what was agreed at the outset. If the scope changes, amend the agreement accordingly.

Most designers recognize that adequate compensation for the artist is in their best interest as it assures the type and level of service needed to fulfill their expectations.

The partnership between artists and designers is an old and honorable one. After too many years of the arts being separated from the design of our environments, we're happy to be part of a renewed interest in collaboration.

# http://www.guild.com

For over a decade, THE GUILD has introduced design professionals to artists through the pages of its annual sourcebooks. Now professionals can reach qualified artists directly, via the 'Commissions Clearinghouse,' a unique on-line service offered by THE GUILD.

The idea behind the Clearinghouse is simplicity itself. Architects and designers can have trouble finding qualified artists for their projects. Conversely, artists may struggle to find opportunities that make use of their particular talents and expertise.

The Commissions Clearinghouse puts it all together.

Through the Clearinghouse, design professionals describe the details of their project (media, size, site, budget, timeline, etc.) and specify how and when the artist should respond. This information is then listed in the Clearinghouse section of THE GUILD's site on the World Wide Web. Qualified artists respond directly to the design professional, and there is no charge to the designer, nor to the artist. Access to Clearinghouse information is limited by password to artists participating in GUILD sourcebooks.

We invite you to list your upcoming commissions, building projects, portfolio requests and competitions in the Commissions Clearinghouse. Call (800-969-1556) or fax (608-256-1938) THE GUILD office to request a listing form, or enter your information directly on-line (http://www.guild.com).

See you in cyberspace!

# FEATURED ARTISTS

*Many of the projects shown on the following pages were commissioned by design professionals for site-specific installation. These ingenious, exhilarating collaborations are an inspiration for future projects.*

# FURNITURE

# Carl Close Jr. Hammersmiths

**Carl and Susan Close Jr.**
558 West Hollis Street
Nashua, NH 03062
FAX 603-889-6301
TEL 888-598-4642

The iron artistry of Carl Close Jr. Hammersmiths is reminiscent of the classical design revival of the first part of this century. Graceful lines, subtle texture, chased and chiseled openwork, repoussé and hand forging bring back a time when design and craftsmanship were king and clients settled for nothing less.

Carl Close Jr. started his study of metal working at the age of ten in his father's forge and knew then that it would be his life-long passion.

Carl Close Jr. Hammersmiths specializes in museum-quality interior furnishings, door knockers, grills, heirloom-quality lighting, forged memorial markers, beds and small decorative personal items.

A  Chased and chiseled lamp with mica shade, 24"H

B  Repoussé door knocker, 11"H

C  Candelabra, forged mild steel, 18"H

A

B

C

Printed in Hong Kong ©1997 THE GUILD: The Designer's Sourcebook

# Peter Mangan

**634-A Guerrero Street**
**San Francisco, CA 94110**
**TEL  415-431-7060**

Peter Mangan creates sculptural lights that engage the viewer and illuminate a space. Glass and metals combine, resulting in unique and contemporary pieces. He enjoys making chandeliers, wall sconces, floor lights, sculptures and panels.

Peter Mangan has worked as an artist for 20 years and exhibits internationally. He has created lighting for numerous restaurants and homes.

A  *Fireworks on the Moon*, glass and metals, 36" x 24" x 6"

B  *Ridged Chandelier*, glass and metals, 34" x 34" x 24"

A

B

Photos: Charles Maier

# Material Plane

**Jeff and Laurel Allbritten**
PO Box 389
2504 Rosicky Avenue
Malin, OR 97632
FAX 541-723-2610
TEL  541-723-2750
E-Mail: matplane@aol.com

Jeff and Laurel Allbritten find passion in the power of fire and spirit to transform living materials such as copper, bronze and glass into functional art pieces used and cherished for generations.

The Allbrittens are distinguished by meticulous attention to authenticity, craftsmanship and the unrelenting standard of quality found in their hammered copper, forged bronze, custom slumped or blown glass, mica and semi-precious stones.

With a national roster of clients, their work is found in restaurants, clubs, hotels, corporate headquarters, churches and private residences.

Recent commissions include:
Lucasfilm
Safeway Corporation
Hilton Hotels

Prices start at $500.

A  *Sol,* forged bronze and copper with repoussé detailing, hand-painted slumped glass, 50" x 48"

B  *Gothique,* forged bronze, 33" x 12¹/₂"

A

B

# Angelika Traylor

100 Poinciana Drive
Indian Harbour Beach, FL 32937
FAX 407-779-3612
TEL   407-773-7640

Specializing in one-of-a-kind lamps, autonomous panels and architectural designs, Traylor's award-winning work can be recognized by its intricate, jewel-like composition.

Often referred to as having painterly qualities, Traylor's work — like the exquisite lamp and charming autonomous panel shown here — reflect an original and intensive design process, implemented with meticulous craftsmanship and an unusually beautiful selection of glass.

Her work has been featured in many publications, and she has been recognized with her inclusion in seven different *Who's Who* reference books.

Please inquire for more information on available work, commissions and pricing.

Also see these GUILD publications:
*THE GUILD: 2, 3, 4, 5*
*Designer's Edition: 7, 8, 9, 10, 11*
*Architect's Edition: 6*
*Gallery Edition: 2*

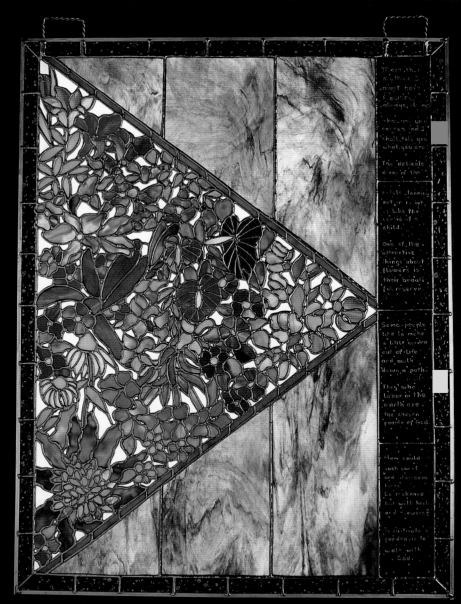

Photos: Randall Smith

# A Working Artist's Outlook

Ask New Hampshire furniture maker Peter Maynard to describe his style, and he has to think long and hard. Unlike artisans who work in a single signature motif, Maynard's designs run the gamut from simple Shaker pieces to exquisite neo-classical creations.

Maynard says his wide range is mainly a response to the challenge of selling handmade furniture in today's marketplace. But it's also part of discovering himself. Find the common elements in the artist's carefully crafted pieces, and there you have the essence of the craftsman.

"My style has evolved in the face of the very workaday demands of making a living," Maynard says. "I try to stay open to every opportunity, while still finding unique ways to express myself."

Maynard finds that THE GUILD fits in perfectly with his working-artist's attitude of combining creativity and commerce. A GUILD-inspired commission from a Chicago homeowner included three very specific pieces of furniture. In this regard, the commission was typical.

"People seldom come to me and say, 'You make all the aesthetic decisions,'" Maynard says. "They want to have some significant input. I work very closely with people to be sure they get what they want."

James Prinz

**Artist:** Peter Maynard
**Liaison:** Robert Turner, Design Source Inc., Chicago, IL
**Type of Work:** Sideboard
**Site:** Private Residence, Chicago, IL

# John Arenskov

**Cloudlift Studio**
**634 Cherry Drive**
**Prescott, AZ 86303**
**TEL   520-776-4638**

John Arenskov designs and builds furniture that bridges the boundary between craft and art. His designs integrate Art Deco and contemporary elements, combining wood, metal and glass.

His work has been featured in *Fine Woodworking Design Book Six* and *Design Book Seven*.

John enjoys collaborating with clients, decorators and architects. Commissions are welcome.

A   Table, satin wood, macasser ebony, aluminum, 48" x36" x 29"

B   Stereo console, satiné, pau ferro, 44" x 30" x 20"

A

B

Photos: Ross Hilmoe

# Matthew Healey

**Tree To Treasure**
**PO Box 466**
**Hartland, VT 05048**
**FAX 802-436-3666**
**TEL  802-436-3666**

Matthew Healey accepts commissions for furniture and wooden architectural embellishments for public, corporate and private environments.

Each one-of-a-kind piece addresses the specific parameters of the application and frequently involves collaboration with the architect or interior designer, along with the individual client. A custom design, firm price estimate and completion schedule are presented prior to execution and installation.

Healey received his B.F.A. degree from the School for American Craftsmen, Rochester Institute of Technology, and has been creating distinctive furniture and architectural woodwork for 12 years. With attention to detail and integrity of craftsmanship, each piece becomes a treasure.

Portfolio and prices are available upon request.

A  Bedside tables, curly maple, ebony inlay,
    18" x 18" x 26"

B  Queen bed, black walnut, 68" x 88" x 62"

A

Rich Frutchey

B

Printed in Hong Kong ©1997 THE GUILD: The Designer's Sourcebook

# Maynard & Maynard Furnituremakers

Peter Maynard
PO Box 77, Beryl Mtn. Road
South Acworth, NH 03607
FAX 603-835-2892
TEL   603-835-2969
E-Mail: pmaynard@cyberportal.net

For 23 years, Maynard & Maynard has been custom designing and building museum quality furniture in a broad range of styles for designers and collectors throughout North America.

Their work has been featured in numerous publications, including *Architectural Digest*, *Interior Design* and *Traditional Home*, which featured Peter and his work in the article "Twentieth Century Masters: Five of the Country's Best Furnituremakers".

Also see these GUILD publications:
*THE GUILD: 5*
*Designer's Edition: 6, 8*

A   Walnut sideboard (detail)

B   Walnut sideboard, rosewood tea cart, with wave motif, curly maple dropleaf table with elliptical top.

A

B

Photos: James Prinz

# Jon Sutter

**Jon Sutter Woodworking**
**One Worman's Mill Court, Suite #9**
**Frederick, MD 21701**
**FAX 301-698-2517**
**TEL  301-698-5517**

Inspired by mechanical forms, Jon Sutter creates custom-designed furnishings that are imbued with life, energy and playfulness. He considers the mechanical world — the world of bridges, towers and buildings — a subset of the natural one. "If nature did not provide us with electro-magnetism," he says, "not only would there be no bridges, there would be no us."

A former artist in residence at the Appalachian Center for Crafts, and a recent recipient of the Emerging Artist Award at the Philadelphia Furniture Show, Jon Sutter is a new artist with a growing reputation for fresh and exciting work.

Commissions accepted.

All images © 1996 Jon Sutter.

Hall tree, 24"Dia x 67"H

Compact disk cabinet with antenna, 16"W x 67"H x 15"D

Table clock, 21"W x 24"H x 7"D

*The Safe*, hall clock, 32"W x 69"H x 14"D          Photos: David Egan

# Jon Uidl

**Hardwood Design Studios**
**902 Wicker Street**
**Woodstock, IL 60098**
**FAX 815-338-6167**
**TEL  815-338-6157**

The benefits of a traditional, time-honored apprenticeship are clear in Jon Uidl's extreme attention to detail and quality craftsmanship. With over ten years of woodworking experience, he is comfortable with any style or material, but is most sought after for his elegant interpretations of historical designs.

Jon's work is distinguished by a bold use of highly figured hardwoods and veneers. Commissions range from humidors to conference tables and formal libraries. Pricing and scheduling are available upon request.

Entertainment center, flame-grained sweet birch

Rich Sistos

# Glenn W.S. Ward

Eidos Design Studio
553 Paradise Crescent
Waterloo, ON
Canada, N2T 2J8
FAX 519-884-6405
TEL  519-745-9835
E-Mail: Eidos@DGI.CA
http://www.dgi.ca/~eidos

"Language is the means of communicating idea or feeling by use of conventionalized sign, sound, question or marks having understood meaning."
*Webster's Dictionary*

Verbal language is used to communicate idea and concept from one person to another. Visual language embodies the experience of who we are and what we believe, and is a signifier of our social fabric.

In his designs, Glenn Ward has sought to make pieces that are both functional and artistically pleasing. While enhancing their environment, these pieces also serve as an expression of the personality of their users. To customize these furnishings for their future surroundings various combinations of woods, glass, marble, veneer and inlay can be selected.

Commissions are welcome. Prices are available upon request.

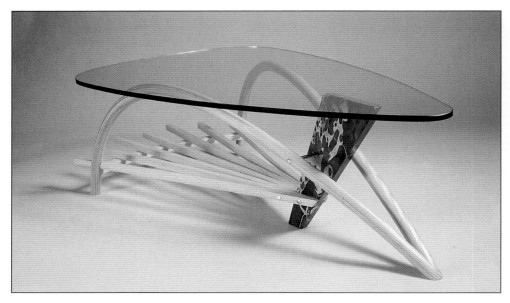

John Good

Ontario Craft Council

Printed in Hong Kong ©1997 THE GUILD: The Designer's Sourcebook

# Michael A. Burns

**Works in Metal**
602 Clemons Avenue
Madison, WI 53704
FAX 608-258-8944
TEL 608-241-7544

Michael Burns combines stone, metal and glass in sculptural furniture. With elements of iron working, stone carving, sculpture and jewelry making, each piece is a work of grace and functionality. Styles are crafted and scaled to fit into home or office, indoors or out. These one-of-a-kind pieces are shown at craft exhibitions and galleries across the United States. Michael Burns collaborates closely with clients on each custom design. With 20 years of experience, he captures the natural harmony of the metal and stone in every detail.

Also see this GUILD publication:
*Designer's Edition: 11*

A  Park coffee table, steel and granite, 17" x 60" x 40"

B  Spiral console table, steel and granite, 29" x 52" x 12"

C  Mahogany drawers console, steel, wood, granite, 31" x 48" x 14"

D  Corn console table, steel, silver, gold, granite, 29" x 60" x 14"

A

B

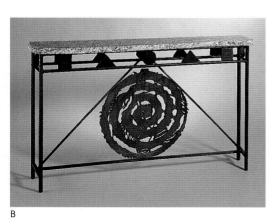

C

D

Photos: Jim Carman

# York Ast

**635 East 6th Street #4E**
**New York, NY 10009**
**TEL  212-674-4085**

Self-taught artist York Ast creates furniture with a strong emphasis on form that interacts with its surroundings in a harmonious way.

His specialty is finding creative solutions that are not only beautiful, but also highly functional and practical.

In the late 1980s, when Ast lived in Vienna, he started to design and build sculptural furniture using steel and scrap metal. Since then, the range of materials he works with has stretched to include copper, wood, leather and concrete.

A *Hot Seat*, 1995, patinated copper, wood and upholstery radiator cover, 36"W x 12"D x 23"H

B *Tideless*, 1996, modular copper and wood bar at Glorious Food, New York, NY, 16'L

A

B

Printed in Hong Kong ©1997 THE GUILD: The Designer's Sourcebook

# Ikeru Ltd.
# Design Workshop

**Andrea Dasha Reich**
**466 Washington Street**
**New York, NY 10013**
**FAX 212-274-0115**
**TEL 212-219-3757**

Taking original art several steps further, Czech-born artist and designer Andrea Dasha Reich helps redefine functional art. Using many media — including oils, acrylic, metal and others — she unites art and furniture design. By using a polymer resin of extraordinary depth, she achieves a high gloss or satinesque finish, resulting in an exhilarating experience of vibrant color and depth. Lace-like legs of laser-scrolled steel give the tables a majestic resting place. This concept has also been applied to hanging panels, paintings and screens.

Ms. Reich's work is shown in public, private and corporate collections in the U.S., Europe and Asia. She offers customized concepts for architects and decorators because, she says, "the world is our archive and inspiration."

A Wall art, 30"W x 38"H

B Lamp, 48"H

C Round table, 54"Dia x 27"H

D Square table, 48"W x 48"L x 17"H

A

B

C

D

# Toni Putnam

Route 9D, RR #2
Garrison, NY 10524
TEL 914-424-3416

Sculptor Toni Putnam creates furniture using imagery from medieval herbals and alchemy. These evocative bronzes can be used outdoors or inside. Each is a unique piece. The lost-wax casting process is used to create them. They are beautifully crafted and patinated using touches of gold and silver wax or leaf.

Putnam's work is represented in collections and prestigeous exhibitions across the U.S. and abroad.

Commissions are welcomed. More information is available upon request.

Pieces on this page range from $2,000 to $6,000.

Also see these GUILD publications:
*Architect's Edition: 12*
*Designer's Edition: 10*
*Gallery Edition: 3*

A  *Medieval Potato Plant Table*, 29"H x 12" x 21"

B  *Sun/Moon Chair*, 4$^1/_2$'H x 2' x 2'

C  *Leaf Coffee Table*, 18" x 3$^1/_2$' x 3$^1/_2$'

A

B

C

# Paul Knoblauch

45 Beacon Street
Rochester, NY 14607
FAX 716-271-3520
TEL 716-442-3381

Paul creates functional art utilizing metal, glass and wood. While constantly involved with producing new work, he also enjoys the challenges that commissions bring.

A  Coffee table, 36"

B  Gate, 168"

C  Lamps, 91"

D  Pedestals, 40" to 45"

E  Chair, 49"

F  Chair, 53"

A

B

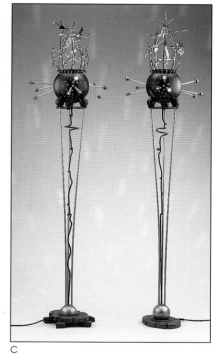

C

D

E

F

# Allen Root

**Allen Root Architectural Metals**
**PO Box 288**
**San Luis Obispo, CA 93406**
**TEL   805-544-7960**

Allen Root and his staff have practiced their craft for twenty years amidst the gentle hills of California's Central Coast. From there they have forged a client base that spans the nation. With an uncommonly high level of craftsmanship and a fine eye for detail, they produce tables, seating, lighting and accessories for homes and public spaces. Applying aesthetic sensibilities to the dreams and parameters of their clients, the consistent results are pieces that delight and satisfy.

All inquires are welcome.

Also see these GUILD publications:
*Architect's Edition: 9, 10*

Lobby seating, Performing Arts Center, San Luis Obispo, CA, 30" x 72"

Dining table, Swain residence, San Luis Obispo, CA, 66" x 84"

Photos: Josef Kasparowitz

# Doug Weigel

**Steel Sculptures by Doug Weigel**
PO Box 92408
Albuquerque, NM 87199-2408
FAX 505-821-9696
TEL 505-821-6600

Doug Weigel designs and produces two- and three-dimensional sculptures and furniture in steel. Styles include Southwestern, Western and Art Deco, as well as client-commissioned ideas.

Allow four to eight weeks from design approval and contract to completion. Shipping and handling, FOB Albuquerque. Selected commissions include the collection of President George Bush, Petrified National Forest, Scottsdale Airport, Sandia Laboratories and the Hyatt Aruba.

A Powder-coated Hopi game table: 42"; four denim-covered chairs

B Frog bar stool; powder-coated frog pot holders; powder-coated, glass-topped frog and cactus tables: 24"Dia and 30"Dia; frog mirror: 48" x 14"

C Steel petroglyph floor lamp; heartline bear mirror: 20" x 30"; men on a cornstalk bench with leather seat; petroglyph glass-topped coffee table: 30"Dia

Printed in Hong Kong ©1997 THE GUILD: The Designer's Sourcebook

A

B

C

# Fish of Fancy

While THE GUILD offers many benefits to artists, immediate gratification usually is not one of them. More often, GUILD sourcebooks generate a steady, but moderate, flow of inquiries over several years of use.

Don't tell that to Elizabeth Van Riper, however. The Texas artist's ad in *The Designer's Sourcebook 11* produced contacts and sales within weeks of the book's publication. Those sales included a large standing screen for a vacation lodge in Colorado and a pair of headboards for a private home in the Canadian woods. Both are perfect settings for Van Riper's whimsical, fantastically colored fish figures.

A former banker and spare-time painter, Van Riper started focusing on furniture with fish imagery two years ago. "It was just something that I had in my head for the longest time," she explains.

That inspiration has ballooned into a full-time career. While Van Riper works in many styles, her durable, meticulously crafted fish pieces have found the most enthusiastic audience — thanks, in part, to a growing market of discerning anglers. And, as Van Riper is quick to point out, "I make fish art that doesn't have to be relegated to the den."

Monty Swift

**Artist:** Elizabeth Van Riper
**Liaison:** Hugh Newell Jacobsen, FIA; Washington, DC (Architect)
**Type of Work:** Twin Headboards
**Site:** Private Residence, Canada

# Freefall Designs

**Suzanne Donazetti**
**Kenneth Payne**
PO Box 797
Carrizozo, NM 88301
TEL   505-648-2313

Suzanne Donazetti and Kenneth Payne work together to create abstract images in copper. Suzanne gilds, paints and weaves onto the structures, which Kenneth designs and builds of copper tubing, wood or plexiglas.

Elegant mirrors, clocks, tables, water fountains and wall sculptures are entirely handcrafted by the artists. Their unique two- and three-dimensional forms are commissioned by private and corporate collectors and are represented in many galleries.

Pieces by Kenneth and Suzanne are easy to install, lightfast, and coated to insure low maintenance. The artists enjoy working with clients on color preferences, and provide sketches or samples for specific client needs. Call or write for additional information.

Also see these GUILD publications:
*Designer's Edition: 9*
*Gallery Edition: 3*

Three-panel folding screen, copper, 4$\frac{1}{2}$' x 6'

John Yost, Marble Street Studio

# Illuminations

**Margaret Oldman**
71 Delano Avenue
San Francisco, CA 94112
FAX 415-469-9789
TEL   415-469-9789
E-Mail: Slumper@aol.com

Margaret Oldman has been creating sand-carved crystal and glass for over 15 years. She is a graduate of the California College of Arts and Crafts. Her work is represented in collections worldwide, including the Erte Estate in Paris and the Imperial Palace in Tokyo.

Ms. Oldman works with architects, interior design professionals and homeowners to incorporate her artful and functional glass carvings into public and private settings. Her implementation of both representational and abstract styles is unique and adaptable to any size project. Carved or frosted glass serves to separate spaces aesthetically, and to create privacy.

Margaret's work includes slumped sculptures and finely carved European crystal. Both are ideal for gallery and corporate office displays.

A professional brochure is available.

*Conversation Piece*, 1996, slumped, sand-carved bowl, 18"Dia

Paul Margolies

*Sun Goddess*, 1996, sand-carved triptych, collection: Imperial Palace, Tokyo, Japan, 61" x 61"

Amyx Photography

# Edith Morgan

2101 La Mesa Drive
Santa Monica, CA 90402
FAX 310-395-6257
TEL 310-395-6257

Edith Morgan is a California artist who started painting as a child in Mississippi. Before graduating from Otis Parson's School of Design in 1983.

She painted large abstractions for many years and has now turned to nature. Her special love for animals and oriental art has led her to these exquisite screens of gold leaf and oil, her favorite medium. Her passion for tigers has been incorporated into 78" x 64" free-standing screens . Commissions considered.

# Originals by Win

**Win Peterman**
**PO Box 1866**
**161 Windcliff Road**
**Prince Frederick, MD 20678**
**FAX 410-535-4976**
**TEL   410-535-3419**

Win has been painting for 15 years. Her canvas of choice for the past five years has been silk. She uses French fabric dyes to attain strong, permanent color and to capture depth and motion.

Her pictures, wall hangings and room divider screens are influenced by the grandeur of the mountains where she grew up, and the power of the ocean, near her present home.

The strength, weight and durability of silk make it ideal for large-scale commissions.

Prices start at $50.

Photos: David Egan

# Elizabeth Van Riper

**Van Riper Designs**
1411 East Campbell Road #700
Richardson, TX 75081
FAX 972-783-2227
TEL  972-783-2525

Fresh, sophisticated and whimsical best describe the art furnishings created by Elizabeth Van Riper. A legacy of four generations of female artists precedes Elizabeth into the fine arts. Her unusual heritage and experiences have culminated in the formation of Van Riper Designs.

Elizabeth's decorative and functional art furnishings are inspired by the creative extravagance of nature's flora and fauna. Room divider and fireplace screens, tables, chests, headboards and boxes, as well as custom works, all share a unique artistic interpretation of the natural world. A strong sense of color and style has helped Elizabeth build successful relationships with galleries, museums, designers and clients.

A single Van Riper work stands out as a conversation piece, while complementary elements can create an entire vignette. All major works are signed and numbered.

Dolphin fish room divider screen, acrylic on wood, 6' x 6'

Blanket chest, 38" x 18" x 19"

Fruit swivel stools

Dragonfly room divider screen, acrylic on wood, 6' x 6'

Photos: Monty Swift

Furniture  39

ACCESSORIES

# Jennifer Mackey

**Chia Jen Studio**
**PO Box 469**
**Scotia, CA 95565**
**FAX 707-764-2505**
**TEL 707-764-5877**
**E-Mail: suziraz@aol.com**

Jennifer Mackey of Chia Jen Studio uses sponging, painting, screen printing and appliqué techniques to fashion unique designs. Mackey's works blend European, Mediterranean and Eastern influences.

Mackey, who strives for a creative and fresh look, applies her talents to upholstery fabrics, drapery material, floor coverings and hangings. Her clients are in both the design community and the general public.

Chia Jen Studio offers its designs in natural fiber textiles, such as linen, silk, hemp, wool and cotton. Non-toxic, water-based pigments are used; they are colorfast and environmentally sensitive.

Color brochure available.

Also see these GUILD publications:
*Designer's Edition: 6, 11*
*Architect's Edition: 12*
*Gallery Edition: 3*

A  Side chairs, gold foil and wash

B  Hand-finished bench, foil accents

C  Black linen slip chairs, metallic wash inks

A  Mark Guerra

B  Robin Robin

C  Robin Robin

# Barker-Schwartz Designs

**Joyce Barker-Schwartz**
**915 Spring Garden Street #315**
**Philadelphia, PA 19123**
**TEL 215-236-0745**

Joyce Barker-Schwartz designs and produces the most innovative and exciting alternatives in floor or wall treatments.

Each rug is a functional work of art that is carefully constructed with woven painted canvas strips and appliquéd canvas shapes, which are then hand stitched and sealed for durability and a unique look. Our woven rugs and wall hangings require minimum care and are highly resistant to scratches and stains.

Information regarding commissions and prices is available upon request.

Also see this GUILD publication:
*Designer's Edition: 9*

A *Fire Flower II*, 7' x 6'

B *Slightly Off-Center*, 8' x 8'

A                                          Karen Mauch

B                                          Barry Halkin

# Gloria E. Crouse

**Fiber Arts**
4325 John Luhr Road NE
Olympia, WA 98516-2320
**TEL** 360-491-1980

Gloria Crouse creates highly textured art rugs and wall works, using unique variations of hand hooking and sculpting. Her work is shown in many collections, including Weyerhaeuser, SAFECO Insurance, Sea-Tac International Airport, Western State Hospital and the Tacoma Art Museum.

Additional works may be seen in Ms. Crouse's recently published book, *Hooked Rugs: New Materials/ New Techniques,* with accompanying video (Taunton Press).

A  *Ragtime*, hand tufted, 7' x 8'

B  *Fusion*, hooked and sculpted wools and metal, 7' x 9'

A

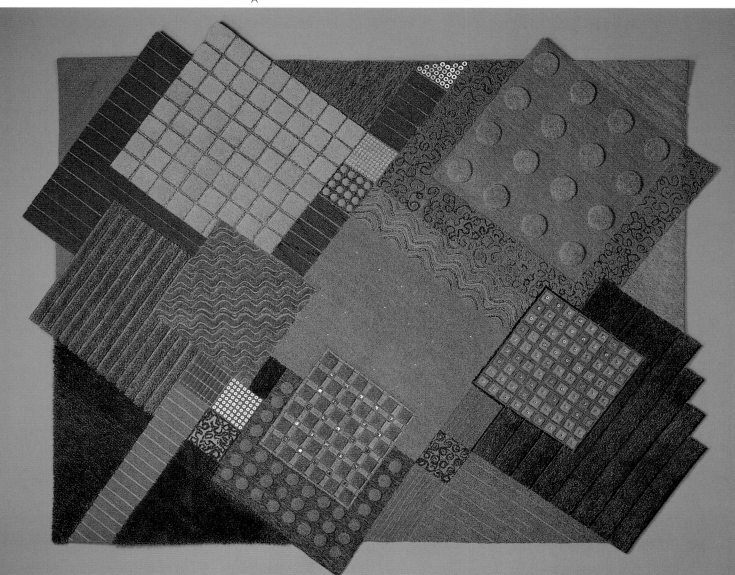

B

Photos: Roger Schreiber

# Mary Zicafoose

3323 South 104th Avenue
Omaha, NE 68124-2512
FAX 402-343-1590
TEL   402-343-1589

Mary Zicafoose uses color boldly, creating powerful visual statements in fiber. Her internationally collected tapestries and rugs blend universal symbols with multi-cultural themes. All pieces are custom-designed, custom-dyed handwoven wool on linen warp. Quality materials and a dense weave structure ensure that the tapestries will withstand environmental exposure.

Prices start at $125 per square foot. Commission packet available upon request.

Recent commissions include:
Mobil Corporation
Norwest Banks
Tenaska-Canada
The U.S. Embassy in Accra, Ghana

Also see this GUILD publication:
*Designer's Edition: 9*

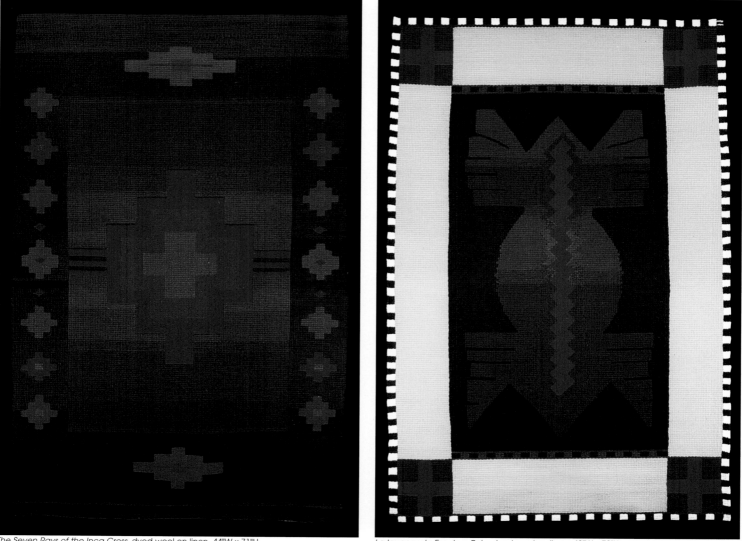

*The Seven Rays of the Inca Cross*, dyed wool on linen, 44"W x 71"H

*La Iguana y la Escalera Roja*, dyed wool on linen, 48"W x 72"H          Photos: Kirby Zicafoose

# Maya & Terry Balle

**Balle Arts Inc.**
**46 Waltham Street #108**
**Boston, MA 02118**
**FAX 617-338-3884**
**TEL 617-338-3883**

One-of-a-kind acrylic sculptures and limited-edition vessels, vases and bowls are hand carved by Maya and Terry Balle in their Boston-based studio. The Balles are pioneering proprietary techniques for the carving and coloring of acrylic. Geometric concepts create beautiful optical effects such as rainbows, internal mirrors, and phantom images that interact and become more dramatic with changing light.

The Balle Accessory Collection has gained an international reputation for its use of colors that harmonize with any environment.

Public collections and commissions include:
Hasbro Children's Hospital, Providence, RI
Hyatt Hotels, worldwide
Royal Caribbean Cruiselines, Miami, FL
Nynex, Boston, MA
Swiss Hotels, Atlanta, GA
IBM, Chicago, IL

*Optical Vessel*, 6"H x 15"W, *Double V*, 22"H x 8"W

*Butterfly*, 11"H x 20"W x 15"D

Photos: Steve Dunwell

# Cohn-Stone Studios

**Michael Cohn**
**Molly Stone**
**5755 Landregan Street**
**Emeryville, CA 94608**
**FAX 510-654-9706**
**TEL  510-654-9690**

Michael Cohn and Molly Stone are internationally acknowledged by museum, corporate and private collections for their unique sculptural works of glass art.

A whirlwind of air, light and glass reflect the forces of nature in the *Tornado Series*, pictured on the top of this page. These large-scale pieces, 20 inches high and 14 inches deep, glow with simple elegance in a vortex of 23-karat gold leaf.

The *Tortoise Shell Athena Series*, pictured at the bottom of this page, combines classical forms with bold elegant color. The 20-inch-deep *Athena Bowl* radiates light with a gold luster glass interior. The stately *Athena Vase* stands 27 inches in height.

Cohn-Stone Studios also produces a wide variety of functional forms of hand-blown art glass.

Brochure available upon request.

A  *Tornado Series*

B  *Tortoise Shell Athena Series*

A

B

Photos: Charles Frizzell

# Bill Hopen

**Hopen Studio**
**268 North Hill Road**
**Sutton, WV 26601**
**FAX 800-872-8578**
**TEL  800-872-8578**

Sculpture by Hopen is well known throughout the eastern United States. His large commissioned bronzes are placed in churches, hospitals, universities, public buildings, museums and parks.

Designers employ Hopen's small expressive works as potent accent pieces; collectors acquire them because of the value founded upon Hopen's major works.

You are invited to call the artist directly to discuss your project or to obtain a video brochure.

Also see these GUILD publications:
*Architect's Edition: 9, 10, 11*

A  Portrait of Senator Byrd for the Capitol Rotunda (work in progress), bronze, 10'H

B & C  Selection of 8" figures in bronze and crystal

A

Cathy Brunt

B

Jurgin Lorenzen

C

Jurgin Lorenzen

# Jonathon Winfisky

**Potter Road/Legate Hill**
**Charlemont, MA 01339**
**TEL   413-339-8319**

Jonathon Winfisky has been designing and producing unique and original blown and cast sculptural glass vessel forms since 1976.

The *Sculptural Design Series* and the *Cast Design Series* are examples of forms which are designed to work collectively or individually when displayed in private residences and public spaces.

Larger pieces are available by commission and all designs can be produced in a wide variety of sizes and colors. Please call or write for further information.

A  *Cast Design Series*, 1991, bowl: 15"; vase: 14"; vial: 6"; bud vase: 8"; ming vessel: 8"

B  *Sculptural Design Series*, ©1991, bowl: 15"; vase: 12"; fluted vase: 8"; perfume vial: 5¹/₂"; tapered vase: 10"

A

B

# Christopher Bennett

Rt. 2, Box 242A
Keosauqua, IA 52565
FAX 319-592-3463
TEL 319-592-3228

Christopher Bennett specializes in classically rendered sculptures of human figures and animal wildlife. Over the years, Chris has created more than 45 public works of art for parks, liturgical settings, memorial monuments, private residences, hospitals and college settings. When creating a commissioned work of art for a particular community, Chris draws inspiration from nature and local history, creating site-specific works which relate to and inspire the community of origin.

Commissions include:
Marshalltown Medical and Surgical Center,
  Marshalltown, IA
Indian Hills Community College, Ottumwa, IA
Veteran's Memorial Auditorium, Des Moines, IA
Rockford Park District, Loves Park, IL

Additional information and pricing upon request.

Also see this GUILD publication:
*Architect's Edition: 13*

A  *Hawk and Mole*, 1996, bronze and cedar
   shadow box, copies available, 3¹/₂' x 2¹/₂' x 6"

B  *Donor Recognition Wall*, 1996, cast ceramic and
   carved oak, 11' x 4¹/₂' x 8"

A

Ed Vinson, Keokuk, IA

B

Vickie Sanborn, C.P.P., Waterloo, IA

# Matt Kowollik

**Matt Kowollik Wildlife Art**
**5892 Whippoorwill Hollow**
**Milford, OH 45150**
**TEL  513-575-0795**

Matt Kowollik carves and paints North American birds and game fish. Born in Berlin, Germany, and a design graduate from the University of Cincinnati, the artist brings a contemporary approach to the old tradition of the wooden bird. Since 1975, the artist's carvings have been decorating homes and offices from coast to coast.

Each piece is individually sculpted and polished from hardwoods — such as cherry, walnut, maple, oak or ebony — using a bandsaw, grinder, rasps, knives and chisels. Colors are achieved with artist oils and brushes.

The artist's signature style is a self-taught technique using glazes of artist oils applied on the polished hardwood. This staining technique blends the essence of the subject with the figuring in the wood, giving a spontaneous freshness to even familiar subjects.

Please feel free to contact the artist. Slides, photographs and flyer available upon request.

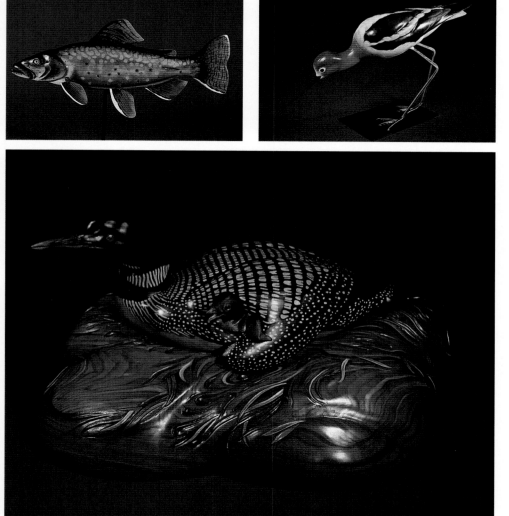

# Longfellow Bronzes "Poetry You Can Touch"

Irene Wilkins Longfellow
HC 85, Box 4268
Livingston, MT 59047
FAX 406-222-6665 (Gateway Office Supply)
TEL 406-222-2332
E-Mail: toothphd@aol.com

Known for her attention to detail and knowledge of both human and animal anatomy, Irene Longfellow's bronzes are exciting and varied in subject. Her sculptures of African people and animals are in great demand.

Now seventy-one, Ms. Longfellow came late to sculpture. She has works in private collections, has won several awards and has been juried into many prestigious shows.

Commissions welcomed.

Prices range from $500 to $6,000.

A *The Beginning of the End,* dodo bird, extinct, bronze, 13 1/2"L x 11"H

B *Old Survivor,* white rhino with birds, 1994, bronze,

A

B

# Elsbeth C. McLeod

**Magus Studios**
1934 Ptarmigan Lane NW
Poulsbo, WA 98370
TEL  360-697-6557

Elsbeth McLeod has been incorporating portraiture into her professional work for over 20 years, with ceramic sculpture becoming her primary medium for the last twelve. Her work is collected internationally and is noted for its characteristic appearance of aged ivory.

A creative process that often spans several weeks for more complex pieces begins with preliminary sketches and template design and ends with a glaze of oil pigments after the final kiln-firing. Brass or wood are often incorporated into the finished form.

Retail prices range from $250 to $2,500. Please write for slides of available work.

A  *Harvest*, stoneware and brass, 26" x 10" x 6"

B  *Cocooned*, stoneware, steel and walnut, 20" x 21" x 10"

C  *Monk Series*, stoneware, 19"H to 23"H

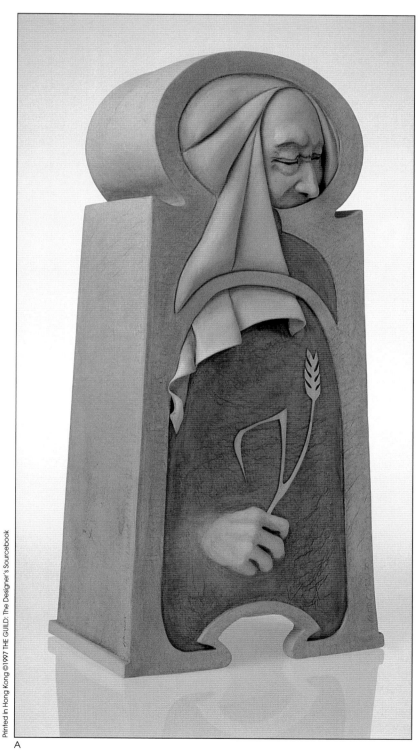

A

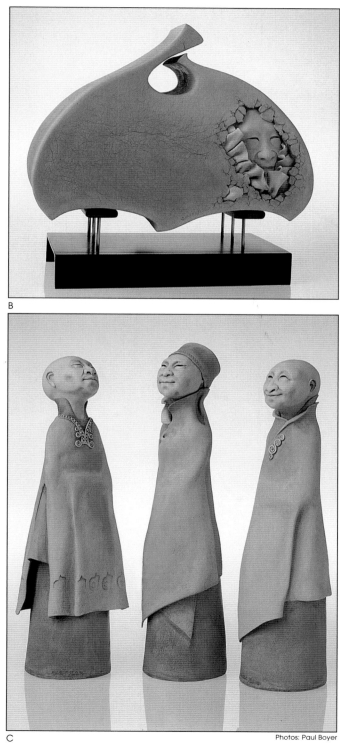

B

C

Photos: Paul Boyer

# Lawrence Northey

9580 Kirkmond Crescent
Richmond, BC V7E 1M8
FAX 604-275-9594
TEL  604-275-9594

Lawrence Northey is an accomplished technician as well as an inspired designer. His work expertly combines his passions for technology and art. Northey's vibrant and engaging creations have delighted both commercial and private clients in the United States and Canada. Actress Kristie Alley purchased two musical automata for her private collection in 1993.

Site-specific commissions guaranteed on time and within budget.

A  *Rocket Lamp*, 1996, fiberglass, lights, wood, chromed metal, 36" x 16"

B  *Courier*, 1995, fiberglass, chromed metal, 29" x 15"

C  *Heavy K and the Turtlenecks*, 1994, musical light automata, 35" x 27" x 72"

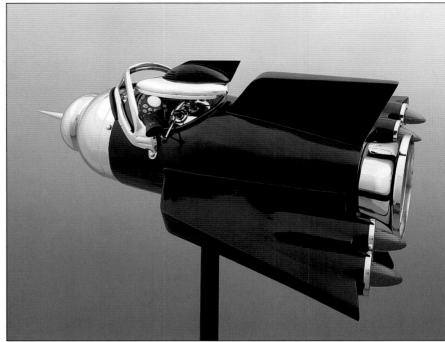

A

B

C

Photos: Ivan Hunter Photography

# Martin Sturman

Martin Sturman Sculptures
416 Cricketfield Court
Westlake Village, CA 91361
FAX 805-381-1116
TEL 805-381-0032

Martin Sturman creates original steel sculptures in floral, figurative and abstract designs. These sculptures are executed in stainless or carbon steel suitable for indoor or outdoor placement.

Each stainless steel sculpture is burnished to achieve a beautiful shimmering surface. Carbon steel sculptures are painted with acrylic and coated with polyurethane to preserve their vitality.

Martin often has sculptures available for delivery but encourages site-specific and collaborative efforts. Photographs and prices upon request.

Also see these GUILD publications:
*Designer's Edition: 7, 8, 9, 10, 11*

A  *Circle Dancers*, 1996, stainless steel, 53" x 108" x 108"

B  Coffee table, 1996, acrylic and steel, 21" x 20" x 20"

C  *Circle Dancers* (detail)

A

B

C

Photos: Barry Michlin

# Paul Henry Wilton

131 Weyand Avenue
Buffalo, NY 14210
TEL 716-824-4087
E-Mail: PAULWILTON@aol.com

Paul Henry Wilton takes you into the past using Old World techniques. Step back in time to a world your ancestors knew.

Copper, brass, exotic woods, semi-precious and precious stones, and a variety of other materials are brought to life with metal forming, hollow forming, raising, chasing, etching, etc. The work visits the past and creates a legacy for the future.

Each work is highly durable, functional and one-of-a-kind, personally created by Paul Henry. Sculptures may be obtained from a small inventory for immediate delivery or commissioned for a more personal and site-specific piece of antiquity.

Photos: Myers Studio, Buffalo, NY

# Nancy J. Young
# Allen Young

11416 Brussels NE
Albuquerque, NM 87111
FAX 505-299-2238
TEL  505-299-6108

The Youngs create two-and three-dimensional free-standing sculptures and mixed media wall art. Color preferences and commissions are accepted. Prices range from $200 to $3,000, depending on size and complexity.

Photos, pricing and scheduling upon request.

Selected commissions include: the U.S. State Department for embassies in Port Moresby, New Guinea, and Caracas, Venezuela; IBM; AT&T; and American Express.

Also see these GUILD publications:
*THE GUILD: 1, 2, 3, 4, 5*
*Designer's Edition: 6, 7, 8, 9, 10, 11*

A  Hand-cast paper plate, 25"Dia x 2"D

B  Wood sculpture, left: 26"H x 3"W x 7"D; right: 59"H x 8"W x 3"D; hand-cast paper vessel, center: 18"Dia x 13"H

A

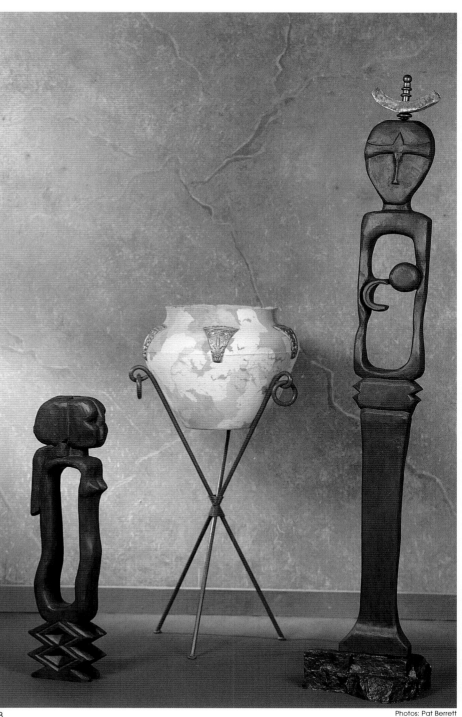

B

Photos: Pat Berrett

ART FOR THE WALL

# Leonard Baron

**3320 Quebec Place NW**
**Washington, DC 20008**
**FAX 202-363-3767 (Call first)**
**TEL  202-362-5905**

Leonard Baron is a New York-born artist now residing in Washington, DC. He has exhibited his work in galleries in New York, Washington and the Midwest. Mr. Baron is known for large, vibrant colorfield paintings and constructions which convey a sense of positive, rhythmic energy in motion.

The artist's work is featured in commercial and residential environments. It can be found in many prominent private collections, as well as numerous business facilities throughout the U.S. and abroad. A complete portfolio of constructions and paintings is available. Commissions are welcomed.

Also see this GUILD publication:
*Designer's Edition: 11*

A *Trillium*, acrylic on canvas, 6' x 6'

B *Band of the Sun*, acrylic on canvas, 44" x 84"

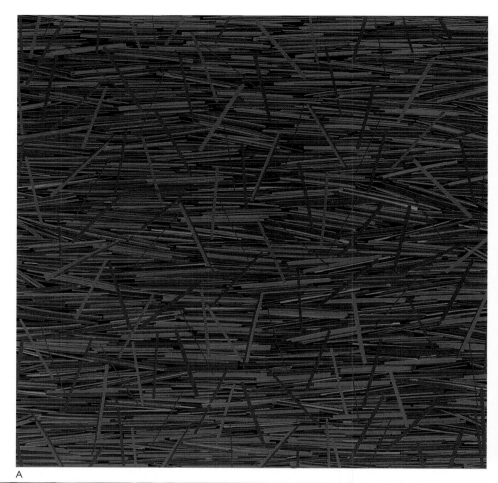

A

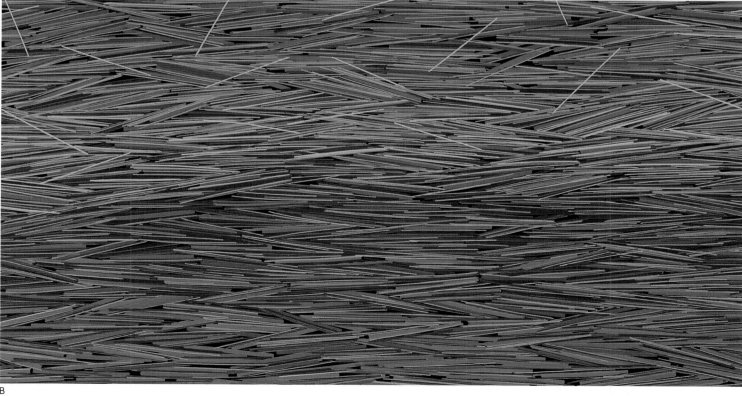

B

Printed in Hong Kong ©1997 THE GUILD: The Designer's Sourcebook

# Rita Blitt

Rita Blitt Inc.
6 Commodore Drive #334
Emeryville, CA 94608-1620
FAX 913-381-5624
TEL 913-381-3840
TEL 510-654-6536

"I feel like I'm dancing on paper." Rita Blitt, 1978

"Rita Blitt's paintings are reflective on both a visual and intellectual level, inviting the viewer to share in their simple beauty."

Program notes
Atlanta Ballet's Dance Technology Project — 1996
An arts-meets-science collaboration with the
Georgia Institute of Technology

Blitt, listed in *Who's Who in America*, has drawings, paintings and sculptures in museums and other collections throughout America, in Germany, Israel and Singapore.

SHOWN: *After the Ballet*, 1997, acrylic on paper, 30" x 22" (each)

Nancy Bundt

Malcolm Lubliner

# Brian L. Chapman

PO Box 905
Orange, VA 22960
TEL 540-672-5047

Brian Chapman's contemplative paintings layer jewel-like colors over sensuous textures, creating rich yet subtle surfaces. Archetypal animals and human figures appear in these works, evoking the timeless bonds between psyche and spirit.

Chapman's paintings are represented nationwide at galleries in Los Angeles, Seattle, Atlanta, Santa Fe, Dallas, Louisville and Bozeman, Montana. Sizes range from 12 by18 inches to 36 by 86 inches. Prices range from $500 to $5,000. Larger work available by commission. Slides available by request.

A  *Living in Mid-Air*, oil on wood panel, 18" x 24" x 3"

B  *Flight 206*, oil on wood, 17" x 20¹/₂" x 3"

A

B

Photos: Don Mason

# James C. Leonard

**401 Sutton Circle**
**Danville, CA 94526**
**FAX 510-736-5968**
**TEL  510-736-1399**

James C. Leonard is a contemporary artist who
shows nationally and internationally. He works
with art consultants who feature his work in many
important national projects. The focus of James's
work falls into three different series — landscape,
figurative and abstract. His work is characterized
as strong yet sensitive, expressive yet structured.

Please feel free to contact the artist. Slides,
photographs and a catalog are available
upon request.

A *Memories Made Clear*, acrylic on canvas, 60" x 72"

B *Once Seen Never Forgotten*, acrylic on canvas,
48" x 66¹/₂"

A

B

# René Levy

**40 Mayflower Drive**
**Tenafly, NJ 07670**
**FAX 201-569-4670**
**TEL  201-569-3934**
**E-Mail: ReneLevy@aol.com**

René Levy's paintings are lush with texture, patterning and colorful layers of paint that are coordinated into an expressionistic unity. The imagery is either landscape or figurative, mostly representational and some abstract.

Exhibitions include the Sylvia White Galleries in Santa Monica and New York.

National juried exhibitions include:
St. John's University Art Gallery, NY
Viridian Gallery, NY
Art Center of Northern New Jersey

She has also had a one-woman show at the Tanner Gallery in Westwood, New Jersey. Many works are included in corporate and residential collections.

Slides and prices are available upon request.

Also see this GUILD publication:
*Designer's Edition: 11*

A  *A House Divided*, oil on canvas, 42" x 48"

B  *Poses*, monoprint with woodcuts on paper, 37" x 49"

C  *Provence Hilltop*, oil on canvas, 42" x 50"

A                                                    John Ferrentino

B                                                    John Ferrentino

C                                                    Eric Landsberg

# Ginny Lohr

**Greedy for Color — Designs by Ginny Lohr**
52 Woodshire North
Getzville, NY 14068
TEL   716-689-4752

Ginny Lohr's designs include lively abstract interpretations of flowers, leaves and other motifs inspired by nature. Using color to define imagery in a dramatic way, this painter and fiber artist has recently completed commission work based on the themes 'leafscape' and wildflowers.

Designs are available as batiks, using wax resists and fiber reactive dyes hand painted on silk or cotton cloth, or as watercolor paintings on archival board. Works are suitable for framing.

SHOWN: *Fly Away Home*, 1996, dyes, pigment on cotton, $600, 40"H x 40"W

# Christopher H. Martin

**The Christopher H. Martin Art Gallery**
**2805 Allen Street #213**
**Dallas, TX 75204**
**FAX 214-969-0234 (Call first)**
**TEL   214-969-0234**

Christopher Martin's abstract expressions convey an undeniable source of energy and excitement. His use of brilliant colors and intriguing shapes creates a dynamic synergy that captivates viewers of these images.

Christopher's works are in corporate and private collections throughout the United States, Mexico and Europe.

Prices range from $600-10,000.

A  *Native Narcissism,* $1,200, 27" x 48"

B  *To Believe in Yourself,* $2,700, 72" x 32"

C  *A New Beginning,* $1,850, 40" x 48"

B

A

C

# John Mominee

Represented by Andrew Baumann Graphics
595 West Madison Street
Platteville, WI 53818
FAX 608-348-2787 (call first)
TEL  608-348-2787
E-Mail: Baumann@pcii.net

John Mominee is a Wisconsin artist known for his handsome, large-format monotypes. Collectors respond to the extraordinary color, sensuous texture and relationship of light to dark.

Created by painting on a plexiglass plate, the monotype is printed with an etching press on Arches 100% cotton paper. Subtle nuances, unattainable with any other process, appear in the finished work.

John earned an M.F.A. in painting from Southern Illinois University in 1967. He taught at the university level until 1994, when he decided to become a full-time painter.

He has a long list of exhibitions and his work can be found in numerous prominent corporate and private collections.

Information and artwork available. Dealer inquires welcome. Commissions accepted.

Prices: $1,000-$5,000

A  *Red Romance*, 1996, monotype, 58$^1$/$_2$" x 39$^1$/$_4$"

B  *Figaro's Secret*, 1997, monotype, 22$^1$/$_2$" x 42"

A

B

Photos: Andrew Baumann

# Jerry Skibell

**Originator of Modular Murals™**
**Skibell Art**
**7 Wooded Gate Drive**
**Dallas, TX 75230**
**FAX 972-233-5252**
**TEL  972-233-3838**

This Texas artist introduces an exciting contemporary concept, ideal for working horizontally or vertically in large spaces.

Skibell paints each one-of-a-kind creation using acrylic on gallerywrap, square canvases arranged in unique configurations, designed specifically for the intended wall space.

From a photograph of the proposed space, Skibell can provide a scale rendering of the future painting,

Sizes of square modules range from 12 to 24 inches with prices based on the number and module sizes used. Minimum price is $1,500.

A *Expectations*, 1996, twelve-piece Modular Mural™, mixed media on canvas, 6' x 3'

B *Stacked Diamonds*, 1996, eight-piece Modular Mural™, acrylic on canvas, 6' x 6'

A

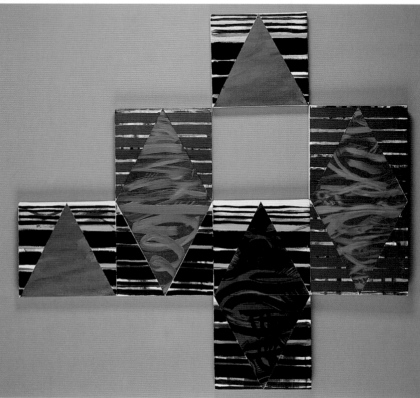

B

# Leroy Wheeler Parker M.F.A.

**40 Meek Place**
**Lafayette, CA 94549**
**TEL   510-937-7336**

Leroy Wheeler Parker is a very accomplished professional artist who creates in many disciplines. Here he focuses on his paintings on canvas and paper. Some works are 30 feet by 12 feet. He works on walls also.

Parker's works are in national and international corporate and private collections.

Prices start at $500.

Commissions include:
The Koll Co.
Quantum of Milpitas, CA
Cleeman Realty, New York, NY
The Gensler Co., Los Angeles, CA
Sacramento Metro Light Rail, Sacramento, CA
Schulman Liles Clinic, Oakland, CA

Also see these GUILD publications:
*THE GUILD: 3, 4, 5*
*Designer's Edition: 6*
*Gallery Edition: 3*

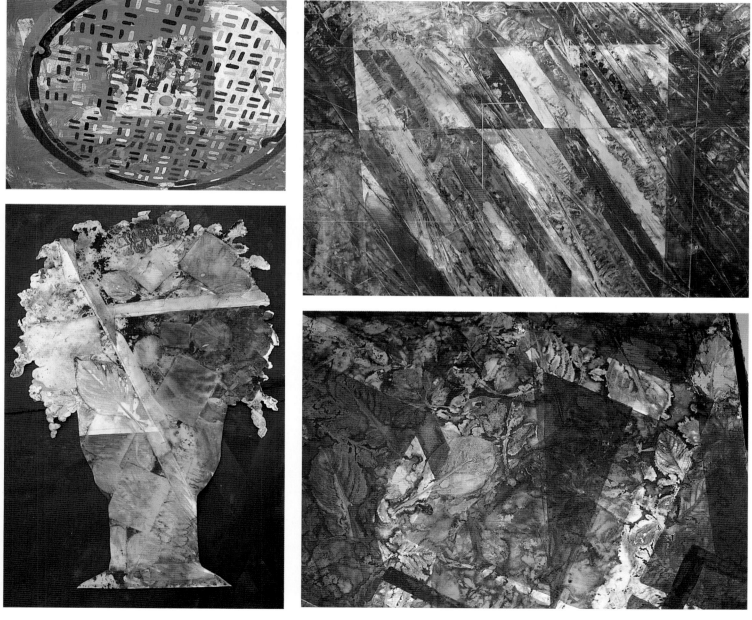

# Showing Different Facets

California painter James Leonard never quite knows what he'll be working on next. One day, he might finish a boldly colored abstract composition, and the next, begin an evocative landscape or figurative painting.

"At the real heart of all artists is a little child who likes to explore a lot of different types of expression. I've tried not to lose that feeling," Leonard says. "The way I work is very instinctual. I don't pre-sketch or anything like that. For me, that undercuts the very element of creativity."

Leonard has found THE GUILD an ideal partner for his expansive approach to art. While his ad in last year's *Designer's Sourcebook* highlighted his abstract work — leading to a sale to a corporate client in California — he looks forward to featuring his landscape work this year, and still other expressions of his vision in future editions.

"One nice thing about THE GUILD is that it offers you the opportunity to show different facets of your work," he says. "Usually a gallery wants to pin you down to one specific identity, but THE GUILD really gives you the freedom to show more of who you are."

Allon Pickard

**Artist:** James Leonard
**Liaison:** Joe Cannon, Design Consultant
**Type of Work:** Acrylic on Canvas
**Title:** *Diva Bardo*
**Site:** Conference Room, B.H. Miller, Santa Ana, CA

# L. Kristin Dahlgren

PO Box 38
Temple, NH 03084
FAX 603-654-6107
TEL  603-654-2080
E-Mail: dblack@jlc.net

The jewel-like color of Kristin Dahlgren's oil paintings is derived from techniques of the Old Masters.

Striving to express the essence of each subject — from a single piece of fruit, to the human being behind the portrait, to liturgical paintings and murals — the artist delights in such subtleties as luminosity within shadow and emphasized light play to encourage the awakening of greater perception.

With 15 years of graphic arts experience and art direction with an AAAA advertising agency before turning exclusively to fine arts, Ms. Dahlgren has a thorough understanding of the design process and the ability to work well with clients and professionals.

A  *Apricots, Plums, Grapes*, oil on canvas, 7" x 11"

B  *Pear*, oil on canvas, 8" x 8"

C  *Jason and Ping*, oil on canvas, 22" x 28"

Frank Cordelle

A

B

Frank Cordelle

C

# Charmaine Caire

Greg Smith — Smith/Isaacs Fine Art, Inc.
160 Mercer Street
New York, NY 10012
FAX 212-343-0795
TEL 212-343-9713

Charmaine Caire creates one-of-a-kind, privately commissioned, hand-painted photographs in both intimate sizes and murals. The subject may be photographed in Ms. Caire's studios in New York City and Philadelphia, or at any client location. Alternately, the image may be selected from a client's cherished collection. Ms. Caire then reworks the image using a proprietary technique which includes the liberal use of tints, inks, paints, oils and pastels.

According to Caire, "Layering darkroom, painting and photographic processes is a multidisciplinary process, and my clients can see my passion in the final product."

Private placements are in New York; Philadelphia; Dallas; Palm Beach; Washington, DC; and London. Her work is also included in prominent corporate collections.

References are available upon request.

Private commission, 1996, 40" x 40"

Private commission, 1996, 40" x 40"

# Pamela Joseph

MA Nose Studios, Inc.
407 Aspen Oak Drive
Aspen, CO 81611
FAX 970-920-2242
TEL  970-920-4098
TEL  970-920-6820 (Studio)
E-Mail: manose@rof.net
http://www.pamopoly.com

Pamela Joseph had 3 one-person shows in 1996, in New York, Los Angeles and Aspen.

"Humor can get the message across without blunting it...Ms. Joseph suggests that the ladies have a few uniquely effective strategies for gaining yardage."

*The New York Times,* April 1996

"Hang on to your libido. Lust meets linoleum, Betty Page meets Martha Stewart, and female sexuality is met with complete and total acceptance in artist Pamela Joseph's self-titled solo exhibition. Playfully celebrating unbridled female lust in a delightfully un-P.C. manner, Joseph's work contrasts images of pin-up queens with everyday clichés in an attempt to delineate the many faces of the modern woman."

*Los Angeles Reader,* April 1996

*Chicken Inspector,* 1995, mixed media and collage on wallpaper, 49" x 37"

*Monotype Series: Bridle,* 1996, monotype with Chine Collé, 24" x 16"

*Monotype Series: Laundry Day,* 1996, monotype with Chine Collé, 24" x 16"

# Yoshi Hayashi

255 Kansas Street #330
San Francisco, CA 94103
TEL  415-552-0755

Yoshi Hayashi's designs range from very traditional 17th century Japanese lacquer art themes that are delicate with intricate detail to those that are boldly geometric and contemporary. By skillfully applying metallic leaf and bronzing powders, he adds illumination and contrast to the network of color, pattern and texture. His original designs include screens, wall panels, furniture and decorative objects.

Hayashi's pieces have been commissioned for private collections, hotels, restaurants and offices in the United States and Japan. Prices upon request.

Also see these GUILD publications:
*THE GUILD 3, 4, 5*
*Designer's Edition: 6, 7, 8, 9, 10, 11*

Barbara Boissevain

Ira D. Schrank

# Barry Masteller

**Lisa Parker Fine Art**
584 Broadway, Suite 308
New York, NY 10012
FAX 212-334-5682
TEL   408-726-2500 (Artist's Studio)
TEL   212-925-6145

Barry Masteller's work has a living quality that touches the spirit. In the studio, he combines 35 years experience with inspiration he finds as witness to life's cycle of beginnings, endings and renewal. With landscape as a reference, Masteller paints multiple layers and achieves a potent luminosity.

Barry Masteller's work has been featured in extensive museum and gallery exhibitions and is owned by numerous museum, private and corporate collections around the world. He can be found in *Who's Who in American Art* and *New American Paintings, Volume 6.*

Color catalog $20. Additional information and visuals upon request.

A  *Earth and Sky 92*, 1996. oil on canvas, 48" x 30"

B  *Time and Place 16*, 1996, oil on canvas, 30" x 40"

A

B

Photos: Dennis Wyszynski

# Kathleen Parr McKenna

**McKenna Design**
**2918 Dolomite Springs**
**Blue Mounds, WI 53517**
**FAX 608-437-4222**
**TEL  608-437-6358**

Kathleen paints in the truest form of the water-color media. Her work is distinctive in color, definitive yet delicate in line, and holds a stylized quality. Her compositions are lively, yet convey a sense of serenity. The involved use of lights and darks contributes to a dynamic display of color.

A graduate of the American Academy of Art, Kathleen has painted professionally for over 20 years. Her works are represented in galleries across the country and in corporate and private collections. She enjoys personalizing compositions for specific clients and environments.

Prices and slides are available upon request.

A  *Night Solo*, watercolor, 30" x 22"

B  *Apples In Season*, 1993, watercolor, WHA-TV Arts
   & Antique Auction, 22" x 30"

A

B

# Glenn C. Rudderow

**Glenn C. Rudderow Fine Art Paintings**
**370 Barrett's Run Road**
**Bridgeton, NJ 08302**
**FAX 609-453-7611**
**TEL  609-451-8791**

A representational painter working in oil and watercolor, Glenn Rudderow paints with an emotion and color sense uniquely his own.

Rudderow has received awards in regional, national and international competitions, and has been featured in numerous group and solo exhibitions. His work is represented in corporate and private collections throughout North America.

Since 1986, Glenn has been an instructor in painting and drawing at the Pennsylvania Academy of Fine Arts.

Slides and resumé are available upon request. Prices start at $1,200. Landscape and portrait commissions accepted.

A  *Sunflowers and Gray*, oil on panel, 22" x 30"

B  *Buck Run*, oil on panel, 18" x 24"

C  *Burcham's, A Winter Snow*, water media on paper, winner of the Fred Albrecht Memorial Award, AWS, 1996, 29" x 40"

A

B

C

Photos: Will Brown

# Constance Tenhawks

Represented by: Debra Thorne
Piece of Mind Productions™
415 North Baldwin Street
Madison, WI 53703
FAX 608-256-1086
TEL  608-256-1015
E-Mail: pomdthor@mailbag.com

Constance Tenhawks paints in boldly colored acrylics that create a feeling of excitement, and radiate energetic layers of mosaic-like, intensely patterned designs. Her highly textured work includes both representative and abstract paintings that impart warmth and drama in both private and corporate settings.

Constance's current work is an explosive culmination of professional fine-arts training, heartfelt emotion and passionate interest in inlaid designs.

Commissions are welcome, and both site-specific and collaborative efforts are encouraged. Depending upon scale, most paintings can be shipped within eight weeks of commission.

A  *Horses*, 1995, acrylic on canvas, 30"H x 40"W

B  *Eggplants*, 1995, acrylic on canvas, 23"W x 36"H

A

B

# Claudia Wagar

301 First Street West
Sonoma, CA 95476
FAX 707-996-7054
TEL  707-996-7054
E-Mail: Bonnemort@aol.com

Claudia Wagar creates rich watercolors of the California wine country and related subjects. She is also widely recognized for her hotel and winery murals. (See page 142 of *The Architects Sourcebook 8* for her murals.) In addition, she publishes her own limited edition and open edition prints, notecards and winery posters.

Also see these GUILD publications:
*Designer's Edition: 11*
*Architect's Edition: 8*

A  *Grape Jam*, 1996, watercolor, 20" x 15"

B  *Peace in the Valley*, 1996, watercolor, 40" x 20"

A

Custom Image

B

Costill Graphics

# Tina Zanetti

908-1395 Beach Avenue
Vancouver, BC V6E 1V7
Canada
FAX 604-685-6518
TEL  604-685-6518

7 De La Marquise
St-Sauveur-Des-Monts, PQ JOR 1R4
Canada
TEL  514-227-4876

A self-taught artist, Tina Zanetti paints a universe
where a multitude of symbols come alive in the
creative form. Through Tina's art, we learn to
see invisible worlds in which the miracle of
beauty is innate.

While born a Roman Catholic to an Italian family,
her cross-cultural dreams of love, harmony and
freedom are accentuated by the bold colors she
employs.

Her work is enjoyed by people from all walks
of life — children and adults. It needs not be a
subject to intellectualize but rather creates a
sense of universal connection.

Completed works are available. Commissions
are welcomed.

Also see this GUILD publication:
*Designer's Edition: 9*

A  Untitled #18, 1995, acrylic, pastel on hard paper
   board, 11" x 14"

B  Untitled #20, 1995, acrylic, pastel on hard paper
   board, 24" x 20"

A

B

# PAINTED FINISHES & MURALS

# Creation Design Studios

**Krassi Gatev**
**1565 Vendola Drive, Studio 1**
**San Rafael, CA 94903**
**TEL  415-472-2216**

Krassi Gatev has worked extensively in art conservation in the U.S. and in Europe. He has collaborated with designers, architects, and directly with clients in designing and executing wall and ceiling decorations, furniture and accessories for historic and commercial buildings, as well as residences.

His deep knowledge and broad understanding of ancient and contemporary styles, materials and techniques combine with an artistic vision, allowing him to create perfect environments for both commercial and residential settings.

A  Design for ceiling

B  Breakfast room, 10' x 10'

A

Photos: Martin Takigawa

B

Printed in Hong Kong ©1997 THE GUILD: The Designer's Sourcebook

# John J. DeVlieger

John J. DeVlieger, Artist/Muralist
3914 Cedar Lane
Drexel Hill, PA 19026
TEL 215-232-8073 (Philadelphia)
TEL 610-446-2115 (Drexel Hill)

John DeVlieger has pushed the boundaries of his classical training to produce current works with vibrant colors, brilliant light quality and contemporary themes. His oil paintings and trompe l'oeil murals reflect both the legacy of his traditional craft and his dynamic, imaginative perspective on life.

John welcomes commissions internationally. He has the versatility to produce on-site works or works on canvas for subsequent installation.

Please call to request additional literature, pricing and scheduling.

A *Cherub Rotunda*, oil on canvas mural, 9'Dia

B *Bello's Capri Vista*, oil on canvas mural, 20' x 9'

A

B

Photos: Todd Murray Photography

# Classical and Contemporary

An artist never knows when advertising will pay off. The elegant screens and wall panels of San Francisco artist Yoshi Hayashi have graced the pages of THE GUILD for many years. One of those early pages caught the attention of art advisor Cathy Baum, who recalled Hayashi's work years later when an appropriate opportunity arose. "She remembered my work," Hayashi says, "but we never talked until this commission came up."

Baum's client, a San Francisco import firm, was so pleased with the first piece Hayashi produced for them that they followed up with a second commission. According to Hayashi, the company, which imports many Asian products, identified with his juxtaposition of classical Japanese techniques and contemporary images.

"My screens and paintings are classically Oriental," Hayashi says of his work. "At the same time, I include very strong modern images. But in all my work — even the most contemporary pieces — there's an Oriental feeling."

The credit for that goes largely to Hayashi's father, a craftsman devoted to classical Japanese styles and techniques. Though Hayashi paid little attention to his father's work as a child, he's found that a knowledge of traditional technique is ingrained. "I never thought I had learned anything from him," the artist says, "but my body knew what he was doing."

Barbara Boissevain

**Artist:** Yoshi Hayashi
**Liaison:** Cathy Baum, Art Advisor
**Type of Work:** Wall-Hanging Screen
**Title:** *Spring Moon*
**Site:** DFS-West, San Francisco, CA

# FEE FI FAUX

**Karen Jacobsen**

**PO Box 773**
**Sun Valley, ID 83353**
**TEL   208-726-3702**

**PO Box 1934**
**Mill Valley, CA 94942**
**TEL   415-568-6774**

Karen Jacobsen creates exquisite murals and unique impasto finishes for residential and commercial spaces throughout the U.S. and abroad. Her experience with designers, architects and contractors over the last decade provides for a level of professionalism and creative insight complementary to any project.

With an extensive imagination and sharp eye for color and design, Ms. Jacobsen shapes each project to reflect the true individuality of the client and his or her surroundings.

Portfolio and references available upon request.

Photos: Michael Hewes

# David Flett

23R Atlantic Avenue
Toronto, ON M6K 3E7
Canada
FAX 416-516-4649
TEL  416-516-4649

David Flett, painting since the early 1970s, can reproduce any existing photograph or image. He can also be directed to assemble his own composition, from three to 100 feet long, on canvas or wall.

There are no tariff charges on paintings crossing the United States-Canada border.

Commissions include:
Marilyn Monroe on the set of *The Seven Year Itch,* for Paramount Pictures, 30' x 10'
Cafe scene of 21 movie stars, for Paramount Pictures, 14' x 8'
Montage from *The Wall* video, by Pink Floyd, for HMV Retail Music Chain, 30' x 10'

A *Mid-July,* 1996, acrylic, 3' x 4'

B Reproduction of Guido Reni, 1620 original, 1995, acrylic, from the private collection of Vincent Labraico, Toronto, 7' x 5'

A

B

# David E. Garrison
# PSA

Garrison Art Studio
831 South Garfield
Burlington, IA 52601
TEL   319-753-0809 (Studio)
TEL   319-372-5473 (Agent)

Discover the past. Envision the future.

David Garrison invites viewers to stroll through history via his fascinating murals. With a career spanning 30 years, his masterful scenes breathe life and feeling into the past.

David's interior and exterior works are permanently installed in private collections as well as in public and corporate facilities. He encourages client interaction from the initial design through the installation process.

The quality and durability of David's work were proven when portions of the Iowa Welcome Center mural survived extreme humidity and water immersion during the great Iowa floods of 1993.

His most recent commission for the Iowa Sesquicentennial Celebration is a monumental outdoor history of Fort Madison, Iowa, on the banks of the Mississippi River.

Dave Richter

Dave Richter

# John Pugh

PO Box 1332
Los Gatos, CA 95031
FAX 408-353-3370
TEL  408-353-3370
http://www.illusion~art.com

Imagine, if you will, opening a door into quite a different room. You are moving into a deceptive land where reality ends and illusion begins. It's a dimension of both shadows and substances — of time and place, You have crossed over into the art of John Pugh.

A master of architectural trompe l'oeil, John integrates his work into each site to further perplex the viewer. John's creative energy, easy manner, and ability to articulate the client's concepts make him a favorite choice among private collectors, as well as architects and designers who serve discriminating clients.

Attention to detail — from design through final installation — is John's hallmark.

Brochures available upon request.

Also see these GUILD publications:
*Architect's Edition: 7, 8, 9, 11, 12*
*Designer's Edition: 11*

*Pompeian Niche with Krater*, private wine cellar, Los Gatos, CA, 36" x 55"

Calypso Imaging

*Art Imitating Life Imitating Art Imitating Life*, Cafe Trompe L'Oeil, San Jose, CA, 13' x 20'

Brian Brumley

# R&R Muto

**Decorative Arts Studio by R&R Muto**
83 Linden Street
Rochester, NY 14620
TEL  716-232-6030
E-Mail: Muto2@aol.com

Rick and Robin Muto opened their studio in 1977 and have become leading practitioners of the decorative arts in upstate New York. Their specialty is illusionary and decorative painting, ranging from murals to a myriad of painted finishes. An intuitive sense of color and composition enables the Mutos to create environments ranging from classic to contemporary.

Their collaborations with designers, architects and clients help to bring ideas and concepts to a concrete visual statement.

Projects include:
Monroe Golf Club, Pittsford, NY
Eastman Theater, Rochester, NY
Mann's Jewelers, Brighton, NY

A  Trompe l'oeil Italian villa with landscape

B & C  Trompe l'oeil television cabinet

D  Roman ruin with trompe l'oeil frame and ceiling ornament, wood-grained doors, glazed walls and marbled moldings

A                                      John Griebsch

B                                      John Griebsch

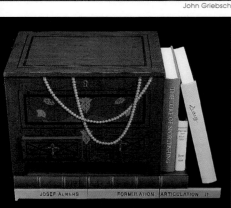
C                                      John Griebsch

D                                      Dave Brennan

# Gary Von Vradenburg

Fine Art Interiors by Gary
PO Box 3829
San Rafael, CA 94912
TEL 415-453-9865

Gary Vradenburg has been creating special interiors for 20 years, working in New York, New Orleans and San Francisco. His artistry goes beyond faux finishing to designing and creating a total environment. His masterful skill enables him to create a one-of-a-kind look for furniture, homes, hotels, restaurants or businesses.

Renovating on a budget becomes feasible with Vradenburg's expert use of color and paint, eliminating the need for structural changes. He can transform a structural handicap into a working visual statement.

"I love taking anything — old or new — and transferring it into unique visual art," says Vradenburg. "And when you love your work, it shows."

Call the artist for more information about his award-winning designs.

Photos: Bruce Lazarini

# OTHER MEDIA

# Bruce R. Bleach

**146 Coleman Road**
**Goshen, NY 10924**
**TEL 914-294-8945**

Bruce R. Bleach has been creating works for the wall for the past 23 years. The most recent and exciting works on metal are etched and painted bronze wall sculptures, as shown in this 4¹/₂ by 8 foot installation mounted on black wood. His wall sculptures, created in bronze, zinc, copper and aluminum, are maintenance-free and ready to hang for corporate and residential installations. Also shown are paintings on handmade paper, rich in color and texture. *The Wall*, below, measures 30 by 70 inches.

Bruce R. Bleach is listed in *Who's Who In American Art*. He is recognized internationally for his etchings, monoprints and paintings Selected collections include Motorola, Xerox, IBM, AT&T, Dupont, Merck, RCA, Trump Tower, Yamaha and Hyatt.

Drawings and samples available.

Also see this GUILD publication:
*Designer's Edition: 8*

Nick Saraco

Gregory Staley

# Barbara Brotherton

**Barbro Designs**
**56 Canyon Road**
**Fairfax, CA 94930**
**FAX 415-256-1763**
**TEL   415-485-0242**

Barbara Brotherton's unique wall sculptures are inspired by crusty building surfaces seen in her travels to Italy, Turkey, Egypt, China and Japan.

She combines materials such as distressed wood, earthy pigments, gold, silver, copper leaf, cast stone and patinas to create contemporary wall pieces that reflect her deep appreciation of Mediterranean and Far Eastern design.

Her work is widely represented in private and corporate collections. Slides and pricing available upon request. Site-specific commissions are welcomed.

Also see this GUILD publication:
*Designer's Edition: 10*

A  *Small Japanese Paths*, each panel 4' x 1'

B  *Aztec Sunrise*, 2' x 4'

A

B

Photos: Gugger Petter

# Jeff Easley

215 8th Avenue South
PO Box 502
Wellman, IA 52356-0129
FAX 319-628-4766
TEL 319-646-2521

Since establishing a studio in 1979, Easley has received many awards for his design capabilities and high standards of craftsmanship. The sculptures are constructed using non-endangered woods and are chosen for their natural colors. Dimensions can be adjusted to fit specific locations, large or small. Other designs available upon request. Abstract and progressive, these wall sculptures add warmth and richness to public spaces, private residences and the corporate environment. Prices begin at $650 and vary with size and complexity.

Selected commissions include:
University of Northern Iowa
International Center, Kofu, Japan

A *The Future Is Uncertain*, ©1996, 24"H x 41"W

B *Elbow Room*, ©1997, 31"H x 40"W

C *The One That Got a Way*, ©1997, 66"H x 60"W

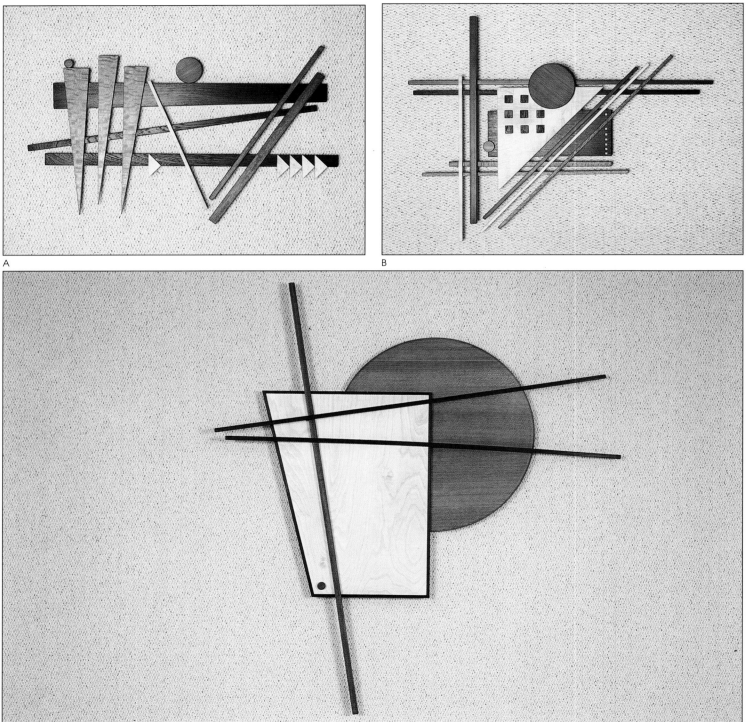

A

B

C

# Giordano Studios

**Joan Giordano**
**136 Grand Street**
**New York, NY 10013**
**FAX 212-431-6244**
**TEL  212-431-6244**

Internationally acclaimed artist Joan Giordano has created a highly personal technique, employing such disparate elements as hand-made paper, copper, aluminum and acrylic. Giordano's use of tactile surfaces is unique; the dramatic contrasting of metals and fibers amplifies the interplay of light and shadow in her wall sculptures. By employing a broad array of elements and textures, her sculpture can be adapted and adjusted to accommodate an unlimited number of design and decorating challenges.

Commissions and site-specific projects are welcome. Contact Giordano Studios for an initial consultation or photographs of available work.

A *Moving Out*, 60"H x 42"W x 8"D

B *Dancing With Shadows*, 36"H x 45"W x 12"D

C *Three Oceans*, 90"H x 50"W x 8"D

A

B

C

# Home Shopping

It's a familiar conundrum for art patrons: you like the piece, but you're not sure how it will look in your home. No problem, if you're dealing with Pittsburgh artist Kurt Shaw. When a Virginia couple contacted him through his most recent page in THE GUILD, Shaw was happy to take them on a tour of everything he had in stock.

"I store things all around town, at relatives' places and wherever I can get some room," Shaw says, "so I was driving them all over." When the clients still couldn't decide which of Shaw's paint-on-steel fixtures would work best in their home, Shaw cheerfully drove out with their favorites and let them try the art on for size.

"It wasn't really a problem for me," Shaw says. "One thing that's nice about being in Pittsburgh is that I'm within a day's drive of half the population in America. And I like being involved with the clients, going to their homes and getting a feel for how a piece will fit into their lives."

Ultimately, Shaw not only sold four pieces, but built an ongoing relationship that has led to further sales to the clients' friends and associates. "It's great," he says. "I kind of have my own cheerleaders now."

**Artist:** Kurt Shaw
**Type of Work:** Enamel on Steel
**Title:** *Xiphias*
**Site:** Private Residence, Richmond, VA

# Katherine Holzknecht

22828 57th Avenue SE
Woodinville, WA 98072
TEL 206-481-7788

Katherine Holzknecht creates unique mixed-media artworks for architectural spaces. Site-specific art results from collaboration with design professionals, producing innovative artworks that are ideal for interiors because of their durability and lightfastness. Katherine specializes in full-spectrum colors and visual textures to enhance existing design features.

Commissions are welcomed with a design fee. Design work includes scale drawings and samples. Holzknecht's work has been exhibited extensively in the Northwest and is included in over 50 corporate, public and private collections.

Further information available upon request.

Also see these GUILD publications:
*THE GUILD: 5*
*Designer's Edition: 8, 10, 11*

A & B *Dynamic Concurrence*, commissioned for the Decatur Apartments, Seattle, WA

C *Symbolia Educere*, commissioned through the Washington State Art in Public Places Program, Mountain View Middle School, Bremerton, WA

A

B

C

Jim Mannino, Landreth Studios

# Silja Lahtinen

**Silja's Fine Art Studio**
**5220 Sunset Trail**
**Marietta, GA 30068**
**FAX 770-992-0350**
**TEL  770-993-3409**

Silja Talikka Lahtinen uses images from the myths and landscapes of her native Finland in her large wall panels. With striking combinations of colors and materials, her collages address the "poetry and spirituality missing from our modern life."

Lahtinen's other work — paintings of acrylic and oil on canvas, and drums of wood, rope, plywood and fiber — are well known to collectors in the United States and Europe. She exhibits regularly in New York and other U.S. cities, as well as in Paris, France and Helsinki, Finland.

Commissions are accepted. For more information, please contact the artist.

Also see these GUILD publications:
*Designer's Edition: 9, 10, 11*
*Gallery Edition: 1, 2, 3*

A  *Everybody Knows I Am a Karelian Girl*, 1996, linen, wool, acrylic, wood, overall: 77" x 61", individual pieces, left: 67" x 19"; middle: 77" x 21"; right: 62" x 15"

B & C  *Everybody Knows I Am a Karelian Girl* (details)

A

B

C

# Linda R. Lhermite

**Les Insolites**
**3111 Clint Moore Road #205**
**Boca Raton, FL 33496**
**TEL   561-989-0361**

Using a material long esteemed for its intrinsic beauty, Linda Lhermite creates stunning and unique wall hangings.

These works join a love of color with suede's tactile sensuousness, culminating in a way that is both reflective and visually appealing.

Each hanging is composed of hundreds of pieces of the finest suedes. Fused and stitched together, they form glorious, intoxicating abstracts or deeply moving representational pieces.

To obtain a complete portfolio of available works, please contact the artist.

A   *Fireflies*, 54³/₄" x 48¹/₂"

B   *Maggali, La Femme du Policier*, from the series: *Broken Goddesses*, 63¹/₂" x 51¹/₄"

A

B

Photos: Miguel Martin, Miami, FL

# Bernard J. Roberts

W1952 Roosevelt Road
Oconomowoc, WI 53066
TEL 414-474-4103

Bernard Roberts is an established professional sculptor with a B.S., M.S. and M.F.A., who works in hand-carved wood.

His forms are inspired by nature and combine the rich character of wood with softly textured, painted areas. These beautiful, sensuous sculptures are durable and may be customized for any interior setting.

He is pleased with the response he received from *The Designer's Sourcebook 11* and looks forward to further interest in his work.

Portfolio available.

Also see this GUILD publication:
*Designer's Edition: 11*

A *Emergence*, 36"H x 24"W x 2¹/₂"D

B *Atman*, 36"H x 24"W x 2¹/₂"D

C *Seed Pod*, 16"H x 24"W x 2¹/₂"D

A

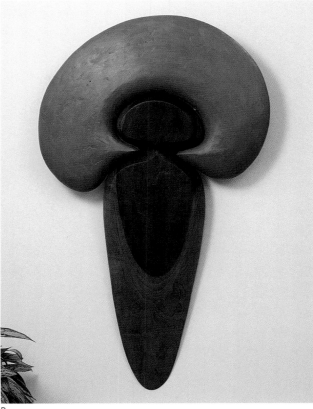

B

C

# Susan Starr & Co.

Susan Starr
1580 Jones Road
Roswell, GA 30075
FAX 770-993-5683
TEL 770-993-3980
TEL 770-992-1697

Tapestry, wall and free-hanging constructions by Susan Starr are rich in color and texture. Wide varieties of materials are used, including hand-dyed wools, silk, cotton, rayon, plexiglass, wooden rods and handmade papers. Starr's work has been featured in publications such as *USA Today*, *Interior Design* and *Contract*. AT&T, Bank of America, and the Marriott and Hyatt Hotels are among her many corporate clients.

Works are available in a range of sizes; the largest to date measures 50 feet by 27 inches. Designed for specific sites in consultation with architects, interior designers, galleries and individuals, her wall pieces hang in hospitals, office lobbies, hotels, residences and restaurants.

Types of work available include flat and dimensional tapestries, stick constructions, kite forms and handmade-paper constructions.

A Handmade-paper construction, 5' x 7'

B Ceremonial robe, 6' x 6'

C Stick construction, 5' x 8'

D Handmade-paper and stick construction, 4' x 12'

A

B

C

D

Photos: Mike Granberry

# Susan Venable

**Venable Studio**
**214 South Venice Boulevard**
**Venice, CA 90291**
**FAX 310-822-0050**
**TEL  310-827-7233**

Susan Venable's work is non-objective – an exploration of structure and surface. The reliefs are constructed of steel grids and twisted copper wire. The paintings are encaustic and oil.

In both, layers are stacked to create a rich and complex surface, maximizing the physicality of the materials.

Venable's wall reliefs have been installed in public spaces, as well as homes and museums in the United States, Europe, Asia and Australia. Site-specific commissions and collaborations are welcomed. The materials are durable, low maintenance and suitable to installation in public areas.

Also see these GUILD publications:
*Designer's Edition: 9, 10, 11*
*Architect's Edition: 12*

A *Zona Rosa*, 36" x 72"

B *Miami Mambo*, 30" x 60"

C *Mistral*, 65" x 120"

A

B

C

Photos: William Nettles

Printed in Hong Kong ©1997 THE GUILD: The Designer's Sourcebook

# Mary Boone Wellington

**M.B. Wellington**
**88 Boston Post Road**
**Amherst, NH 03031**
**FAX 603-673-2311**
**TEL  603-673-2311**
**E-Mail: MRYBOONE@aol.com**

Mary Boone Wellington has completed numerous commissions for public, private and corporate environments. An expert at working out the final details with architects, designers and owners, she creates a completed work that fulfills esthetic criteria and expresses the highest vision.

Commissions and collections include:
American Embassy, Belize
Bank of Georgia, Atlanta, GA
Coca Cola, Salem, NH
Concord Hospital, Concord, NH
Gillette Inc., Boston, MA
Kaiser Medical, San Diego, CA
Kintetsu, Nara, Japan
MCI, Denver, CO
Millipore Inc., Molsheim, France
International Group Inc., Hong Kong
Shiva Corporation, Bedford, MA
State of New Hampshire

Also see these GUILD publications:
*Architect's Edition: 11*
*Designer's Edition: 11*

A & B  *Leaf 1 and 2*, 1996, oil and gold leaf on canvas, Cross Point, Lowell, MA, 20" x 30"

C  *Dance* Series, relief, painted aluminum, 1997, private collection, 14' x 5' x 4"

A

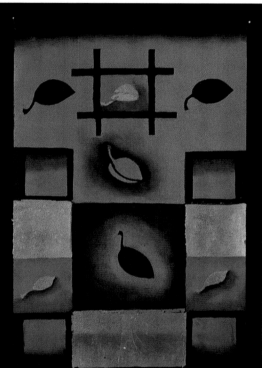
B

C

# Bill Wheeler

Studio 1617
1617 Silver Lake Boulevard
Los Angeles, CA 90026
FAX 213-660-7991
TEL 213-660-7991
E-Mail: studio1617@Leonardo.net

Bill Wheeler has been creating limited-edition original prints and paintings for public and private commissions since 1970. He also has nearly 20 years experience working in collaboration with designers and architects to create site-specific installations. His security-mounted wall constructions are made of masonite and/or archival plastics incorporating iridescent and metallic surfaces. They are designed to the client's color and size specifications; commissioned works have ranged from 2 by 2 feet to 10 by 164 feet.

Mr. Wheeler is a versatile artist, able to accept and incorporate the client's suggestions and modifications into his artwork. Such teamwork results in an installation that becomes an integral part of the interior space.

Also see these GUILD publications:
*THE GUILD: 4*
*Designer's Edition: 6, 7, 9*

METAL

# Eric Boyer

**Eric Boyer Sculptures in Wire Mesh**
**72 Cotton Mill Hill #A-12**
**Brattleboro, VT 05301**
**TEL** 802-257-2027
**E-Mail: eboyer@sover.net**
http//www.brattleboro.com/boyer

Eric Boyer creates original sculptures in woven wire mesh. The work juxtaposes classical nudes with an exciting industrial material. Formed by hand, these lightweight and resilient figures have been exhibited nationally and collected internationally since 1989.

Works are created for wall-hanging from a single point or free-standing with a wood or masonry base. Sculptures are black, rusted or patinated, and powder-coated for an extremely durable finish. Work may be commissioned in a wide range of sizes and scales with prices starting at around $1,000.

Male torso (left), 1995, rusted steel wire mesh on patinated masonry base, 24" x 8" x 8";
draped female torso (right), 1995, black steel wire mesh, 62" x 40" x 8"

Jeff Baird

# Lois Key Giffen

1600 79th Street Ocean
Marathon, FL 33050
TEL   305-743-3546

Lois Giffen has lived and worked on five continents, and her paintings are collected worldwide. In recent years, she has turned her attention to sculpture. Working in clay, stone, bronze and steel she creates an atmosphere of calm, serenity and well-being. Her works are best suited to intimate spaces, and she enjoys commissions for specific rooms, walls, and gardens.

Ms. Giffen's work is included in collections — mostly private — in Australia, Austria, Cyprus, Great Britain, East and West Malaysia, Malta, Sweden, and the United States.

A *Moon Mirror*, 1996, steel and bronze, 19"Dia

B *Reef*, 1996, steel with enamel, 42" x 31" x 4"

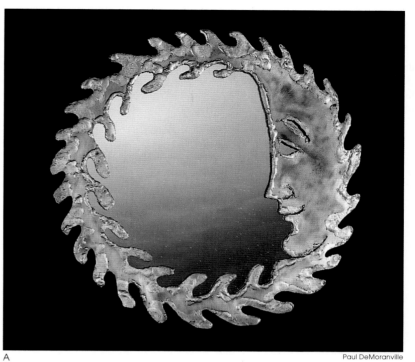

A

Paul DeMoranville

B

Larry Lipsky

# Marsha Lega

**Marsha Lega Studio**
**1819 North Center Street**
**Joliet, IL 60435**
**FAX 815-727-5255**
**TEL   815-727-5255**

Marsha Lega loves the stability of metal and
its intrinsic beauty that can also meet many
needs. She believes that the beauty of metal
opens possibilities to good design. Her interests
in furniture, sculpture and functional artifacts
are all facets of her work, which functions in
both residential and corporate settings.

Marsha Lega sells her work nationwide through
galleries, art consultants and designers. She has
exhibited both nationally and internationally. Custom orders are welcomed. A catalog is available.

Also see this GUILD publication:
*Designer's Edition: 8*

A  *Stainless Steel Sculpture #102*, stainless steel
   F table

B  Wall sculpture in stainless steel and black,
   Sprint Corporate Headquarters, 6'$1/2$' x 14'

A

Paul Kozal

B

Tatjana Alvegard

# Susan McGehee

**Metallic Strands**
**540 23rd Street**
**Manhattan Beach, CA 90266**
**FAX 310-546-7152**
**TEL  310-545-4112**
**E-Mail: metlstrnds@aol.com**

Susan McGehee is a weaver who uses metals instead of fiber, while incorporating traditional weaving techniques and patterns. She weaves on a floor loom with anodized aluminum wire and metals. Her technique creates lightweight contemporary wall hangings that complement both residential and commercial spaces.

Prices range from $150 to $190 per square foot.

Additional information available upon request.

A  *Zig Zag II*, woven anodized aluminum wire, 16" x 38"

B  *Renaissance*, woven anodized aluminum wire with copper, 8" x 32"

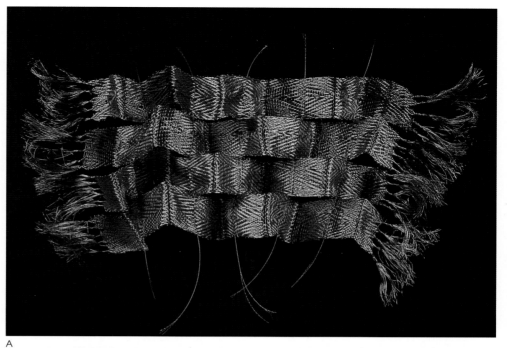

A

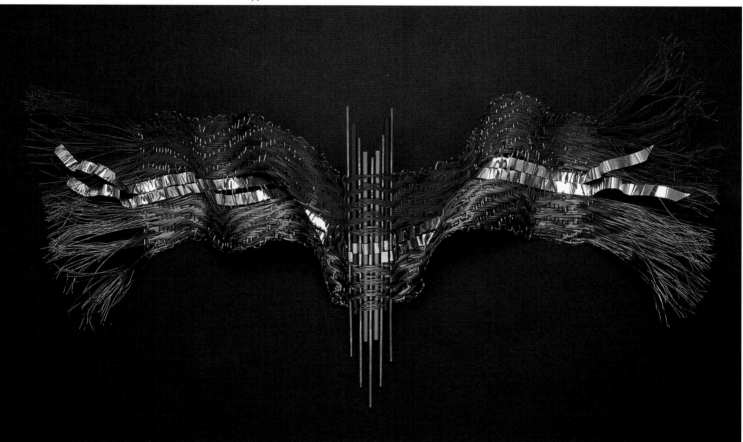

B

George Post

# James Mitchell

**Mitchell Sculpture**
**4564 West Mission Boulevard**
**Montclair, CA 91763**
**FAX 909-628-9923**
**TEL 909-590-0393**

Jim Mitchell's wall-mounted sculptures have
evolved from his much larger free-standing
work as the culmination of his desire to expand
the manipulation of three-dimensional sculptural
space. Materials are stainless steel, bronze and
aluminum. Many are painted in bright, emotional
colors. The careful attention to detail and design
creates a work of enduring quality to be enjoyed
for generations.

Photos, prices and references are available.

*Stainless Abstraction IV*, painted stainless steel, 32" x 60"

*Stainless Abstraction I*, painted stainless steel, 23" x 28"

*Bronze Abstraction IV*, bronze with patina, 23" x 28"

*Stainless Abstraction II*, painted stainless steel, 23" x 28"

*Stainless Abstraction VII*, painted stainless steel, 32" x 60"

# Pierre Riche

**Pierre Riche Art Enterprises**
**PO Box 736**
**Bearsville, NY 12409**
**TEL 914-679-5930**
**E-Mail: gvplan@bigfoot.com**

Designing a dazzling mirror for a client is what metal sculptor Pierre Riche does best. Whether spicing up a restaurant or reflecting on a new look for a home, these mirrors add life to any interior.

These completely unique works of functional art are available as shown here, or can illustrate scenes such as landscapes, horses, mermaids, angels, etc. Drawings and colors are approved before commissioning, and strong attention is paid to craftsmanship. Prices range from $350 to $1,500.

A  Floor mirror, 1996 residence, metal, 11" x 21" x 69"

B  Wall mirror, 1996 restaurant, metal, 2' x 4' x 2"

A

B

Photos: Larry Fine

# Kurt Shaw

**12 Coulter Street**
**Pittsburgh, PA 15205**
**FAX 412-922-5818**
**TEL  800-524-7429**
**E-Mail: kurtshaw@ix.netcom.com**

Kurt Shaw's intriguing works, made from painted sheet metal, are unique in color, depth and impact. Wall-hung sculptures make an impressive focal point in airy spaces and complement any type of environment.

Lightweight and easy to hang, Shaw's durable wall sculptures require only occasional dusting. Sizes range from small to architectural scale. The artist offers site-specific solutions for unusual spaces or special design needs.

To see more sculptures, plus paintings and collages, call for full-color catalog.

Also see these GUILD publications:
*Designer's Edition: 9, 10*

A  *Koan*, 60"H x 90"W x 9¹⁄₂"D

B  *Cycasin*, 19"H x 22"W x 6¹⁄₂"D

C  *Catalpa*, 44"H x 51"W x 9"D

D  *Deucalion*, 63"H x 28"W x 8³⁄₄"D

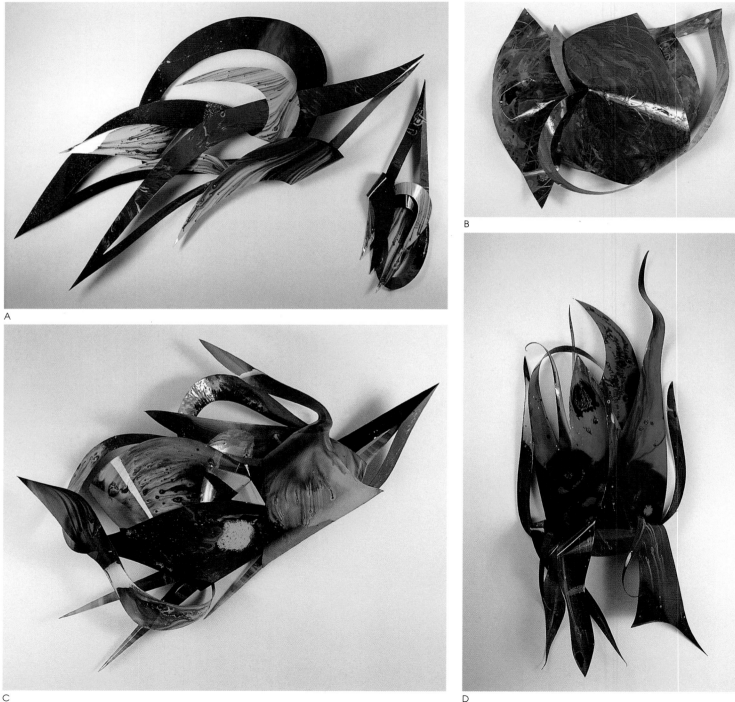

A

B

C

D

Printed in Hong Kong ©1997 THE GUILD: The Designer's Sourcebook

# GLASS

# Shawn Athari

**Shawn Athari's, Inc.**
**14332 Mulholland Drive**
**Los Angeles, CA 90077**
**FAX 888-886-MASK**
**TEL   310-476-0066**
**E-Mail: glassmaker@aol.com**

Shawn Athari's world in the glass field started in 1975, and it has given her the opportunity to perfect a variety of glass techniques. The combination of these techniques results in glass sculptures unique in her field. Athari has created a chronology of work depicting an ever-changing evolution of both her skills and techniques. She brings historical artifacts and contemporary images alive in a glass form.

Using ancient methods of taking molten glass and reforming it into desired shapes, Shawn simultaneously does color mixing, creating colors unique to her work.

Galleries include:
The Art of Disney, Walt Disney World, FL
Little Switzerland, AK
Pismo, Denver, CO
Neiman Marcus, selected stores

Also see these GUILD publications:
*THE GUILD: 5*
*Designer's Edition: 6, 7, 8, 9, 10, 11*

A  *Large Oars*, 40" x 12" x 4"

B  *Eagle Pole*, 21" x 43" x 5"

C  *Skidegate Pole*, 21" x 43" x 5"

A

B

C

# Shawn Athari

Shawn Athari's, Inc.
14332 Mulholland Drive
Los Angeles, CA 90077
FAX 888-886-MASK
TEL 310-476-0066
E-Mail: glassmaker@aol.com

A *Aleutian Oars*, these oars from the Bearing Strait are representative of those used in the late 1800s, 60" x 24" x 3"

B *Hokhokw*, Pacific Northwest bird of prey, 28" x 27" x 4"

C *Geeksam*, the original is thought to be the father of all totem poles, 15" x 33" x 5"

Photos: Robert W. Baumbach

# Deborah Goldhaft

**Fire & Ice Glass Studio**
**PO Box 2292**
**11933 SW Cove Road**
**Vashon Island, WA 98070**
**FAX 206-463-1859**
**TEL  206-463-3601**
**E-Mail: fireice@pdsnorth.com**
**http://www.psdnorth.com/~fireice**

Deborah Goldhaft's unique glass design work reflects her varied life experience. She incorporates elements of anthropology, Tai Chi, geometric design and Feng Shuei into all her work. Universal archetypes are her aim. Fifteen years of experience in glass art gives Deborah's work an extremely three-dimensional and visually satisfying feel.

Goldhaft offers custom designed art glass for the designer or architect who requires a unique and personal touch. Her specialities are double-sided deep carving and innovative use of etched mirror. She creates windows, tabletops, standing panels and sculptural pieces. Gallery work is also available.

The artist welcomes commissions and enjoys working personally with clients. More information is available upon request.

Also see this GUILD publication:
*Designer's Edition: 11*

A  *Sea Turtle Table*, carved blue and clear plate glass, brushed steel frame, 12" x 12"

B  *Plains Indian Choke Cherry*, carved plate glass, sash window, 4' x 3'

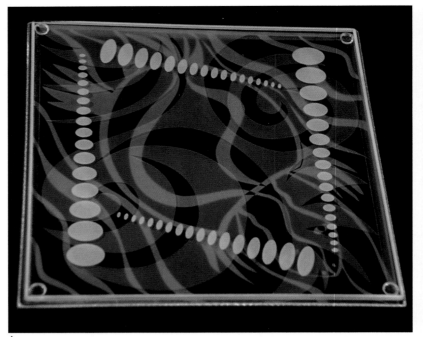

A

B

Springate Photography

# Charles Gray

14425 North 42nd Place
Phoenix, AZ 85032
FAX 602-493-7304
TEL  602-996-2319
E-Mail: artistgray@aol.com

. . . FOR MULTI-DIMENSIONAL SPATIAL
AND THEMATIC SOLUTIONS.

Also see these GUILD publications:
*Designer's Edition: 9*
*Architect's Edition: 11, 12*

A  *Still Waters Run* (detail and installation), GTE
collection, California, 97,000+ glass marbles,
14" x 66" x 3" and 9' x 66" x 3", with *Silent Gift of Curl,*
wall sculpture, custom acrylic hand rails, 20' x 9'

B  *Ode to Georgia O* (detail and installation),
GTE collection, 70,000+ glass marbles 9' x 9' x 9'

C  *Don's Thoughts* (three views), sound and ultraviolet-
activated light sculpture, AMC Theatres collection,
Florida, 24' x 4'

A

Dennis Tannen

B

Dennis Tannen

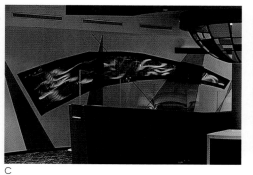

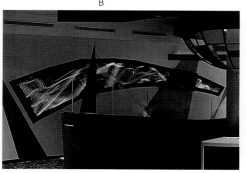

C

Mickey Adair

# THE GUILD REGISTER®
## of Glass Art for the Wall

**A.R.T. GLASS BY VICTORIA STREET**

VICTORIA STREET
5701 ANDREWS RD
MEDFORD, OR 97501
TEL 541-770-1141
FAX 541-770-2030
Established: 1980

**Products:** murals, lighting, wall reliefs **Techniques:** leaded or copper-foiled, painted or enameled, bent, fused or kiln-formed **Specialization:** stained and fused glass **Size Range:** no size limit **Price Range:** $500 to $5,000 for 2D, 3D stained, fused glass art pieces; $100 to $150/sq. ft.

**ABOUT FACE GLASS STUDIO**

SHELLY SZEKELY
317 OCEANO STE F
SANTA BARBARA, CA 93109
TEL 805-564-1806
E-Mail: dbrit@west.net
Established: 1994

**Products:** tiles, masks and fish **Techniques:** sandcarved or etched, bent, fused or kiln-formed, lamp worked beads **Specialization:** residential **Size Range:** 5" × 5" to 18" × 11" **Price Range:** $90 to $550 for fish, masks or tile

**ACACIA ART GLASS STUDIOS**

LUCINDA SHAW
3000 CHESTNUT AVE #336
BALTIMORE, MD 21211-2751
TEL 410-467-4038
FAX 410-366-6472
Established: 1980

**Products:** tiles, panels or screens, murals **Techniques:** leaded or copper-foiled, sandcarved or etched, beveled, painted or enameled, bent, fused or kiln-formed **Specialization:** liturgical, residential **Size Range:** 4" × 3" to 2' × 12.6' **Price Range:** $150 to $3,000 for murals, panels

**ALEXANDER STUDIO**

ALEXANDER V. MANDRADJIEV
12756 MOORPARK ST #204
STUDIO CITY, CA 91604
TEL 818-762-5598
FAX 818-762-5598
Established: 1978

**Products:** mosaics, murals, wall reliefs **Techniques:** painted or enameled, hand-cut smalti and glass **Specialization:** liturgical, residential, commercial **Size Range:** 12" × 16" to 3' × 21' **Price Range:** $340 and up for panels, etc.; $150 to $500/sq. ft.

**TOBEY ARCHER**

TOBEY ARCHER STUDIO
6521 SW 20TH ST
PLANTATION, FL 33317-5102
TEL 954-525-4344
FAX 954-525-4377
Established: 1978

**Products:** lighting, wall reliefs, neon and fiber optics **Techniques:** painted or enameled, neon, sculpted mixed media **Specialization:** public art and design **Size Range:** 18" × 18" to 125' × 50' **Price Range:** $1,200 to $300,000 for architectural art & design

**ARCHITECTURAL STAINED GLASS, INC.**

JEFF G. SMITH
PO BOX 9092
DALLAS, TX 75209
TEL 214-352-5050
FAX 214-827-5000
E-Mail: jeff_g_smith@acd.org
Established: 1977

**Products:** panels or screens, wall-mounted stained **Techniques:** sandcarved or etched, leaded or copper-foiled, mirror-lit stained glass **Specialization:** commercial, residential, religious **Size Range:** 48" × 48" to 15' × 72' **Price Range:** $74 to $140/sq. ft.

**ARTISTIC GLASS WORKS**

JACQUELINE GARDNER
313 1100 MEMORIAL AVE
THUNDER BAY, ON P7B 4A3
CANADA
TEL 807-344-1863
FAX 807-623-5122
Established: 1993

**Products:** glass, mirrored surfaces **Techniques:** sandcarved or etched, carved, airbrushed **Specialization:** residential, commercial **Size Range:** 1" × 1" to 8' × 6' **Price Range:** $500 to $2,000 for panels; $200 to $500/sq. ft.

**★ SHAWN ATHARI**

**SHAWN ATHARI'S, INC.**
**14332 MULHOLLAND DR**
**LOS ANGELES, CA 90077**
**TEL 310-476-0066**
**FAX 888-886-MASK**
**E-Mail: glassmaker@aol.com**
**Established: 1975**

**Products:** 3D glass sculpture **Techniques:** bent, fused or kiln-formed, cast, blown **Specialization:** commercial, residential **Size Range:** 13" × 9" to 4' × 2' **Price Range:** $800 and up

**See pages 114-115 for photographs and additional information.**

**JOHN BASSETT**

26 SEARLE AVE
BROOKLINE, MA 02146
TEL 617-739-1160
FAX 617-739-0288
Established: 1985

**Products:** panels or screens, mixed media **Techniques:** leaded or copper-foiled, painted or enameled, bent, fused or kiln-formed, slumped **Specialization:** recycled and found glass, carved pine **Size Range:** 12" × 9" to 7' × 3' **Price Range:** $300 to $3,000 for panels

**SANDRA C.Q. BERGÉR**

QUINTAL UNLIMITED
100 EL CAMINO REAL #202
BURLINGAME, CA 94010-5225
TEL 415-348-0310
FAX 415-340-0198
Established: 1980

**Products:** panels or screens, lighting, wall reliefs **Techniques:** leaded or copper-foiled, sandcarved or etched, laminated, cast, neon **Specialization:** commercial, public, residential **Size Range:** 40" × 20" **Price Range:** $150 to $400/sq. ft.

**LAURIE BIEZE**

BIEZE'S CITY CENTER GALLERY & STUDIO
216 S BARSTOW
EAU CLAIRE, WI 54701
TEL 715-833-0007
Established: 1963

**Products:** panels or screens, wall reliefs, sculpture **Techniques:** leaded or copper-foiled, sandcarved or etched, beveled **Specialization:** Art Nouveau **Size Range:** 30" × 23" to 13' × 25' **Price Range:** $120 to $240/sq. ft.

**JAY BLAZEK**

WESTERN NEON INC.
2700 1ST AVE S
SEATTLE, WA 98134
TEL 206-682-7738
FAX 206-682-8159
Established: 1989

**Products:** lighting, wall reliefs, free-standing sculpture **Techniques:** sandcarved or etched, painted or enameled, engraved, bent, fused or kiln-formed, neon **Specialization:** public, commercial sculpture **Size Range:** 6" × 3" to 20' × 10' **Price Range:** $400 to $250,000 for free-standing or wall sculpture; $20 to $200/sq. ft.

## ANNA CABO

2003 6TH ST
SANTA MONICA, CA 90405
TEL 310-450-1011
FAX 310-450-1011
Established: 1990

**Products:** tiles, panels or screens, murals **Techniques:** painted or enameled, bent, fused or kiln-formed **Specialization:** residential, commercial **Size Range:** 2" × 2" to 20" × 40" per tile **Price Range:** $300 and up for platters, panels, murals; $90 to $360/sq. ft.

## ★ ANDI CALLAHAN

**COYOTE STUDIO**
**76 ASPEN RD**
**PLACITAS, NM 87043**
**TEL 505-771-1117**
**FAX 505-771-1117**
**Established: 1987**

**Products:** tiles, platters, masks and figures **Techniques:** bent, fused or kiln-formed **Size Range:** 4" × 4" to 15" × 15" **Price Range:** $85 to $225 for platters, masks, figures

**See photograph this page and page 137.**

## JILL CASTY

JCD
494 ALVARADO ST
MONTEREY, CA 93940
TEL 408-649-0923
FAX 408-649-0713
Established: 1971

**Products:** murals, lighting, wall reliefs **Techniques:** sandcarved or etched, painted or enameled, bent, fused or kiln-formed, laminated, cast **Specialization:** commercial **Size Range:** 3' × 4' to 8' × 6' **Price Range:** $2,500 to $10,000 for wall reliefs

## CELESTIAL STAINED GLASS AND DAGAZ STUDIO

CYNTHIA BOOKER-BINGLER AND
ROGER BINGLER
PO BOX 43
SARGENTVILLE, ME 04673
TEL 207-359-2558
FAX 207-359-2558
**Products:** tiles, panels or screens, wall/furniture combo **Techniques:** leaded or copper-foiled, sandcarved or etched, beveled, bent, fused or kiln-formed, painted or enameled **Size Range:** 2' × 3' to 20' × 40' **Price Range:** $800 to $30,000 for murals

## CLASSICAL GLASS

DAVID DUFF
1333 MAIN ST
CINCINNATI, OH 45210
TEL 513-381-4334
Established: 1972

**Products:** panels or screens, lighting, clocks **Techniques:** leaded or copper-foiled, beveled, painted or enameled **Specialization:** Victorian to contemporary **Size Range:** 12" × 12" to 12' × 12' **Price Range:** $20 to $200/sq. ft.

## CRISTTLE GLASS

RICHARD CRISP
RT 3 BOX 178
SPRUCE PINE, NC 28777
TEL 704-765-5301
Established: 1989

**Products:** ornaments **Techniques:** blown **Size Range:** 3" to 18" Dia **Price Range:** $8.50 to $100 for ornaments, flowers

## CULTUS BAG GLASS

MEREDITH MACLEOD
7712 HELLMAN RD
CLINTON, WA 98236
TEL 360-579-3079
FAX 360-579-1060
Established: 1980

**Products:** tiles, mosaics, murals **Techniques:** painted or enameled, bent, fused or kiln-formed **Specialization:** commercial, residential **Size Range:** 1" × 1" to 8" × 8" tiles **Price Range:** $2 to $38 per individual tile; $28 to $432/sq. ft.

## CHAR AND KEVIN EAGLETON

118 W MARKET ST
MOUNT CARROLL, IL 61053
TEL 815-244-3554
Established: 1978

**Products:** tiles, lighting, wall reliefs, sculptures **Techniques:** sandcarved or etched, painted or enameled, bent, fused or kiln-formed, laminated, cast **Specialization:** residential **Size Range:** 10" × 8" to 8' × 4' **Price Range:** $500 to $700 for 24" × 24" wall relief

## THOMAS H. EMERSON

SANDMAN
166 S BROAD ST
MERIDEN, CT 06450
TEL 203-237-3216
FAX 203-237-3216
Established: 1978

**Products:** panels or screens, mirrors, windows **Techniques:** sandcarved or etched, painted or enameled, glue chip **Size Range:** 8" × 10" to 6' × 10' **Price Range:** $40 to $350/sq. ft.

## LONNIE FEATHER

1528 SE HOLGATE
PORTLAND, OR 97202
TEL 503-234-6642
Established: 1980

**Products:** panels or screens, murals **Techniques:** sandcarved or etched, painted or enameled, mixed media, collage **Specialization:** commercial **Size Range:** 16" × 12" to 10' × 10' **Price Range:** $1,000 to $30,000 for murals, panels; $100 to $300/sq. ft.

## KEVIN FULTON

KEVIN FULTON GLASS SCULPTOR
PO BOX 7033
BEND, OR 97708
TEL 541-382-8636
FAX 541-389-2031
Established: 1974

**Products:** murals, platters, wall reliefs **Techniques:** bent, fused or kiln-formed, cast, blown, lampwork **Size Range:** 12" × 12" to 5' × 15' **Price Range:** $250 to $15,000 for platters to large murals; $100 to $500/sq. ft.

## GIFTED ART

CHARLES DORKA
PO BOX 2573
MANSFIELD, OH 44906
TEL 800-575-5108
Established: 1995

**Products:** panels or screens, gallery windows **Techniques:** leaded or copper-foiled **Specialization:** residential **Size Range:** 10" × 8" to 6' × 3' **Price Range:** $80 to $2,500 for portable "gallery windows"; $150 to $250/sq. ft.

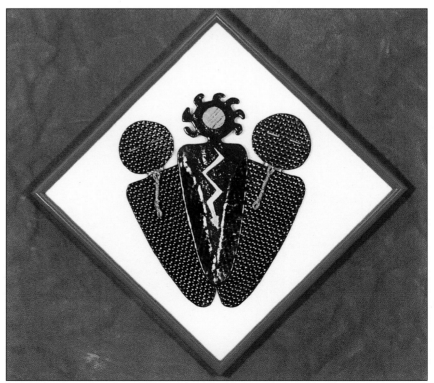

Andi Callahan, *Ancient Sisters Series*, 1997, fused glass, 16" × 16", photo: Charles Callahan Photography

# GLASS ART FOR THE WALL

## ★ DEBORAH GOLDHAFT

**FIRE & ICE GLASS STUDIO**
PO BOX 2292
11933 SW COVE RD
VASHON ISLAND, WA 98070
TEL 206-463-3601
FAX 206-463-1859
E-Mail: fireice@wolfenet.com
Established: 1991

**Products:** panels or screens, platters, mirrors **Techniques:** sandcarved or etched, double-sided deep carving **Specialization:** custom design **Size Range:** 8" × 10" to unlimited **Price Range:** $150 to $200/sq. ft.

See page 116 for photographs and additional information.

## NANCY GONG

GONG GLASS WORKS
42 PARKVIEW DR
ROCHESTER, NY 14625-1034
TEL 716-288-5520
FAX 716-288-2503
Established: 1979

**Products:** panels or screen, murals, tiles **Techniques:** leaded or copper-foiled, sandcarved or etched, painted or enameled, laminated **Specialization:** freestyle, geometric, abstract **Size Range:** no limit **Price Range:** $255 and up for large-scale architectural art; $100 and up/sq. ft.

## ★ CHARLES GRAY

14425 N 42ND PL
PHOENIX, AZ 85032-5403
TEL 602-996-2319
FAX 602-493-7304
E-Mail: artistgray@aol.com
Established: 1976

**Products:** panels or screens, lighting, wall reliefs **Techniques:** neon, marbles, UV responsive **Specialization:** site specific **Size Range:** 4' × 8' to 6' × 75' **Price Range:** $350 to $500/sq. ft.

See page 117 for photographs and additional information.

## ★ CAROLE HABERKORN

320 ISLAND WAY #112
CLEARWATER, FL 34630
TEL 813-796-5979
Established: 1980

**Products:** mosaics, murals, wall reliefs **Techniques:** painted or enameled, bent, fused or kiln-formed **Specialization:** residential, commercial **Size Range:** 10' × 12' to 7' × 25' **Price Range:** $25 to $6,000 for bas relief, sculpture; $60 to $125/sq. ft.

See photograph page 121.

## RICHARD HARNED

ABSTRACT GLASS
2723 BRANDON RD
UPPER ARLINGTON, OH 43221-3336
TEL 614-488-3688
Established: 1973

**Products:** panels or screens, lighting, wall reliefs **Techniques:** leaded or copper-foiled, sandcarved or etched, cast, blown, neon **Size Range:** 2' × 3' to 10' × 10' **Price Range:** $3,500 to $14,000 for sculpture relief, panels

## HAWKSTEAD STUDIOS

JOHN K. AND CYNTHIA RAY HAWK
4902 LONGFORD DR
RICHMOND, VA 23228
TEL 804-747-5305
FAX 804-747-5305

**Products:** panels or screens, clocks, mirrors **Techniques:** leaded or copper-foiled, stained, watercolors in glass **Size Range:** 8" × 10" to 4' × 8' **Price Range:** $225 to $5,000 for clocks, mirrors to panels and windows; $120 to $200/sq. ft.

## HEATHER GLASS

HEATHER ROBYN MATTHEWS
4401 B SOQUEL DR
SOQUEL, CA 95073
TEL 408-462-3231
FAX 408-462-2306
Established: 1980

**Products:** panels or screens, wall reliefs **Techniques:** sandcarved or etched **Size Range:** 6" × 6" to 96" × 144" **Price Range:** $150 to $400/sq. ft.

## HOLLY SOWLES FINE ARTS

HOLLY M. SOWLES
PO BOX 955
MARSING, ID 83639
TEL 208-896-5006
FAX 208-896-4071
Established: 1992

**Products:** panels or screens, wall reliefs **Techniques:** leaded or copper-foiled, painted or enameled, laminated **Specialization:** commercial, residential **Size Range:** 20" × 30" to 60" × 80" **Price Range:** $400 to $3,000 for wall reliefs

## HOT FLASH DESIGNS

BERNADETTE MAHFOOD
RR3 BOX 32
ST CHARLES, MN 55972
TEL 507-932-3913
Established: 1982

**Products:** tiles, murals, wall reliefs **Techniques:** laminated, sandcarved or etched, flameworked, kiln-formed **Size Range:** 6" × 6" to unlimited **Price Range:** $90 to $5,000 for wall reliefs and framed tile pieces; $100 to $500/sq. ft.

## SIDNEY R. HUTTER

HUTTER GLASS & LIGHT
PO BOX 1168
WALTHAM, MA 02254-1168
TEL 617-647-1923
FAX 617-891-8375
Established: 1979

**Products:** panels or screens, lighting, wall reliefs **Techniques:** sandcarved or etched, beveled, bent, fused or kiln-formed, laminated, cast **Specialization:** laminating **Size Range:** 12" × 12" to 6' × 6' **Price Range:** $3,000 to $20,000

## MARY LADAKH IEMOTO

MU STUDIOS
10208 148TH AVE SE
RENTON, WA 98059
TEL 206-277-9397
Established: 1980

**Products:** wall reliefs **Techniques:** bent, fused or kiln-formed, cast, pate de verre **Size Range:** 4" × 4" to 2' × 2' **Price Range:** $400 to $1,200 for wall reliefs

## KESSLER STUDIOS

BOB AND CINDY KESSLER
273 E BROADWAY
LOVELAND, OH 45140-3121
TEL 513-683-7500
FAX 513-683-7512
Established: 1980

**Products:** mosaics, stained glass **Techniques:** leaded or copper-foiled, sandcarved or etched, painted or enameled, bent, fused or kiln-formed, glass smalti, stone **Specialization:** all types **Size Range:** 4' × 3' to 7' × 30' **Price Range:** $100 to $200 for stained glass; $250 to $500/sq. ft.

## LILI LAKICH

LAKICH STUDIO
704 TRACTION AVE
LOS ANGELES, CA 90013-1814
TEL 213-620-8641
FAX 213-620-8904
Established: 1965

**Products:** neon bas relief sculpture **Techniques:** neon **Specialization:** corporate, private commissions **Size Range:** 24" × 24" to 25' × 85' **Price Range:** $2,750 to $125,000 for neon bas-relief sculpture

## LARANGER STUDIO

RAY AND KATHARYN LARANGER
299 SMADBECK AVE
CARMEL, NY 10512
TEL 914-225-6956
FAX 914-225-6956
Established: 1978

**Products:** panels or screens, mosaics, textural glass reliefs **Techniques:** leaded or copper-foiled, sandcarved or etched, beveled, painted or enameled, dalle de verre **Specialization:** corporate, residential, churches **Size Range:** 1' × 1' to 6' × 18' and up **Price Range:** $75 to $175/sq. ft.

## LINDA LICHTMAN

LICHTMAN STAINED GLASS
17 TUDOR ST
CAMBRIDGE, MA 02139
TEL 617-876-4660
FAX 617-354-1119
Established: 1976

**Products:** panels or screens, murals, glass paintings **Techniques:** painted or enameled, engraved, laminated, acid-etched **Specialization:** corporate, residential, public **Size Range:** 6" × 2" to 12' × 4' **Price Range:** $250 to $3,200 for panels; $150 to $450/sq. ft.

## R. MERCEDES LINDENOAK

PO BOX 18501
BOULDER, CO 80308-1501
TEL 303-545-8798
Established: 1984

**Products:** miniature tapestries **Techniques:** woven glass beads **Specialization:** residential **Size Range:** 6" × 6" to 24" × 30" **Price Range:** $600 to $4,000 for miniature wall-hung works

## MARVIN LIPOFSKY

MARVIN LIPOFSKY STUDIOS
1012 PARDEE ST
BERKELEY, CA 94710-2628
TEL 510-843-7593
FAX 510-843-7594
Established: 1962

**Products:** sculpture **Techniques:** blown **Price Range:** $6,000 to $25,000 for sculpture

## LONGHOUSE WORKS CUSTOM DESIGN GLASS

RICHARD PORTER
1417 OCTOBER WAY
MODESTO, CA 95358
TEL 209-544-2527
Established: 1985

**Products:** tiles, panels or screens, murals, columns, window overlays **Techniques:** sandcarved or etched, painted or enameled, engraved **Specialization:** commercial, residential **Size Range:** 12" × 12" to 8' × 4' **Price Range:** $100 to $1,000 for panels, partitions, overlays; $100 to $300/sq. ft.

## M.B.C. GLASS STUDIO INC.

HOWARD BOWEN
289A STONE SCHOOL HOUSE RD
BLOOMINGBURG, NY 12721
TEL 914-733-4501
FAX 914-733-4502
Established: 1980

**Products:** tiles, panels or screens, murals **Techniques:** leaded or copperfoiled, sandcarved or etched, laminated, cast, 'lifetile' kinetic murals **Specialization:** commercial, residential, liturgical **Size Range:** 4" × 4" to 8' × 20' **Price Range:** $500 to $50,000 for murals/panels; $75 to $350/sq. ft.

## BARBARA MALINOSKI

STAINED GLASS ARTWORKS
8634 BERTHA CT
MANASSAS, VA 22110-7008
TEL 703-330-5119
FAX 800-278-9757
Established: 1976

**Products:** tiles, panels or screens, lighting **Techniques:** leaded or copperfoiled, sandcarved or etched, painted or enameled, bent, fused or kiln-formed, lamp working **Specialization:** commercial, residential, liturgical **Size Range:** 4" × 4" to 48" × 64" **Price Range:** $55 to $145/sq. ft.

## CISSY MCCAA

MCCAA GLASS
PO BOX 5391
FULLERTON, CA 92635
TEL 714-256-1955
FAX 714-671-0608
Established: 1977

**Products:** tiles, wall reliefs **Techniques:** sandcarved or etched, beveled, painted or enameled, bent, fused or kiln-formed, laminated **Size Range:** 15" × 18" to unlimited **Price Range:** $500 to $25,000 for wall reliefs; $100 to $300/sq. ft.

## TOM MCQUAID

TOM MCQUAID GLASS
2005 ALAMEDA PADRE SERRA
SANTA BARBARA, CA 93103
TEL 805-569-2385
Established: 1977

**Products:** tiles, platters **Techniques:** bent, fused or kiln-formed **Size Range:** 4" × 4" to 11" × 17" **Price Range:** $150 to $300 for platters

## MELTDOWN GLASS ART & DESIGN INC.

B.J. KATZ AND MIES GRYBAITIS
1707 EAST WEBER #3
TEMPE, AZ 85281
TEL 602-894-3347
FAX 602-894-4058

**Products:** panels or screens, mosaics, doors, windows **Techniques:** painted or enameled, bent, fused or kiln-formed, cast, deep cast embossing **Specialization:** commercial, residential and liturgical **Size Range:** 10'5" × 5'5" **Price Range:** $150 to $450/sq. ft.

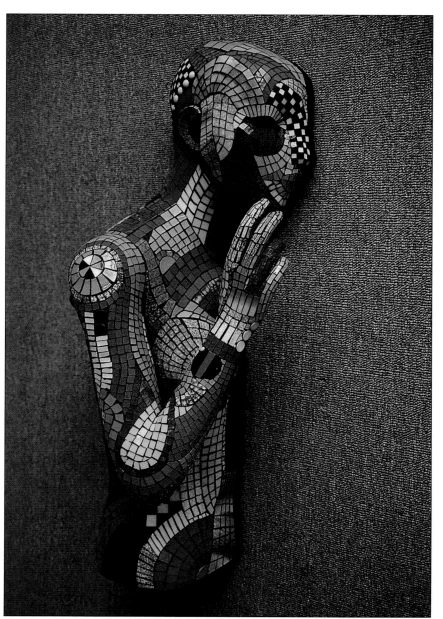

Carole Haberkorn, *She Is Time and Space Itself, High Voltage Goddess Series*, 1996, hand-cut glass mosaics, fused glass, fired lustres, 35"H × 14"W × 10"D

# GLASS ART FOR THE WALL

## THE NEON COMPANY

GREGG BRENNER
858 DEKALB AVE NE
ATLANTA, GA 30307
TEL 404-873-6366
FAX 404-584-6366

**Products:** lighting, signs **Techniques:** painted or enameled, bent, fused or kiln-formed, blown, neon, vinyl application **Specialization:** commercial, custom design **Size Range:** 12" × 12" and up **Price Range:** $200 to $30,000 for project

## ★ MARGARET OLDMAN

**ILLUMINATIONS**
**71 DELANO AVE**
**SAN FRANCISCO, CA 94112-2519**
**TEL 415-469-9789**
**FAX 415-586-8216**
**Established: 1981**

**Products:** panels or screens, illuminated wall pieces **Techniques:** sandcarved or etched, beveled **Specialization:** residential, commercial, corporate gifts **Size Range:** 2" × 2" to 8' × 10' **Price Range:** $150 to $350/sq. ft.

**See page 36 for photographs and additional information.**

Stained Glass Creations, angel fish wall mirror, 1997, stained glass, 15'' × 26'', photo: Taylor Dabney

## WILLIAM COREY PAISLEY

PAISLEY NEON GLASSWORK
650 W COOLIDGE ST
PHOENIX, AZ 85013
TEL 602-230-7857
FAX 602-230-7857
Established: 1987

**Products:** lighting **Techniques:** blown, neon **Specialization:** commercial **Size Range:** 16" × 20" and up **Price Range:** $625 to $50,000; $30 to $60/sq. ft.

## LESLIE PERLIS

LESLIE PERLIS STUDIO
955 CORNISH DR
SAN DIEGO, CA 92107
TEL 619-222-8776
Established: 1972

**Products:** tiles, panels or screens, platters, wall reliefs **Techniques:** bent, fused or kiln-formed, fused glass titanium **Specialization:** commercial, residential, religious **Size Range:** 6" × 6" to 10' × 10' **Price Range:** $100 to $300/sq. ft.

## QUILTS IN GLASS

BRINA B. MELEMED
15 MECHANIC ST #3
PROVINCETOWN, MA 02657
TEL 508-487-5810
FAX 508-487-5815
Established: 1986

**Products:** panels or screens **Techniques:** leaded or copper-foiled, beveled **Specialization:** traditional quilt designs in glass **Size Range:** 12" × 12" to 48" × 48" **Price Range:** $200 to $10,000 for panels or screens

## MAYA RADOCZY

CONTEMPORARY ART GLASS
PO BOX 31422
SEATTLE, WA 98103
TEL 206-527-5022
FAX 206-524-9226
Established: 1982

**Products:** panels or screens, wall pieces and screens **Techniques:** leaded, bent, fused or kiln-formed, laminated, pate de verre **Specialization:** corporate, public art, residential **Size Range:** 4' × 8' to 7' × 60' **Price Range:** $6,000 to $7,000 for 3' × 6' wall piece

## REFLECTIONS

DIANE TOOROIAN
7225 E SYLVANE DR
TUCSON, AZ 85710-5526
TEL 520-886-4063
Established: 1985

**Products:** panels or screens, mosaics, lighting **Techniques:** leaded or copper-foiled, sandcarved or etched, painted or enameled **Specialization:** residential **Size Range:** 18" × 12" to 8' × 4' **Price Range:** $80 to $250 for 3D work; $25 to $150/sq. ft.

## RHONDA'S STAINED GLASS WORKSHOP

RHONDA GEE
1825 BOWNESS RD NW
CALGARY, AB T2N 3K5
CANADA
TEL 403-283-1862

**Products:** panels or screens, murals, lighting **Techniques:** leaded or copper-foiled, beveled **Specialization:** residential **Size Range:** custom **Price Range:** $75 to $500/sq. ft.

## SUSAN RUSSELL

KRAATZ & RUSSELL
UPPER GRAFTON RD
RFD #1 BOX 320C
CANAAN, NH 03741
TEL 603-523-4289
Established: 1976

**Products:** panels or screens, murals, framed-glass plaques **Techniques:** leaded or copper-foiled, blown, decorated blown glass **Size Range:** 12" × 12" to 6' × 3' **Price Range:** $200 to $1,800 for panels; $100 to $400/sq. ft.

## SGO DESIGNER GLASS

DANIELA DIESEL
GARY PARKS
2268 EL CAMINO REAL
MOUNTAIN VIEW, CA 94040
TEL 415-964-4333
FAX 415-964-4032
Established: 1987

**Products:** panels or screens, windows, door inserts **Techniques:** leaded or copper-foiled, sandcarved or etched, beveled, laminated, overlay **Specialization:** custom art design **Size Range:** 1' × 1' to unlimited **Price Range:** $40 to $90/sq. ft.

## SCHAAK'S GLASS & ENGRAVING INC.

KURT J. SCHAAK
207 N MAIN ST
HARTFORD, WI 53027
TEL 800-950-7301
Established: 1986

**Products:** tiles, murals, wall reliefs **Techniques:** sandcarved or etched, engraved, laminated, cast, blown in 1996 **Specialization:** full-service studios/gallery **Size Range:** 6" × 6" to 7½' × 22' **Price Range:** $100 to $50,000 for sculpture; $35 to $300/sq. ft.

## HELLE SCHARLING-TODD

CONTEMPORARY GLASS AND
   MOSAICS
3219 PREBLE AVE
VENTURA, CA 93003
TEL 805-644-6884
FAX 805-644-6884
Established: 1967

**Products:** panels or screens, mosaics, murals **Techniques:** leaded or copper-foiled, sandcarved or etched, painted or enameled, dalle de verre **Specialization:** public art, residential **Size Range:** 1" × 1" to 15' × 15' **Price Range:** $150 to $300/sq. ft.

## JUDE SCHLOTZHAUER

GLASS WORKS
8370 DUSTY LN
MECHANICSVILLE, VA 23111
TEL 804-559-2582
Established: 1973

**Products:** panels or screens, murals, lighting **Techniques:** leaded or copper-foiled, painted or enameled, bent, fused or kiln-formed, pate de verre **Specialization:** custom interiors, private, public **Size Range:** 18" × 14" to 20' × 60' **Price Range:** $300 to $60,000 for mirrors, murals, lighting; $120 to $300/sq. ft.

## KATHRYN AND WALT SCHNABEL

4540 N CLAREMONT AVE
CHICAGO, IL 60625-2112
TEL 773-334-6829
FAX 773-334-6829
E-Mail: schnabe@mail.idt.net
Established: 1984

**Products:** panels or screens, mosaics, lightbox, installation **Techniques:** dalle de verre, hand cut glass & grouted **Specialization:** expressive storytelling designs **Size Range:** 8" × 10" to 6' × 6' **Price Range:** $115 to $165/sq. ft.

## SCHULKIND STUDIO

RIMA SCHULKIND
7412 NEVIS ROAD
BETHESDA, MD 20817-4740
TEL 301-229-2656
FAX 301-229-2656
Established: 1975

**Products:** panels or screens, wall reliefs **Techniques:** neon, assemblage **Specialization:** custom commissions **Size Range:** 30" × 40" to 50" × 150" **Price Range:** $10,000 for 4' × 12' diptych with neon; $150 to $200/sq. ft.

## CAROLE & DAN SCHUPP

ENAMELS, ETC.
2400 E BASELINE #20
APACHE JUNCTION, AZ 85219
TEL 602-982-5720
Established: 1983

**Products:** tiles, panels or screens, wall reliefs **Techniques:** enameled **Specialization:** impressionism art pieces **Size Range:** 6" × 4" to 20" × 12" **Price Range:** $200 to $1,800 for small tiles, multi-piece wall reliefs; $500 to $700/sq. ft.

## MARY SHAFFER

SHAFFER STUDIOS
10001 PRATT PL
SILVER SPRING, MD 20910
TEL 301-588-4388
Established: 1970

**Products:** columns, lighting, free-standing work **Techniques:** bent, fused or kiln-formed, laminated, cast, fiber optics **Specialization:** residential, commercial **Size Range:** 3" × 3" to 50' × 30' **Price Range:** $2,000 to $240,000 for site-specific sculpture; $400 to $1,000/sq. ft.

## ★ STAINED GLASS CREATIONS

**DIANE NAHAN**
**9505 COOL SPRING RD**
**MECHANICSVILLE, VA 23116**
**TEL 804-746-0585**
**FAX 804-746-0240**
**Established: 1979**

**Products:** panels or screens, mirrors **Techniques:** leaded or copper-foiled, beveled **Specialization:** residential **Size Range:** 21" × 12" and up **Price Range:** $85 and up for mirrors and panels; $55 and up/sq. ft.

See photograph page 122.

## WAYNE STRATTMAN

STRATTMAN DESIGN
791 TREMONT ST #E517
BOSTON, MA 02118
TEL 617-266-8821
FAX 617-266-6263
Established: 1983

**Products:** lighting **Techniques:** bent, fused or kiln-formed, neon **Specialization:** commercial **Size Range:** 12" to 12" to 10' × 50' **Price Range:** $200 to $5,000 for fused glass, neon panels; $100 to $300/sq. ft.

## THE 3 OF SWORDS

J.C. HOMOLA
RT 1 BOX 395
AVA, MO 65608
TEL 417-683-3460
FAX 800-282-4818
Established: 1976

**Products:** murals, platters, wall reliefs **Techniques:** sandcarved or etched, engraved, bent, fused or kiln-formed, laminated, lampworked **Size Range:** 13" Dia to 6' × 20' **Price Range:** $180 to $575 for platters, disks; $6 to $15/sq. ft.

## ★ ANGELIKA TRAYLOR

**100 POINCIANA DR**
**INDIAN HARBOUR BEACH, FL**
   **32937-4437**
**TEL 407-773-7640**
**FAX 407-779-3612**
**Established: 1980**

**Products:** panels or screens, lighting **Techniques:** leaded or copper-foiled, painted or enameled **Specialization:** residential **Size Range:** 15" × 20" to 6' × 48" **Price Range:** $1,000 to $8,000 for panels

See page 19 for photographs and additional information.

## FRED VARNEY

VARNEY STUDIOS
BOX 1293 RFD 1
MARSHFIELD, VT 05658-9501
TEL 802-456-7040
Established: 1975

**Products:** panels or screens, lighting, mirrors **Techniques:** leaded or copper-foiled, beveled, painted or enameled, bent, fused or kiln-formed **Size Range:** 12" × 12" and up **Price Range:** $50 to $300/sq. ft.

## WAWRYTKO STUDIOS

MARY FRANCES WAWRYTKO
1945 COLUMBUS RD
CLEVELAND, OH 44113-3540
TEL 216-696-4258
Established: 1975

**Products:** tiles, panels or screens, wall reliefs **Techniques:** painted or enameled, laminated, cast, pate de verre, cameo glass **Specialization:** interior, exterior, site specific **Size Range:** 6" × 6" to 6' × 8' **Price Range:** $250 to $750 for glass panels

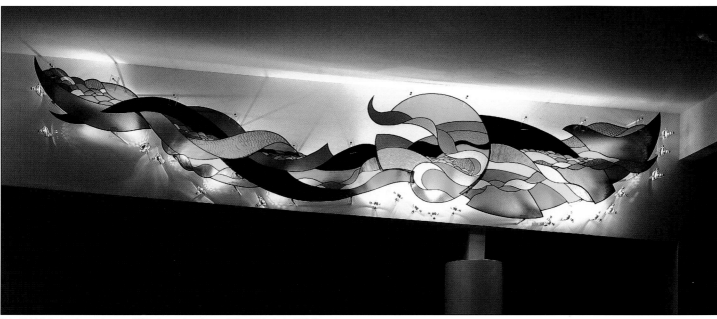

Brian Weidlich, *Acquiescent Journey*, 1996, glass wall sculpture, 15'L × 3'H, photo: M.S. Rezny

# GLASS ART FOR THE WALL

<table>
<tr><th colspan="3">LISTED ARTISTS work at a professional level in the area of glass art for the wall.</th></tr>
<tr><td>Established</td><td>The year the artist began working as a professional.</td><td rowspan="2">Can't find a certain artist?<br>Check the Index of Artists and Companies for a comprehensive listing of every artist in The Designer's Sourcebook 12.</td></tr>
<tr><td>Products</td><td>Types of glass art created by the artist for display on walls.</td></tr>
<tr><td>Techniques</td><td>Techniques typically used by the artist to create the work.</td><td rowspan="3">Need an artist for your project?<br>See the Commissions Clearinghouse on THE GUILD's Web site. List project specs. Artists respond directly.<br>Try it! http://www.guild.com</td></tr>
<tr><td>Size Range</td><td>Range of sizes for the artist's typical art for the wall.</td></tr>
<tr><td>Price Range</td><td>From lowest to highest, typical retail prices for the artist's glass art for the wall. Prices are reported per piece and/or per square foot.</td></tr>
</table>

## HELEN WEBBER

HELEN WEBBER DESIGNS
555 PACIFIC AVE
SAN FRANCISCO, CA 94133-4609
TEL 415-989-5521
FAX 415-989-5746
Established: 1972

**Products:** panels or screens, murals, stained, mirror glass **Techniques:** sandcarved, enameled, leaded, painted, etched leaded, painted, etched **Specialization:** hospitality, religious **Size Range:** 36" x 18" to 7½' x 16' **Price Range:** $100 to $200 and up/sq. ft.

## ★ BRIAN WEIDLICH

**WEIDLICH STUDIOS INC.**
**3385 BOSTON RD**
**LEXINGTON, KY 40503-4303**
**TEL 606-223-2166**
**Established: 1994**

**Products:** panels or screens, wall reliefs, 3D pedestal sculptures **Techniques:** leaded or copper-foiled, laminated, glass and steel **Specialization:** abstract **Size Range:** 42" x 12" to 42" x 15' **Price Range:** $500 to $25,000 for wall and pedestal sculptures

**See photograph page 123.**

## MARY B. WHITE

2327 5TH ST
BERKELEY, CA 94710
TEL 510-848-3932
FAX 510-848-3932
Established: 1975

**Products:** tiles, panels or screens, murals, wall reliefs **Techniques:** painted or enameled, bent, fused or kiln-formed **Specialization:** commercial, residential **Size Range:** 11" x 9" to 8' x 20' **Price Range:** $350 to $20,000 for murals; $100 to $800/sq. ft.

## WINTER GLAS

JOHN WINTER
5924 NW 30TH TERR
GAINESVILLE, FL 32653
TEL 904-335-7327
FAX 904-335-7327
Established: 1972

**Products:** tiles, lighting, wall reliefs **Techniques:** leaded or copper-foiled, sandcarved or etched, bent, fused or kiln-formed, pate de verre **Specialization:** sited residential, commercial **Size Range:** 1' x 1' to unlimited **Price Range:** $100 to $50,000 for sculptural reliefs; $45 to $225/sq. ft.

## WRIGHT'S STAINED GLASS & CUSTOM ART

CARL WRIGHT
330 WINCHESTER AVE
MARTINSBURG, WV 25401-2606
TEL 304-263-2502
Established: 1988

**Products:** mosaics, columns, room dividers, art furniture **Techniques:** leaded or copper-foiled, painted or enameled **Size Range:** 12" x 12" to 4'6" x 6'6" **Price Range:** $95 to $125/sq. ft.

## SCOTT ZOOG

STUDIO 113
991 TYLER ST #113
BENICIA, CA 94510
TEL 707-747-5216
Established: 1992

**Products:** tiles, panels or screens, lighting **Techniques:** bent, fused or kiln-formed, laminated, cast **Specialization:** residential **Size Range:** 1" x 2" to 20' x 6' **Price Range:** $100 to $1,000 for lighting; $50 to $300/sq. ft.

# CERAMICS

# Maureen Burns-Bowie

**9124 West Bush Lake Road**
**Bloomington, MN 55438**
**TEL   612-828-6078**

Dazzling and dramatic porcelain and glass sculptures dance with the light and add elegance and grace to a room. Organic forms are metaphors for psychological and spiritual growth and transformation.

Burns-Bowie has been an artist for over 20 years, and has developed unique tools and techniques to create her complex, unusual works. She has travelled extensively to study under numerous masters. Burns-Bowie has exhibited in universities, museums and galleries nationally and internationally. She is the recipient of prestigious awards, including a number of NEA grants, and is listed in several editions of *Who's Who*.

One-of-a-kind and limited-edition sculptures and fountains.

Commissions welcome

A *Snow Queen: Moonlight's Silent Dream*, freestanding sculpture, porcelain, glass, 24" x 21" x 11"

B *Persephone: Coral Goddess*, wall hanging, porcelain, glass, wood, 42" x 28" x 7"

C *Bold and Tender Daring*, wall hanging, porcelain, glass, wood, 32" x 55" x 12"

A

B

C

Photos: Jerry Mathiason

# Philip Bellomo

3710 Goret Road
Tucson, AZ 85745
TEL   520-743-0815

Twelve years ago, Philip Bellomo embarked on a creative journey that touched on his interest in light and shadow and Middle Eastern architecture. Moorish screens were the inspiration. By combining porcelain and the magic of reduction firing, Bellomo completed the dream.

Changing patterns of light and shadow delight the eye as the sun traces over the tiles' filigree. Both functional window coverings and room dividers are available. Research in Arabic tiles has provided a variety of three-dimensional designs and patterns. The style is Arabic; the mood is soothing and from a different time and distant place.

Photographs and price estimates available upon request.

A & C  Porcelain window, 2'10" x 8'10"

B  Porcelain window, 7'10" x 4'10"

A

B

C

David Burckhalter

# Asking the Right Questions

For Minneapolis artist Sheryl VanderPol, the creative process begins with conversation. Her first priority is to get to know the designers, homeowners and commercial-property owners who want to use her hand-painted ceramic tiles in their kitchens or bathrooms.

From those discussions, VanderPol comes up with a theme that is uniquely personal to the client — perhaps depicting an old family recipe in a kitchen mural, or incorporating favorite flowers in a bathroom sink surround. "People get excited when they realize they can put a little of themselves into the design," says VanderPol, who established her own company, Untapped Resource, six years ago. "Including that personal element is what makes my company unique."

VanderPol has also perfected the art of working long-distance with contractors and designers, as Oakland-based Capstone Cabinetry discovered when they contacted VanderPol recently. By asking the right questions about everything from plumbing fixtures to the appliances she'll have to work around — plus using local tile distributors — VanderPol can usually deliver her original art within three to six weeks.

"After six years of working at this, I've learned how to collaborate with contractors and designers so that things work smoothly and on time," VanderPol says.

**Artist:** Sheryl VanderPol
**Liaison:** Capstone Cabinetry, Oakland, CA
**Type of Work:** Hand-Painted Fruit Mural on Commercial Tile
**Site:** Private Residence, Oakland, CA

# George Fishman

103 NE 99th Street
Miami Shores, FL 33138
FAX 305-751-1770
TEL 305-758-1141
E-Mail: mosaics@bridge.net
http://www.bridge.net/~mosaics

George Fishman's mosaics are commissioned
for a range of commercial and residential settings.
Pictorial or abstract images are incorporated into
walls, floors, sculpture and fountains in classical or
contemporary styles.

*Deco Rugs* combines various materials and was
inserted into a travertine floor. *Theodora's Niche*
uses glass smalti for their richly textured sparkle.
*Clown Fish Medallion*, installed on a cruise ship,
was executed in unglazed porcelains, chosen
for their non-slip and wear-proof qualities.

Also see this GUILD publication:
*Designer's Edition: 10*

A  *Clown Fish Medallion*

B  *Theodora's Niche*

C  *Deco Rugs* (detail)

A

B

C

# Penelope Fleming

**7740 Washington Lane**
**Elkins Park, PA 19027**
**TEL 215-576-6830**

Penelope Fleming designs wall pieces for public spaces, corporate collections and residential environments. The primary material is slate incorporated with modulated black, white and colored clay. Scale and color are unlimited. Pieces are lightweight, easily shipped and installed.

Fleming has worked with many designers, art consultants and galleries for the last 20 years to meet the criteria of design integrity, budget and completion deadlines. Commissioned wall pieces have been installed for many corporations, including Smithe Kline Beckman, Reichhold Chemical Inc., and Ragu Food Inc., as well as private individuals across the U.S. and Europe. Call or write for a catalog, prices and the availability of already completed pieces.

A  *Between Leysin*, 66" x 44" x 4"

B  *Diablerets*, 54" x 44" x 8"

A

B

# Floro Flosi Ceramica

**Floro Flosi**
**5738 North Elston Avenue**
**Chicago, IL 60646**
**FAX 773-631-5688**
**TEL  773-631-2367**

Floro's hand-painted tiles have reached the front covers of *Better Homes and Gardens'* special interest publications. See *Country Kitchen Ideas* (Fall/Winter 1994) and *Kitchen and Bath Ideas* (Spring 1995).

Floro's tiles are literally his canvas, and his canvas becomes your masterpiece, whether painted on factory produced or his own hand-pounded, pressed and cut-to-size tile. Master workmanship and design are his trademark.

With over 10,000 existing designs, Floro's repertoire includes everything from fruit and vegetable baskets to flowers and portraits.

Floro's fully tailored price range will accommodate everyone's budget. Please allow four to eight weeks for delivery.

A *Mary's Little Lamb*, hand-pressed terra cotta tile, 6" x 6"

B *Good Morning Sweetheart*, hand-pounded terra cotta tile

A

B

Photos: Mary Heckman

# Carolyn Payne

**Payne Creations Tile**
4829 North Antioch Road
Kansas City, MO 64119
FAX 816-452-0070
TEL 816-452-8660
TEL 800-880-8660

Carolyn Payne, M. A., owner of Payne Creations Tile, is known for using manufactured tile as her canvas. Designers are impressed with the durability of Payne's artwork, and the ease with which it can be incorporated into their residential, commercial and public works projects.

Her expansive repertoire, designed for interior and exterior applications, includes historic landmarks, signage and murals, which can be applied directly to a surface or hung in panels for potential relocation.

Payne's golf line features signage and mural art to enhance residential and golf course developments.

Also see this GUILD publication
*Designer's Edition: 11*

A  *Back Nine*, 1996, 3¹/₂' x 2¹/₂'

B  *LaQuinta Mansion Fountain*, 1990, Bartlesville, OK

C  *Colorful Tee Marker*, 1996, 24" x 24"

D  *Contemplating the Shot*, 1996, 3¹/₂' x 2¹/₂'

A

B

C

D

# Stewart Specialty Tiles

**Dianne Stewart**
**2899 E. Big Beaver Road #238**
**Troy, MI 48084**
**FAX 810-680-8787**
**TEL 810-680-8453**

Dianne Stewart, owner of Stewart Specialty Tiles, creates unique specialty tile projects including custom-designed, hand-painted tiles and custom handcrafted tiles.

Known for the amount of detail in her work, and her rich, lustrous glazes, Stewart carefully hand paints each tile, bringing life and imagination to an unlimited number of designs. Her color palette is widely diversified, and when kiln-fired, the hand-painted tiles are easily washable and durable.

Also known for her creativity in custom handcrafted tiles, Stewart enjoys creating tiles of custom sizes, shapes and glazes for her clients. Intricate mosaics are among Stewart's specialties, including interlocking, handmade cobblestone shaped tiles, as shown below. Decorative bas-reliefs and custom field tiles are also available.

Visit her on the World Wide Web at:
http:// specialtytiles.com.

# THE GUILD REGISTER®
## *of Ceramic Art for the Wall*

**PAT ABI-SAAB**

SAAB CERAMIC
257 VAN DUYER ST PO BOX 40070
STATEN ISLAND, NY 10304-0002
TEL 718-448-7980
Established: 1989
**Products:** tiles, platters, wall reliefs
**Media:** stoneware, earthenware, inlaid colored clays, metal **Techniques:** cast, constructed, wheel thrown, metal **Size Range:** 8" × 8" to 15" × 24" **Price Range:** $350 to $5,000 for platters, disks; $55 to $280/sq. ft.

**CRISTINA ACOSTA**

CRISTINA ACOSTA DESIGN
PO BOX 923
BEND, OR 97709
TEL 541-388-5157
FAX 541-317-5586
E-Mail: cristina@cristina-acosta.com
Established: 1985
**Products:** tiles, murals **Media:** earthenware **Techniques:** molded, handpainted
**Price Range:** $3.25 to $22 for assorted trims and decos; $180 to $250/sq. ft.

**SUSAN AHLSTROM**

221 PLEASANT PLAINS RD
STIRLING, NJ 07980
TEL 908-580-1319
E-Mail: sujah@aol.com
Established: 1992
**Products:** tiles, wall reliefs **Media:** stoneware, earthenware **Techniques:** constructed, molded **Size Range:** 4" × 4" to 36' × 30' **Price Range:** $225 to $300/sq. ft.

★ **GEORGE ALEXANDER**

**HANDSEL GALLERY**
**112 DON GASPAR**
**SANTA FE, NM 87501**
**TEL 800-821-1261**
**FAX 505-989-9429**
**E-Mail: handselG@aol.com**
**Products:** panels or screens, columns, wall reliefs **Media:** stoneware **Techniques:** constructed, molded, wheel thrown **Size Range:** 12" × 12" to 8' × 8' **Price Range:** $2,000 and up for 3D work; $500 to $700/sq. ft.

**See photograph this page.**

**ALFREDO RATINOFF STUDIO**

ALFREDO RATINOFF
11908 WINTERTHUR LN #106
RESTON, VA 22091-1956
TEL 703-716-2931
Established: 1984
**Products:** tiles, murals, one-of-a-kind pottery **Media:** stoneware, porcelain, earthenware **Techniques:** constructed, wheel thrown, raku fired **Size Range:** 5" × 5" to 10' × 30' **Price Range:** $50 to $3,000 for one-of-a-kind pottery; $40 to $100/sq. ft.

**DALE ALLISON-HARTLEY**

DALE ALLISON-HARTLEY STUDIO
RT5 BOX 83 A
EMPORIA, KS 66801
TEL 316-279-4543
Established: 1976
**Products:** tiles, platters **Media:** stoneware, porcelain, earthenware **Techniques:** constructed, salt or sodium fired, raku fired **Size Range:** 4" × 4" to 2' × 3' **Price Range:** $100 to $1,500 for platters and mixed media clay on glass; $200 to $250/sq. ft.

**ANDERSON'S CERAMICS**

MARK D. ANDERSON
1404 DESCANSO AVE #N
SAN MARCOS, CA 92069
TEL 619-940-9114
E-Mail: mdanderson@aol.com
Established: 1982
**Products:** tiles, wall reliefs, architectural tile **Media:** stoneware **Techniques:** cast, molded, wheel thrown **Size Range:** 2" × 2" and up **Price Range:** $4 to $500 for custom architectural tile; $100 to $200/sq. ft.

**ANTICHITÁ MODERNA**

BARBARA PETRARCA
655 UTICA AVE
BOULDER, CO 80304
TEL 303-444-3626
FAX 303-449-8870
Established: 1993
**Products:** columns, wall reliefs, entryway surrounds **Media:** stoneware, glass, terra cotta **Techniques:** cast, salt or sodium fired, hand-sculpted **Size Range:** 4" × 4" to 20" × 15" **Price Range:** $150 to $400/sq. ft.

**ANTIOCH TILE CO.**

DEBORAH S. ZIMMER
PO BOX 118
1410 DEWITT HENRY DRIVE
BEEBE, AR 72012
TEL 501-882-2024
FAX 501-882-3952
Established: 1984
**Products:** tiles, murals **Media:** stoneware, earthenware **Techniques:** constructed, molded, impressed **Size Range:** 4" × 4" to 20" × 30" **Price Range:** $16 to $48/sq. ft.

**ARCHITILE**

TIFFANY SHERMAN
3109 BEANE DR
RALEIGH, NC 27604
TEL 919-876-2782
E-Mail: gsherman@mindspring.com
Established: 1995
**Products:** tiles, murals, fireplace facades **Media:** stoneware **Techniques:** constructed, molded, wheel thrown **Size Range:** 4" × 4" to 8'2" × 6'7" **Price Range:** $40 to $2,500 for wall murals; $28 to $60/sq. ft.

George Alexander, *Fragment from a Secret Garden*, 1996, stoneware and glaze, 53"H × 15"W × 7"D, $4,850

## ART ON TILES

RITA PAUL
32 WASHINGTON SQ W
NEW YORK, NY 10011-9194
TEL 212-674-6388
FAX 212-979-8373
Established: 1965
**Products:** tiles, panels or screens, murals
**Media:** stoneware, glazed, low-medium fired **Techniques:** constructed **Size Range:** 18" × 12" to 6' × 5' **Price Range:** $500 to $10,000 for murals; $70 to $100/sq. ft.

## ARTFIND TILE COMPANY

143 S MARKET ST
WOOSTER, OH 44691
TEL 330-264-7706
FAX 330-264-7709
**Products:** murals **Media:** white bisque tile **Techniques:** hand slip trail, hand paint **Size Range:** 6" × 6" to 14' × 8' **Price Range:** $28 to $14,000 for murals; $32 to $150/sq. ft.

## ARTISTIC LICENSE

GINIA CLEEVES
ANNE SANGUINETTI
1551 16 ST
SANTA MONICA, CA 90404-3308
TEL 310-453-0932
FAX 310-453-0804
Established: 1980
**Products:** tiles, murals **Price Range:** $7 to $15 for 6" × 6" or 8" × 8" tiles; $50 to $150/sq. ft.

## MELINDA ASHLEY

MELINA ASHLEY STUDIOS
144 MOODY ST BLDG 18
WALTHAM, MA 02154
TEL 617-891-8811
FAX 617-891-8811
Established: 1976
**Products:** tiles, murals, platters **Media:** stoneware, porcelain, earthenware, stained glass **Techniques:** cast, molded, wheel thrown **Size Range:** 2' × 2' to unlimited **Price Range:** $600 to unlimited for murals; $100 to $300/sq. ft.

## AUCIELLO STONE

SHLOMIT AND JOE AUCIELLO
1032 WOTTON MILL RD
WARREN, ME 04864
TEL 207-273-3065
Established: 1083
**Products:** tiles, wall reliefs **Media:** stone **Techniques:** carving, sandblasting **Size Range:** 12" × 12" to unlimited **Price Range:** $85 for 12" × 12" tile; $85/sq. ft.

## BAINBRIDGE TILE STUDIO

NANCY DEPKE
253 ONTARIO ST
OAK PARK, IL 60302
TEL 708-524-2874
Established: 1991
**Products:** tiles, mosaics, murals
**Media:** stoneware, earthenware, marble
**Techniques:** constructed, molded
**Price Range:** $50 to $300/sq. ft.

## ★ NANCY BARBER

**406 RENWICK ST**
**NEW YORK, NY 10013**
**TEL 212-741-8544**
**FAX 212-349-5852**
**Products:** tiles, panels or screens, murals **Media:** stoneware, earthenware **Techniques:** constructed, molded **Size Range:** 14" × 14" to 41" × 82" **Price Range:** $500 to $8,000 for wall pieces; $200 to $400/sq. ft.

**See photograph this page.**

## SALLY BARBIER

ALBERTA COLLEGE OF
ART & DESIGN
1407 14TH AVE NW
CALGARY, AB T2N 1M4
CANADA
TEL 403-277-4580
FAX 403-289-6682
Established: 1975
**Products:** wall reliefs **Media:** earthenware **Techniques:** constructed, glazed, sawdust fired **Size Range:** 20" × 20" to 35" × 35" **Price Range:** $400 to $800 for wall sculptures

## MARVIN BARTEL

1708 LINCOLNWAY E
GOSHEN, IN 46526-5022
TEL 219-533-0171
FAX 219-535-7660
Established: 1965
**Products:** tiles, wall reliefs, fireplace surfaces **Media:** stoneware, porcelain **Techniques:** constructed, wheel thrown, unique tile shapes **Size Range:** 6" × 6" to 8' × 12' **Price Range:** $1,000 to $15,000 for tile murals; $50 to $150/sq. ft.

## ★ BATIK TILE

**JOANNE GIGLIOTTI**
**69 BRALAN CT**
**GAITHERSBURG, MD 20877**
**TEL 888-MY BATIK**
**TEL 301-590-3050**
**FAX 301-990-0009**
**E-Mail:** batiktile@aol.com
**Established:** 1968
**Products:** tiles, murals, custom installations **Media:** earthenware, cuerda seca glazed **Techniques:** painted & printed surface **Size Range:** 1" × 6" and up **Price Range:** $50 to $400/sq. ft.

**See photograph page 136.**

## CHRISTOPHER BECKSTROM

103 READE ST FL 4
NEW YORK, NY 10013
TEL 212-732-0134
**Products:** tiles, lighted panels, 3-D constrctions **Media:** glass, wood, clay **Techniques:** cast, constructed, hand carved **Size Range:** 4" × 4" to unlimited **Price Range:** $50 to $500/sq. ft.

## BARBARA BEDESSEM

NORTHVIEW DESIGNS
544 STORLE AVE
BURLINGTON, WI 53105
TEL 414-763-6545
Established: 1970
**Products:** tiles, murals **Media:** commercial tile **Techniques:** custom painting **Size Range:** 4" × 4" to 4' × 4' **Price Range:** $3 to $20 for single tiles; $30 to $75/sq. ft.

## SUSAN BEERE

CERAMIC TILE ARTIST AND
SCULPTRESS
PO BOX 70
DEL MAR, CA 92014
TEL 619-942-9302
FAX 619-942-1702
Established: 1970
**Products:** tiles, murals, wall reliefs **Media:** ceramic **Techniques:** hand painted, sculpted **Price Range:** $250 and up for bas relief paintings and murals; $150 to $200/sq. ft.

## VICTORIA BELIVEAU

VICTORIA BELIVEAU TILES
RR1 BOX 198 C
JERICHO, VT 05465-9744
TEL 802-899-4543
FAX 802-899-4201
Established: 1988
**Products:** tiles, murals **Media:** earthenware **Techniques:** constructed, formed with leaves and flowers **Size Range:** 2" × 2" to 42" × 48" **Price Range:** $50 to $200/sq. ft.

## ★ PHILIP BELLOMO

**BELLOMO STUDIOS**
**3710 GORET RD**
**TUCSON, AZ 85745**
**TEL 520-743-0815**
**Established:** 1960
**Products:** tiles, panels or screens **Media:** porcelain **Techniques:** cast, molded **Size Range:** 2' × 3' to 10' × 4' **Price Range:** $150 to $350/sq. ft.

**See page 127 for photographs and additional information.**

## SIMI BERMAN

PO BOX 58
CHESTERFIELD, NH 03443-0058
TEL 603-256-8477
FAX 802-257-5119
Established: 1982
**Products:** wall reliefs **Media:** earthenware **Techniques:** constructed **Size Range:** 12" × 10" to 22" × 18" **Price Range:** $110 to $400 for wall sculpture

Nancy Barber, *Round About August* (detail), 1996, glazed terra cotta, overall: 41" × 41", each tile: 6" × 6", photo: Paul Waldman

# CERAMIC ART FOR THE WALL

## BESHEER ART TILE STUDIOS

KENNETH AND JACQUELINE BESHEER
PO BOX 10456
BEDFORD, NH 03110
TEL 603-472-5244
FAX 603-472-2021
Established: 1972
**Products:** tiles, scenic inserts **Media:** ceramic tile **Techniques:** handpainted raised enamel **Size Range:** 4" × 4" to 12" × 12" **Price Range:** $18 to $150 for raised enamel scenic tile; $50 to $200/sq. ft.

## BILL CART TILES, INC.

BILL CART
31 W 21ST ST
NEW YORK, NY 10010
TEL 212-724-7717
FAX 212-727-8566
**Products:** tiles, wall reliefs, trivets **Media:** earthenware **Techniques:** pressed, hand-glazed **Size Range:** 6" × 6" and up **Price Range:** $16 to $19 for trivets, tiles

Batik Tile, *The Dancing Palm* Series, hand-batiked directly on tile, various colors, prices and sizes, photo: Frank LaVelle

## SUSAN O. BLISS

JOPPA CLAYWORKS
114 JOPPA RD E
WARNER, NH 03278
TEL 603-456-3276
Established: 1975
**Products:** tiles, wall reliefs, mirrors, doorways **Media:** earthenware, terra cotta **Techniques:** burnished rolled clay **Size Range:** 2" × 2" to 60" × 30" **Price Range:** $300 to $900 for portrait wall tile; $100 to $300/sq. ft.

## GARY BLOOM

PEACOCK POTTERY
5024 RD 10 SOUTH
ALAMOSA, CO 81101
TEL 719-589-5369
Established: 1976
**Products:** tiles, mosaics, murals **Media:** stoneware, porcelain, earthenware **Techniques:** molded, wheel thrown, hand cut **Size Range:** 1'6" × 1'6" to 12' × 26' **Price Range:** $25 to $200/sq. ft.

## BLUE MOON CERAMIC TILE STUDIO

KATRINA WOLF
PO BOX 22-0964
HOLLYWOOD, FL 33022-0964
TEL 954-927-7900
Established: 1985
**Products:** tiles, murals **Media:** stoneware, porcelain, inlaid colored clays **Techniques:** constructed, molded **Size Range:** 2" × 2" to 10' × 10' **Price Range:** $7 to $25 for feature tiles and accessories; $22 to $44/sq. ft.

## SUSAN BOOMHOUWER

24035 CORMORANT LN
LAGUNA NIGUEL, CA 92677
TEL 714-362-3595
Established: 1978
**Products:** tiles, panels or screens, murals **Media:** stoneware, porcelain, earthenware **Techniques:** cast, constructed, molded **Size Range:** 18" × 18" to 15' × 25' **Price Range:** $75 to $200/sq. ft.

## LINDA BRENDLER

LINDA BRENDLER STUDIOS
428 HACKBERRY AVE
MODESTO, CA 95354
TEL 209-522-3534
Established: 1979
**Products:** murals, platters, wall reliefs **Media:** stoneware, porcelain **Techniques:** constructed, varied techniques **Size Range:** 10" × 30" to 4' × 6' **Price Range:** $150 to $5,000 for platters, wall reliefs

## CYNTHIA BRINGLE

BRINGLE POTTERY STUDIO
PENLAND SCHOOL RD
PENLAND, NC 28765-9999
TEL 704-765-0240
FAX 704-765-0240
Established: 1965
**Products:** murals, platters, wall reliefs **Media:** stoneware, raku fired **Techniques:** constructed, wheel thrown **Size Range:** 1' × 3' to 8' × 10' **Price Range:** $500 to $1,000 for platters; $250 to $600/sq. ft.

## HARRIET E. BRISSON

BRISSON STUDIO
31 POND ST PO BOX 85
REHOBOTH, MA 02769
TEL 508-252-3024
Established: 1955
**Products:** tiles, lighted panels **Media:** earthenware, stoneware **Techniques:** cast, constructed, raku fired **Size Range:** 6" × 6" to 32' × 32' **Price Range:** $100 to $5,000 for murals

## ★ MAUREEN BURNS-BOWIE

MAUREEN BURNS-BOWIE INC.
9124 W BUSH LAKE RD
BLOOMINGTON, MN 55438
TEL 612-828-6078
Established: 1975
**Products:** platters, wall reliefs, wall sculptures **Media:** porcelain, glass **Techniques:** constructed, molded, glass slump **Size Range:** 12" × 7" to 10' × 20' **Price Range:** $500 to $10,000 for wall sculptures

See page 126 for photographs and additional information.

## ANNA CABO

2003 6TH ST
SANTA MONICA, CA 90405
TEL 310-450-1011
FAX 310-450-1011
Established: 1990
**Products:** tiles, panels or screens, murals **Media:** glass **Size Range:** 2" × 2" to 40" × 20" **Price Range:** $330 and up for platters, panels, murals; $90 to $360/sq. ft.

## ★ ANDI CALLAHAN

COYOTE STUDIO
76 ASPEN RD
PLACITAS, NM 87043
TEL 505-771-1117
FAX 505-771-1117
Established: 1987
**Products:** platters, petroglyph figures **Media:** earthenware **Techniques:** constructed **Size Range:** 21" × 21" **Price Range:** $100 to $325 for platters

See photographs pages 119 and 137.

## ROBERT CARLSON
## MARILEE HALL

PRIMUS STUDIO
2350 BROWN'S MILL RD
COOKEVILLE, TN 38506
TEL 615-526-6649
Established: 1971

**Products:** platters, wall reliefs, vessels, sculpture **Media:** stoneware, earthenware, raku, pit fire **Techniques:** cast, constructed, wheel thrown **Size Range:** 10" × 10" to 20' × 30' **Price Range:** $450 for platters (23" to 24"Dia); $250/sq. ft.

## NANCY CARMAN

NANCY CARMAN STUDIO
330 EMILY ST
PHILADELPHIA, PA 19148-2624
TEL 215-389-7160
Established: 1974

**Products:** wall reliefs **Media:** earthenware **Techniques:** constructed, molded **Size Range:** 2' × 2' to 10' × 3' **Price Range:** $1,000 to $12,000 for wall reliefs

## MARY CARROLL

MARY CARROLL CERAMICS
3904 UPTON AVE S
MINNEAPOLIS, MN 55410
TEL 612-922-3914
Established: 1992

**Products:** tiles, mosaics, murals, mirrors **Media:** earthenware **Techniques:** cast, molded, hand built **Size Range:** 10" × 10" to 5' × 8' **Price Range:** $2,500 to $4,000 for commissioned mirrors, murals; $50 to $250/sq. ft.

## VAL CARROLL

VAL CARROLL ENTERPRISES, INC.
6040 SW 28 ST
MIAMI, FL 33155
TEL 305-661-1296
FAX 305-661-1296
Established: 1972

**Products:** mosaics, murals, wall reliefs **Media:** porcelain, glass, marble, mixed media **Techniques:** constructed **Size Range:** 12" × 12" to 150' × 350' **Price Range:** $20,000 to $100,000 for sculpture; $50 to $400/sq. ft.

## CASCADE DESIGN

DY WITT
1136 NITTANY CREST AVE
BELLEFONTE, PA 16823
TEL 800-473-9382
Established: 1985

**Products:** tiles, murals, wall reliefs **Media:** stoneware, porcelain, earthenware **Techniques:** constructed, hand painted **Size Range:** 4" × 4" to 32" × 56" **Price Range:** $10 to $25 for murals

## PATRICK TIMOTHY CAUGHY

20 SOMERSET RD
BALTIMORE, MD 21228-1938
TEL 410-744-8119
Established: 1986

**Products:** platters, wall reliefs, hand built vessels **Media:** stoneware **Techniques:** raku fired **Size Range:** 20" × 20" to 30" × 30" **Price Range:** $550 to $950 for individual pieces

## LYLAMAE T. CHEDSEY

2661 BAHAMAS WAY
GRAND JUNCTION, CO 81506
TEL 303-241-4579
Established: 1980

**Products:** mosaics, table or counter tops **Media:** glass, white clay **Techniques:** constructed hand-cut, fused-glass glaze **Size Range:** 7" × 5" to 3' × 3' **Price Range:** $75 to $1,000 for framed wall hung, table top

## COELHO STUDIOS

JACK M. NEULIST-COELHO
PO BOX 620
6135 W EVANS CREEK RD
ROGUE RIVER, OR 97537
TEL 541-582-0216
FAX 541-432-5109
Established: 1974

**Products:** murals, columns, wall reliefs, tiles, entryway surrounds **Media:** stoneware, porcelain, earthenware, mixed media **Techniques:** constructed, molded, wheel thrown, sculpted **Size Range:** 18" × 16" to unlimited scale **Price Range:** $500 to $10,000 for large, complex pieces

## LOUIS AND CHRISTINE COLOMBARINI

COSMIC CLAY STUDIO
8252 OLD MILL HILL RD
DOWELLTOWN, TN 37059
TEL 615-547-6476
Established: 1978

**Products:** murals, platters, wall reliefs **Media:** low-fired clay bodies **Techniques:** cast, constructed, wheel thrown, primitive fired **Size Range:** 13" × 13" to 12' × 12' **Price Range:** $450 and up for wall pillow series; $150 to $300/sq. ft.

## FRANK COLSON

COLSON SCHOOL OF ART, INC.
1666 HILLVIEW ST
SARASOTA, FL 34239
TEL 941-953-5892
FAX 941-953-5892
Established: 1960

**Products:** tiles, wall reliefs **Media:** stoneware, earthenware **Techniques:** constructed, molded, wheel thrown **Size Range:** 10" × 10" to 18' × 12' **Price Range:** $25 to $60 for mural composits; $35 to $60/sq. ft.

## RAY CONNORS

CUSTOM TILE CREATIONS
6449 WILLOW DR
HAMBURG, NY 14075
TEL 716-648-9742
Established: 1989

**Products:** tiles, mosaics, wall reliefs **Media:** stoneware, earthenware **Techniques:** constructed, molded **Size Range:** 4" × 8" to 16 1/2" × 32" **Price Range:** $500 to $5,000 for mosaics; $100 to $350/sq. ft.

## SUSAN CONWAY

FINE ART TILE
3381 KIHAPAI PLACE
PUKALANI, HI 96768-8813
TEL 808-572-5956
FAX 808-572-5956
Established: 1978

**Products:** tiles, murals, columns **Media:** ceramic tile **Techniques:** hand painted **Size Range:** 6" × 6" and up **Price Range:** $100 to $300/sq. ft.

## LAYAH N. COTTONWOOD
## HILDA HAROLD

UNITY! TILES
786 E RESERVE DR
KALISPELL, MT 59901
TEL 406-257-5056
FAX 406-755-7838
E-Mail: 2084117@mcimail.com
Established: 1976

**Products:** tiles, murals, wall reliefs **Media:** porcelain, earthenware **Techniques:** cast, constructed, molded **Size Range:** 4" × 4" and up **Price Range:** $18 to $175 for individual designer art tiles; $75 to $500/sq. ft.

## COUNTRY FLOORS

15 E 16TH ST
NEW YORK, NY 10003
TEL 212-627-8300
FAX 212-627-7742
**Products:** tiles, panels or screens, mosaics **Media:** earthenware, inlaid colored clays, etc. **Techniques:** molded, hand-painted

## DIANA CRAIN

DIANA CRAIN PORCELAINS
173 LIVE OAK DR
PETALUMA, CA 94952-1016
TEL 707-795-2451
FAX 707-795-2451
**Products:** wall reliefs wall vases and tables **Media:** porcelain, terra cotta, colored painted porcelain **Techniques:** constructed **Size Range:** 10" × 5" to 22" × 10" **Price Range:** $30 to $410 for wall vase

## LYNDA CURTIS

L. CURTIS DESIGNS
145 HUDSON ST
NEW YORK, NY 10013-2103
TEL 212-966-1720
FAX 212-966-1720
Established: 1991
**Products:** tiles, murals, furniture **Media:** stoneware **Techniques:** cast, constructed, molded **Size Range:** 4" × 4" to 7' × 15' **Price Range:** $10 to $20,000 for tile, custom murals and furniture; $35 to $300/sq. ft.

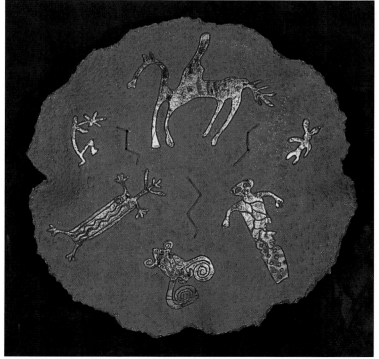

Andi Callahan, *Red Rock Platter*, 1997, micaceous clay and metallic leaf, approximately 20" × 20", photo: Charles Callahan

# CERAMIC ART FOR THE WALL

## DABBERT STUDIO

DAVE AND PAT DABBERT
3009 MAYFIELD WY
MICHIGAN CITY, IN 46360
TEL 219-879-7201
TEL 813-925-9929
Established: 1970
**Products:** tiles wall sculptures **Media:** porcelain **Techniques:** constructed, wheel thrown **Size Range:** 3.5" × 10" to unlimited **Price Range:** $200 to $300/sq. ft.

## PHILLIP DANZIG

GET CRACKIN'!
70 E 10TH ST
NEW YORK, NY 10003
TEL 212-674-3721
Established: 1970
**Products:** mosaics, murals, tiles **Media:** porcelain, stoneware, hand-cracked tile **Techniques:** constructed, shaped **Size Range:** 2' × 2' to 20' × 40' **Price Range:** $75 to $150/sq. ft.

## LYNN BLACKWELL DENTON

607 S 9TH ST
PHILADELPHIA, PA 19147
TEL 215-923-6192
Established: 1968
**Products:** tiles, mosaics, murals **Media:** stoneware, porcelain, earthenware **Techniques:** constructed **Size Range:** 3' × 4' to 10' × 30' **Price Range:** $2,000 to $25,000 for murals

## DESIGN TILES OF MIFFLINBURG

JOANNAH SKUCEK
508 CHESTNUT ST
MIFFLINBURG, PA 17844
TEL 717-966-3373
FAX 717-966-3128
Established: 1983
**Products:** tiles, murals **Media:** earthenware **Techniques:** molded **Size Range:** 3" × 3" to 12' × 12' **Price Range:** $50 to $2,000 for ceramic tile murals; $22 to $100/sq. ft.

## NELL DEVITT

NELL DEVITT POTTERY
RR3 BOX 84
BLOOMFIELD, IN 47424
TEL 812-384-3012
Established: 1985
**Products:** tiles, murals, wall reliefs **Media:** earthenware **Techniques:** constructed **Size Range:** 8" × 8" to 7' × 9' **Price Range:** $200 to $6,000 for clay tiles, murals

## JOE DIFIORE

ARCHITECTURAL TILE
8120 ROLL RD
E. AMHERST, NY 14051
TEL 716-688-9319
Established: 1991
**Products:** panels or screens, mosaics, wall reliefs, tables, mirrors **Media:** porcelain, glass, marble, ceramic **Techniques:** constructed **Size Range:** 12" × 12" and up **Price Range:** $200 and up for mosaic panels; $100 to $300/sq. ft.

## ERIC DOCTORS

CERAMIC TILES, VESSELS AND SCULPTURE
123 KEDZIE AVE
EVANSTON, IL 60202
TEL 708-864-4288
FAX 312-609-9839
Established: 1983
**Products:** panels or screens, tiles, murals **Media:** stoneware **Techniques:** slab built, scored **Size Range:** 4" × 4" to 6' × 10' **Price Range:** $40 to $120/sq. ft.

## DOCUMENTARY MURALS

ELAINE ODLAND CAIN
1559 DOROTHEA RD
LA HABRA HEIGHTS, CA 90631
TEL 310-691-4701
Established: 1976
**Products:** tiles, panels or screens, murals **Media:** earthenware **Size Range:** 8' × 8' to 12' × 12' **Price Range:** up to $100/sq. ft.

## LIBBY DONOHOE

LD TILE
124 WATTS ST
NEW YORK, NY 10013
TEL 212-941-5489
FAX 212-941-5489
Established: 1992
**Products:** tiles, mosaics, murals **Media:** stoneware **Techniques:** molded, hand cut **Price Range:** $50 to $150/sq. ft.

## STEVEN DONEGAN

915 SPRING GARDEN ST
PHILADELPHIA, PA 19123-2605
TEL 215-232-5459
FAX 215-232-5664
Established: 1976
**Products:** tiles, murals **Media:** earthenware **Techniques:** constructed **Size Range:** 31" × 22" to 11' × 12' **Price Range:** $250/sq. ft.

## MAUREEN ELLIS

ELLIS CERAMICS
3070 KERNER BLVD #N
SAN RAFAEL, CA 94901-5419
TEL 415-453-2116
FAX 415-485-4305
Established: 1980
**Products:** tiles, murals, platters **Media:** earthenware **Techniques:** constructed, molded **Size Range:** 4" × 4" to 30' × 500' **Price Range:** $5 to $500/sq. ft.

## MELANIE ENDERLE

HAND PAINTED ART TILES
8048 10TH AVE NW
SEATTLE, WA 98117
TEL 206-782-5982
FAX 206-782-5982
Established: 1990
**Products:** tiles, murals **Media:** stoneware **Techniques:** hand glazed **Price Range:** $8 to $15 for individual tiles; $100 to $130/sq. ft.

## RANDY FEIN

MOUNTAIN STUDIO
4163 YOUNGSTOWN RD
LINCOLNVILLE, ME 04849
TEL 207-763-3433
Established: 1975
**Products:** murals, columns, house portraits **Media:** clay, colored glass **Techniques:** constructed one-of-a-kind constructions **Size Range:** 24" × 24" to unlimited **Price Range:** $1,000 to $50,000 for relief sculpture installations

## JEROME FERRETTI

CUSTOM MASONRY
2000 BROOKLYN
DETROIT, MI 48226-1010
TEL 313-965-3697
Established: 1952
**Products:** panels or screens, murals, columns, fireplaces **Media:** brick **Techniques:** cast, constructed **Size Range:** 12" × 12" to 12' × 12' **Price Range:** $200 to $500/sq. ft.

## FINE ART TILE

STEVE EICHENBERGER
JACKIE HURLBERT
301 E COLUMBIA DR #23
NEWBERG, OR 97132
TEL 503-538-6030
FAX 503-538-6030
Established: 1977
**Products:** murals, hand made relief tile **Media:** stoneware **Techniques:** hand press molds **Size Range:** 2" × 2" to 1'6" × 3' **Price Range:** $7 to $900 for field tile and relief mural; $28 to $200/sq. ft.

## FIRECLAY TILE

PAUL BURNS
495 W JULIAN ST
SAN JOSE, CA 95110-2337
TEL 408-275-1182
FAX 408-275-1187
Established: 1986
**Products:** tiles **Media:** stoneware, porcelain, earthenware **Techniques:** molded **Size Range:** 1" × 1" to 12" × 12" **Price Range:** $6 to $20 for relief decorative tiles; $9 to $16/sq. ft.

## ★ GEORGE FISHMAN

103 NE 99TH ST
MIAMI SHORES, FL 33138
TEL 305-758-1141
FAX 305-751-1770
Established: 1986
**Products:** mosaics, murals, columns **Media:** porcelain, glass, glazed tile and stone **Techniques:** cast, constructed **Size Range:** 18" × 24" to 10' × 20' **Price Range:** $150 to $1,000 for cast mosaic plaques; $50 to $250/sq. ft.

See page 129 for photographs and additional information.

## ★ PENELOPE FLEMING

7740 WASHINGTON LN
ELKINS PARK, PA 19027
TEL 215-576-6830
Established: 1972
**Products:** wall reliefs, tiles **Media:** earthenware, stoneware, slate **Techniques:** constructed, raku fired **Size Range:** 12" × 12" to 96" × 170" **Price Range:** $400 to $20,000 for wall reliefs

See page 130 for photographs and additional information.

## ★ FLORO FLOSI CERAMICA

**FLORO FLOSI**
**5738 N ELSTON AVE**
**CHICAGO, IL 60646**
**TEL 773-631-2367**
**FAX 773-631-5688**
**Established: 1980**
**Products:** tiles, murals **Media:** porcelain, bisque tile **Techniques:** custom hand painted tile **Size Range:** 4¹/₄" × 4¹/₄" to 8' × 40' **Price Range:** $10 to $300/sq. ft.

See page 131 for photographs and additional information.

## DIANE E. FOULDS

PO BOX 117
BURLINGTON, VT 05402-0117
TEL 802-658-0900
FAX 802-658-0900
Established: 1991
**Products:** wall hangings **Media:** painted or enameled **Size Range:** 10" × 12" to 30" × 40" **Price Range:** $300 to $2,500 for wall hangings; $250 to $300/sq. ft.

## FOUR CORNERS TILES FEATURING TILES BY VOLATILE!™

ELENA EIDELBERG
916-A W 3RD ST
AUSTIN, TX 78703
TEL 512-320-0705
FAX 512-320-0705
Established: 1990
**Products:** tiles, mosaics, murals **Media:** stoneware, porcelain, earthenware **Techniques:** cast, constructed, molded **Size Range:** 6" × 6" to 20' × 20' **Price Range:** $15 to $20 for tiles; $65 to $125/sq. ft.

## FOX TILE STUDIO INC.

CATHERINE AND GARY FOX
5665 S VALLEY VIEW VISTA SUITE 3
LAS VEGAS, NV 89118
TEL 702-454-5776
**Products:** tiles, panels or screens, murals, columns, wall reliefs **Media:** stoneware, porcelain, earthenware **Techniques:** constructed, molded, raku fired **Size Range:** variable **Price Range:** $12 and up/sq. ft.

## ★ FRESH FISH CERAMIC TILE

**NORMA AND KIRSTEN HANLON**
**4728 ALDRICH AVE S**
**MINNEAPOLIS, MN 55409**
**TEL 612-824-3325**
**FAX 612-824-1235**
**Established: 1972**
**Products:** tiles **Media:** earthenware **Techniques:** constructed, molded **Size Range:** 3" × 3" to 10" × 10" **Price Range:** $3 to $50 for relief tiles; $25 to $100/sq. ft.

See photograph page 151.

## FULPER TILE

ANNE FULPER
BOX 373
YARDLEY, PA 19067
TEL 215-736-8512
Established: 1987
**Products:** tiles **Media:** stoneware **Techniques:** molded, extruded **Size Range:** 1" × 1" to 12" × 12" **Price Range:** $60 to $93/sq. ft.

## GIFTED ART

TOM BACHELDER
PO BOX 2573
MANSFIELD, OH 44906
TEL 800-575-5108
Established: 1995
**Products:** panels or screens, mosaics, mosaic furniture tops **Media:** porcelain **Techniques:** constructed **Size Range:** 5" × 7" to 2' × 8' **Price Range:** $40 to $4,600 for panels; $150 to $250/sq. ft.

## FRANK GIORGINI

GIORGINI DESIGN, UDU INC.
RT 67 BOX 126
FREEHOLD, NY 12431
TEL 518-634-2559
FAX 518-634-2488
Established: 1971
**Products:** tiles, murals, wall reliefs **Media:** stoneware, earthenware **Techniques:** constructed, salt or sodium fired, molded **Size Range:** 2" × 1" to 8' × 34' **Price Range:** $1,000 to $20,000 for wall plaques, murals; $100 to $400/sq. ft.

## ELIZABETH GRAJALES

ELIZABETH GRAJALES ARCHITECTURAL CERAMICS
667 CARROLL ST
BROOKLYN, NY 11215
TEL 718-857-0729
FAX 718-857-0729
Established: 1978
**Products:** tiles, mosaics, wall reliefs **Media:** stoneware, brick **Techniques:** constructed, molded, glazed **Size Range:** 8" × 8" to 15' × 15' **Price Range:** $200 to $400/sq. ft.

## MICHELLE GREGOR

812 E 24TH ST
OAKLAND, CA 94606
TEL 510-834-1324
Established: 1985
**Products:** wall reliefs, fireplace surrounds **Media:** stoneware **Techniques:** constructed, colored slips **Size Range:** 2' × 2' to 9' × 3' **Price Range:** $500 to $10,000 for sculpted wall reliefs, mostly figurative; $200 to $350/sq. ft.

## KAREN M. GUNDERMAN

11618 N COUNTRY LN
MEQUON, WI 53092
TEL 414-229-6351
FAX 414-229-6154
Established: 1975
**Products:** mosaics, murals, wall reliefs **Media:** earthenware, glass **Techniques:** constructed **Size Range:** 30" × 48" to 9' × 15' **Price Range:** $2,800 to $18,000 for murals

## PETER HALLADAY

PARADISE POTTERY
3374 J80 RD
HOTCHKISS, CO 81419
TEL 970-872-3461
Established: 1985
**Products:** tiles, murals, sinks, fountains **Media:** stoneware, earthenware **Techniques:** constructed, molded, wheel thrown **Size Range:** 4" × 4" and up **Price Range:** $125 and up for sinks and fountains; $50 to $200/sq. ft.

## LARRY HALVORSEN

LARRY HALVORSEN CERAMICS
335 NW 51
SEATTLE, WA 98107
TEL 206-781-1434
Established: 1981
**Products:** tiles, platters, wall reliefs **Media:** stoneware **Techniques:** constructed **Size Range:** 14" × 14" to unlimited **Price Range:** $75 to $125/sq. ft.

## KATHY A. HARRIS

5113 NEWHALL ST
PHILADELPHIA, PA 19144-4019
TEL 215-843-6959
Established: 1973
**Products:** tiles, mirror frames **Media:** stoneware, porcelain, earthenware **Techniques:** cast, molded **Size Range:** 2¹/₂" × 5¹/₄" to 3' × 4' **Price Range:** $150 to $1,000 for interlocking geometric tiles

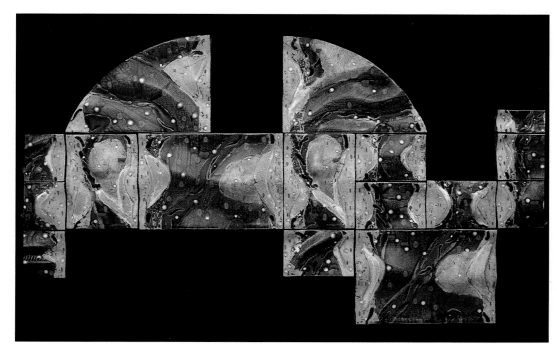

Beverlee Lehr, *Priscilla's Wall: 106 Seasons*, 1995, handbuilt stoneware, 48"H × 144"W × 3"D (shown: 72"W), photo: Socolow Photography

# CERAMIC ART FOR THE WALL

## ★ PHILLIP HARRIS

**ASH WORKS**
**PO BOX 275**
**WEST PARK, NY 12493**
**TEL 914-384-6396**
**Established: 1981**
**Products:** tiles, murals, wall reliefs **Media:** porcelain, stains, glazes, inlaid textures **Techniques:** constructed, slab built, oxidation **Size Range:** 12" × 12" to 16" × 16" **Price Range:** $95 to $225 for individual mural units; $95 to $150/sq. ft.

See photograph page 151.

## DEBORAH HECHT

CUSTOM DESIGN ON TILE
1865 HARVEST LN
BLOOMFIELD HILLS, MI 48302
TEL 810-333-2168
**Products:** tiles, murals, wall reliefs **Media:** stoneware, earthenware, overglaze painting **Techniques:** constructed, molded, opus sectile **Size Range:** 5" × 8" to 4' × 10' **Price Range:** $100 to $400/sq. ft.

## HEINZ KOSSLER ARCHITECTURAL CERAMICS

HEINZ KOSSLER
PO BOX 18525
ASHEVILLE, NC 28814-8525
TEL 704-252-4161
E-Mail: drtile@aol.com
Established: 1984
**Products:** tiles, platters, wall reliefs **Media:** stoneware, earthenware **Techniques:** constructed, molded, slab built **Size Range:** 6" × 6" to 10' × 15' **Price Range:** $20 to $500 for single tiles to wall platters; $25 to $500/sq. ft.

## HENNING PORCELAIN

MICHELLE M. HENNING
RR 1 BOX 620
HARPSWELL, ME 04079-9720
TEL 207-833-5556
FAX 207-833-5719
Established: 1989
**Products:** wall reliefs **Media:** porcelain **Techniques:** constructed **Size Range:** 2" × 1½" to 1' × 1' **Price Range:** $50 to $650 for wall reliefs

## GRETCHEN HEUGES
## MARGARET HEUGES

HEUGES TILES
RR 1 BOX 1020
SUGARLOAF, PA 18249
TEL 717-788-0628
**Products:** tiles, mosaics, wall reliefs **Media:** earthenware **Techniques:** constructed, molded **Size Range:** 4" × 4" to unlimited **Price Range:** $25 for hand-cast relief tile, 4" × 4"; $75 and up/sq. ft.

## HICKORY TREE STUDIO

WALT SCHMIDT
5745 N MURAT RD
BLOOMINGTON, IN 47408
TEL 812-332-9004
Established: 1972
**Products:** wall reliefs **Media:** stoneware **Techniques:** constructed, molded, wheel thrown **Size Range:** 3" × 5" to 10" × 14" **Price Range:** $40 to $80/sq. ft.

## CLAUDIA HOLLISTER

1314 NW IRVING ST #206
PORTLAND, OR 97209-2722
TEL 503-636-6684
FAX 503-226-0429
Established: 1980
**Products:** tiles, murals, wall reliefs **Media:** porcelain, inlaid colored clays **Techniques:** constructed, molded **Size Range:** 12" × 12" to 8' × 10' **Price Range:** $500 to $25,000 for wall constructions; $50 to $300/sq. ft.

## JERI HOLLISTER

801 AMHERST AVE
ANN ARBOR, MI 48105-1652
TEL 313-761-1971
FAX 313-747-4121
Established: 1987
**Products:** panels or screens, wall reliefs **Media:** earthenware **Techniques:** constructed **Size Range:** 18" × 12" to 60" × 72" **Price Range:** $500 to $5,000 for wall reliefs and free-standing panels

## SYLVIA HYMAN

OBJECTS IN CLAY
1112 PARK RIDGE DR
NASHVILLE, TN 32515
TEL 615-665-1143
Established: 1938
**Products:** tiles, panels or screens, wall reliefs **Media:** porcelain **Techniques:** constructed **Size Range:** 17" × 19" to 42" × 62" **Price Range:** $1,000 to $4,500 for irregularly shaped wall relief

## MARY LADAKH IEMOTO

MU STUDIOS
10208 148TH AVE SE
RENTON, WA 98059
TEL 206-277-0755
**Products:** murals, wall reliefs, sculpture **Media:** stoneware, earthenware, glass **Techniques:** cast, constructed, wood fired **Size Range:** 5" × 5" to 24" × 24" **Price Range:** $1,000 to $1,500 for wall reliefs

## ★ ILLAHE TILEWORKS

**SUE WERSCHKUL**
**695 MISTLETOE RD #E**
**ASHLAND, OR 97520**
**TEL 541-488-5072**
**FAX 541-488-2741**
**Established: 1974**
**Products:** tiles, murals, wall reliefs **Media:** stoneware, porcelain, inlaid colored clays **Techniques:** constructed, molded, pressed **Size Range:** 4" × 4" to murals **Price Range:** $15 to $100/sq. ft.

See photograph page 151.

## IMPRESSIONS IN CLAY

JUD RANDALL
8705 GARDNER RD #14
TAMPA, FL 33625-3714
TEL 813-920-2410
FAX 813-920-2410
Established: 1981
**Products:** tiles, wall reliefs **Media:** stoneware, earthenware, raku-fired **Techniques:** constructed, wheel thrown, raku fired **Size Range:** 2" × 1" to 10' × 10' **Price Range:** $100 and up for platters, tiles, wall reliefs; $20 to $45/sq. ft.

## INGERSOLL STUDIOS

MARJI AND TOM INGERSOLL
39040 S HIGHWAY ONE
GUALALA, CA 95445-0483
TEL 707-884-4602
E-Mail: mitile@intercoast.com
Established: 1990
**Products:** tiles, murals, platters **Media:** ceramics **Techniques:** constructed, slab, hand painted **Price Range:** $150 to $250 for platters; $125 to $350/sq. ft.

## JEFF IRWIN

JEFF IRWIN CERAMIC ART (STUDIO 1)
3594 3 AVE
SAN DIEGO, CA 92103
TEL 619-544-6420
Established: 1982
**Products:** tiles, platters, wall reliefs **Media:** stoneware, porcelain, earthenware **Techniques:** constructed, molded **Size Range:** 1' × 1' to 8' × 10' **Price Range:** $400 to $600 for 22" platter, hand drawn tiles; $200 to $300/sq. ft.

## J.E. JASEN

JUNE JASEN
36 E 10TH ST
NEW YORK, NY 10003-6219
TEL 212-674-6113
FAX 212-777-6375
Established: 1979
**Products:** tiles, murals, custom design **Media:** enamel **Techniques:** glass on metal **Size Range:** 4" × 4" to unlimited **Price Range:** $175 to $450/sq. ft.

## SHELLIE JACOBSON

RD2 GRANDVIEW RD
SKILLMAN, NJ 08558
TEL 609-466-3612
Established: 1978
**Products:** tiles, platters, wall reliefs **Media:** porcelain **Techniques:** constructed, hand built **Size Range:** 15.5 × 12.75 to 4'2" × 4'2" **Price Range:** $150 to $1,500 for wall reliefs, wall platters

## ANTHONY J. JEROSKI

A.J. DESIGNS INC.
PO BOX 576
MUNCIE, IN 47308-0576
TEL 317-287-1647
Established: 1988
**Products:** tiles, panels or screens, murals **Media:** stoneware, porcelain, mixed media **Techniques:** constructed, hand built **Size Range:** 18" × 10" to 10' × 18' **Price Range:** $150 to $25,000 for sculptural forms/murals

## JOCELYN STUDIO

JOCELYN GOLDMAN
39 OLD TOWN ST
EAST HADDAM, CT 06423
TEL 860-526-1581
Established: 1988
**Products:** tiles, platters, wall relief **Media:** stoneware, earthenware, inlaid colored clays **Techniques:** constructed, molded, raku fired **Size Range:** 4" × 4" to 4' × 4' **Price Range:** $8 to $50/sq. ft.

## TOVE B. JOHANSEN

6613 BRAWNER ST
MCLEAN, VA 22101
TEL 703-893-6728
Established: 1952
**Products:** tiles, panels or screens, mosaics, requests from architects **Media:** brick, refractory clay, marble **Techniques:** cast, constructed, molded **Size Range:** 2' × 3' to 12' × 54'

## JOHNSON POTTERY

LESLIE JOHNSON
745 RIVERSIDE DR
FREDERICTON, NB E3B 5W5
CANADA
TEL 506-455-2062
FAX 506-455-2062
E-Mail: johnsonpottery@msn.com
Established: 1992
**Products:** platters, mirror frames, clocks **Media:** stoneware **Techniques:** constructed, wheel thrown, hand built **Size Range:** 6" × 6" to 3' × 3' **Price Range:** $45 to $195 for mirrors, clocks and platters

## JULIE'S TROPICAL DREAMS

JULIE LEIMAN WEAVER
7101 BAY ST
ST PETE BEACH, FL 33706
TEL 813-367-4578
Established: 1983
**Products:** tiles, mosaics, wall reliefs **Media:** earthenware **Techniques:** cast, constructed **Size Range:** 5" × 5" to 8' × 8' **Price Range:** $175 to $450 for wall reliefs; $36 to $200/sq. ft.

## JACKLYN JURAS ARTIQUITIES

JACKLYN JURAS
627 CAROL VILLA DR
MONTGOMERY, AL 36109
TEL 334-273-0420
FAX 334-832-4449
Established: 1971
**Products:** panels or screens, platters, pottery ceramics **Media:** stoneware, porcelain, earthenware **Techniques:** constructed, molded, kiln **Size Range:** 7" × 6" to 6' × 6' **Price Range:** $35 to $2,200 for platters and vases; $25 to $75/sq. ft.

## SHERRY KARVER

4333 HOLDEN ST #54
EMERYVILLE, CA 94608
TEL 510-653-2524
FAX 510-428-2660
Established: 1980
**Products:** mosaics, murals, wall reliefs **Media:** ceramic, mixed media **Techniques:** constructed, painted, smoke fired **Size Range:** 2' × 2' to 10' to unlimited **Price Range:** $2,000 to $25,000 for wall reliefs, installation

## KATIA MCGUIRK TILE COMPANY

KATIA MCGUIRK
383 W OAKLAND AVE
DOYLESTOWN, PA 18901
TEL 215-348-1562
**Products:** tiles **Media:** earthenware **Techniques:** molded, hand pressed **Size Range:** 2" × 2" to 12" × 12" **Price Range:** $10 to $90 for individual tiles; $54 to $250/sq. ft.

## STEVEN AND SUSAN KEMENYFFY

SWIFT CREEK POTTERY & PRESS
4570 OLD STATE RD
MCKEAN, PA 16426-2239
TEL 814-734-4421
FAX 814-734-4736
Established: 1967
**Products:** tiles, murals, wall reliefs **Media:** raku **Techniques:** constructed raku fired **Size Range:** 7" × 7" to 11' × 12' **Price Range:** $1,500 to $9,000 for wall reliefs, sculpture

## DOUGLAS KENNEY

DOUGLAS KENNEY CERAMICS
700 BOND AVE
SANTA BARBARA, CA 93103
TEL 805-962-3666
FAX 805-962-3666
Established: 1987
**Products:** tiles, platters, wall reliefs **Media:** stoneware, porcelain, earthenware **Techniques:** constructed, molded, wheel thrown **Size Range:** 12" × 12" to 6' × 4' **Price Range:** $150 to $3,400 for platters; $80 to $250/sq. ft.

## KEPPERS POTTERY

KEN KEPPERS
235 US HWY 8
TURTLE LAKE, WI 54889-9110
TEL 715-986-4322
Established: 1975
**Products:** tiles, platters **Media:** stoneware, porcelain **Techniques:** wheel thrown, wood fired **Price Range:** $75 and up for platters; $18 to $24/sq. ft.

## STEPHEN KNAPP

74 COMMODORE RD
WORCESTER, MA 01602-2727
TEL 508-757-2507
FAX 508-797-3228
Established: 1972
**Products:** mosaics, murals, wall reliefs **Media:** glass, inlaid colored clays **Techniques:** mosaics, over-glazed tile **Size Range:** 4' × 8' to 9' × 38' **Price Range:** $200 to $700/sq. ft.

## ★ KŌP DESIGNS

**RODNEY AND LISA COOPER**
**9910 MELROSE**
**LIVONIA, MI 48150-2824**
**TEL 313-917-9006**
**Established: 1995**
**Products:** tiles, mosaics, wall reliefs **Media:** stoneware, earthenware, colored glaze **Techniques:** constructed, molded, hand sculpted **Size Range:** various **Price Range:** $35 and up for existing designs

**See photograph page 151.**

## KRISTENSEN STUDIO

GAIL KRISTENSEN
360 CATHEDRAL ROCK TR
SEDONA, AZ 86336
TEL 520-282-2448
Established: 1960
**Products:** wall reliefs **Media:** stoneware, porcelain, glass **Techniques:** constructed, hand construction **Size Range:** 12" × 12" to 6' × 40' **Price Range:** variable/sq. ft.

## KRYSIA

KRYSIA STRONSKI
1360 LUCERNE
MONTREAL, QB H3R 2H9
CANADA
TEL 514-731-0234
Established: 1985
**Products:** panels or screens, murals, wall reliefs **Media:** stoneware, earthenware, paper clay **Techniques:** cast, constructed, wheel thrown **Size Range:** 1' × 1' to 8'× 1' **Price Range:** $150 to $1,500 for panel; $30 to $100/sq. ft.

## L'ESPERANCE TILE

LINDA ELLETT
237 SHERIDAN AVE
ALBANY, NY 12210
TEL 518-465-5586
FAX 518-465-6563
Established: 1954
**Products:** tiles, mosaics, wall reliefs **Media:** porcelain, earthenware, inlaid colored clays **Techniques:** constructed, molded, hand pressed **Size Range:** 4" × 4" to 6" × 6" **Price Range:** $22 to $300/sq. ft.

Christine Merriman, *Lily Pond*, three-piece fireplace screen, raku-fired, 48"H × 48"W

# CERAMIC ART FOR THE WALL

## LA LUZ CANYON STUDIO

JERRY WELLMAN
NINA MASTRANGELO
PO 10627
ALAMEDA, MN 87184
TEL 505-899-9977
FAX 505-898-8819
Established: 1982
**Products:** tiles, murals, full-room design **Media:** stoneware, porcelain, earthenware **Techniques:** handpainted, glazed **Size Range:** 4.25" × 4.25" to unlimited **Price Range:** $3.50 to $30 for individual tiles; $30 to $270/sq. ft.

## JANE WARREN LARSON

LARSON CERAMICS
6514 BRADLEY BLVD
BETHESDA, MD 20817-3248
TEL 301-365-0686
Established: 1982
**Products:** tiles, murals, columns **Media:** stoneware **Techniques:** constructed, variable reduction **Size Range:** 10" × 10" to 8' × 20' **Price Range:** $80 to $16,000 for mural; $100 to $200/sq. ft.

## LATKA STUDIOS

TOM AND JEAN LATKA
229 MIDWAY AVE
PUEBLO, CO 81004-1912
TEL 710-543-0720
Established: 1965
**Products:** tiles, mosaics, murals, custom extruded clay **Media:** stoneware, earthenware, brick, bronze **Techniques:** constructed, molded, wheel thrown, extruded molding **Size Range:** 1' × 1' to 8' × 8' **Price Range:** $100 to $300, for wall work; $100 to $300 for murals/sq. ft.

## PATRICIA LAY

77 GRAND ST
JERSEY CITY, NJ 07302-4521
TEL 201-333-5437
Established: 1968
**Products:** tiles, murals, wall reliefs **Media:** stoneware, earthenware **Techniques:** cast, constructed, molded **Size Range:** 12" × 12" to 12' × 40' **Price Range:** $300 to $800/sq. ft.

## DEIRDRE LEE

URBAN JUNGLE ART AND DESIGN
244 W BROOKES AVE
SAN DIEGO, CA 92103-4810
TEL 619-299-1644
FAX 619-296-1570
Established: 1971
**Products:** tiles, murals **Media:** ceramic **Techniques:** constructed, molded, reduction fired, hand painted **Size Range:** 6" × 18" and up **Price Range:** $100 and up for murals and borders; $50 to $80/sq. ft.

## ★ BEVERLEE LEHR

**BEVERLEE LEHR CERAMIC SCULPTURE
RR 2 BOX 112
PALMYRA, PA 17078-9711
TEL 717-838-4937
FAX 717-838-6428
Established: 1973
Products:** wall reliefs **Media:** stoneware **Techniques:** molded, hand built **Size Range:** 24" × 36" to 8' × 6' **Price Range:** $200 to $350/sq. ft.

**See photograph page 139.**

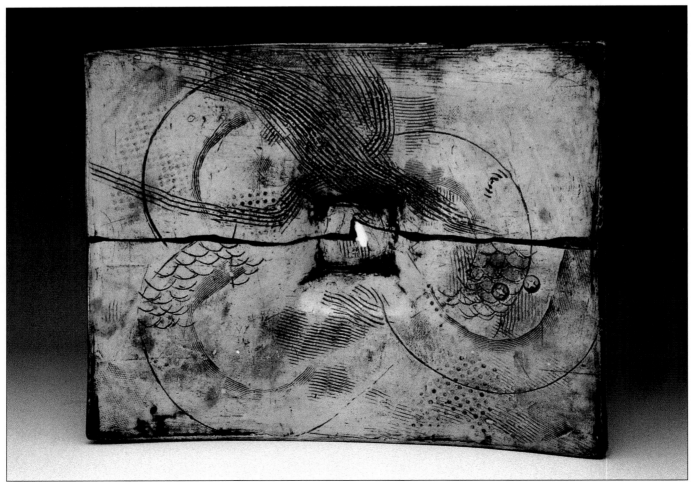

Alena Ort, *Butterfly*, 1994, hand-built stoneware with oxides, 10" × 8" × 2", photo: Theresa A. Schwiendt

## LEUTHOLD CERAMICS

MARC LEUTHOLD
355 CENTRAL PARK WEST
NEW YORK, NY 10025
TEL 212-222-0923
Established: 1988
**Products:** tiles, murals, wall reliefs, sculptures **Media:** stoneware, porcelain, glass **Techniques:** molded, carved ceramics **Size Range:** 2" × 2" to 100" × 200" **Price Range:** $500 to $5,000 for sculptures, one-of-a-kind; $200 to $1,000/sq. ft.

## LIQUID SKY MARBLED TILE

KRISTYN A. WOODLAND
JAMES D. CURRIER
15 DENNISON ST
NEWPORT, RI 02840
TEL 401-847-7018
FAX 401-846-7878
**Products:** tiles, decorative tile **Media:** earthenware **Techniques:** marbling **Size Range:** 4¹/₄" × 4¹/₄" to 12" × 12" **Price Range:** $6 to $150 for individual tile; $54 to $150/sq. ft.

## THOMAS W. LOLLAR

50 W 106TH ST #2A
NEW YORK, NY 10025-3888
TEL 212-362-9117
Established: 1979
**Products:** tiles, panels or screens, murals **Media:** stoneware, earthenware **Techniques:** constructed, slab, bas relief **Size Range:** 24" × 22" to 10' × 10' **Price Range:** $10,000 to $15,000 for 5' × 12' murals; $300 to $500/sq. ft.

## HAROLYN LONG

2115 N BROOKHAVEN DR
EDMOND, OK 73034
TEL 405-348-2205
Established: 1985
**Products:** tiles, wall reliefs **Media:** stoneware **Techniques:** raku fired **Size Range:** 39" × 32" to 12" × 12" **Price Range:** $60 to $750 for wall reliefs

## LUTZ CUSTOM TILE

TERRI LUTZ
12715 133RD AVE E
PUYALLUP, WA 98374
TEL 206-840-5011
FAX 206-840-8545
Established: 1987
**Products:** tiles, mosaics, wall reliefs **Media:** ceramic **Techniques:** molded, pressed **Size Range:** ¹/₂" × ¹/₂" to 16' × 8' **Price Range:** $10 to $42 for molded relief tiles

## ★ ELIZABETH MACDONALD

**BOX 186**
**BRIDGEWATER, CT 06752**
**TEL 860-354-0594**
**FAX 860-350-4052**
**Established: 1972**
**Products:** tiles, murals, wall reliefs **Media:** stoneware **Techniques:** constructed **Size Range:** 8" × 8" to 14' × 72' **Price Range:** $200 to $250/sq. ft.

**See page 152 for photographs and additional information.**

## MARGIE HUGHTO STUDIO

MARGIE HUGHTO
6970 HENDERSON RD
JAMESVILLE, NY 13078
TEL 315-469-8775
Established: 1971
**Products:** tiles, murals **Media:** stoneware, earthenware, inlaid colored clays **Techniques:** constructed, molded **Size Range:** 12" × 12" to 32' × 40' **Price Range:** $3,000 to $100,000 for ceramic tile murals; $300 to $500/sq. ft.

## MARLO BARTELS ARCHITECTURAL CERAMICS

MARLO BARTELS
2307 #7 LAGUNA CANYON RD
LAGUNA BEACH, CA 92651
TEL 714-494-4408
FAX 714-497-0400
ESTABLISHED: 1979
**Products:** tiles, mosaics, murals **Media:** stoneware, earthenware, ceramic/ferro cement **Techniques:** constructed, wheel thrown, custom installation **Size Range:** any size **Price Range:** $40 to $140 for architectural installation; $40 to $140/sq. ft.

## JULIE MATTHEWS

JULIE MATTHEWS STUDIO
131 W KLATT RD
ANCHORAGE, AK 99515
TEL 907-344-2529
FAX 907-344-2529
Established: 1978
**Products:** tiles, murals, columns **Media:** stoneware, porcelain, earthenware **Techniques:** constructed, raku fired **Size Range:** 4" × 4" to 9' × 40' **Price Range:** $1,000 to $25,000 for murals, site specific installation; $100 to $300/sq. ft.

## E. JOSEPH MCCARTHY

CUSTOM TILE STUDIO
39 ELEVENTH ST
TURNERS FALLS, MA 01376
TEL 413-863-3121
FAX 413-863-4913
Established: 1980
**Products:** tiles, murals **Media:** ceramic tile **Techniques:** hand painted **Size Range:** single tiles to large-scale murals **Price Range:** $50 to $200/sq. ft.

## DONNA MCGEE

47 EAST ST
HADLEY, MA 01035
TEL 413-584-0508
Established: 1978
**Products:** tiles, murals, platters **Media:** earthenware **Techniques:** constructed **Size Range:** 19" × 12" to unlimited **Price Range:** $85 and up for plaques, platters, murals

## ★ ELSBETH C. MCLEOD

**MAGUS STUDIOS**
**1934 PTARMIGAN LN NW**
**POULSBO, WA 98370**
**TEL 360-697-6557**
**Established: 1971**
**Products:** murals, wall reliefs **Media:** stoneware **Techniques:** constructed **Size Range:** 1' × 1' to 10' × 10' **Price Range:** $120 to $100,000 for wall reliefs and murals

**See page 53 for photographs and additional information.**

## SUZANNE WALLACE MEARS

GREEN ELK RANCH STUDIO
3690 M 50 ROAD
HOTCHKISS, CO 81419
TEL 970-527-5575
Established: 1980
**Products:** tiles, platters **Media:** porcelain, low fire **Techniques:** constructed **Size Range:** 4" × 4" to 21" × 21" **Price Range:** $140 to $240/sq. ft.

## ★ CHRISTINE MERRIMAN

**MERRY WOMAN STUDIOS**
**PO BOX 18**
**BRIDGEWATER, VT 05034**
**TEL 802-672-5141**
**Established: 1971**
**Products:** tiles, panels or screens, murals **Media:** clay **Techniques:** constructed, raku fired, hand drawn imagery, no molds **Size Range:** 6" × 6" to 8' × 6' **Price Range:** $500 and up for hand welded frames; $65 to $150/sq. ft.

**See photograph page 141.**

Phyllis Pacin, *Cityscape 6: Vacation*, 1996, raku-fired clay, 36" × 69", photo: Gary A. Fox

# CERAMIC ART FOR THE WALL

## BRENDA MINISCI

STUDIO DEL PINETO
PANTRY RD BOX 85
N HATFIELD, MA 01066
TEL 413-247-5262
Established: 1961
**Products:** panels or screens, murals, wall reliefs **Media:** stoneware, porcelain, earthenware, cold-cast porcelain **Techniques:** cast, constructed, molded, hand formed **Size Range:** no limits **Price Range:** $350 and up for panels, etc.; $150 to $500/sq. ft.

## MISSION VISTA STUDIOS

LIZ HUNNICUTT
812 GIN ROAD
ENNIS, TX 75119
TEL 972-878-0548
Established: 1987
**Products:** tiles, murals, wall reliefs **Media:** stoneware, earthenware **Techniques:** constructed, molded, hand painted **Size Range:** 4" × 4" and up **Price Range:** $500 and up for wall reliefs; $65 to $540/sq. ft.

## PATRICIA NAYLOR

PO BOX 2701
SANTA FE, NM 87504
TEL 505-473-9414
Established: 1982
**Products:** tiles, wall reliefs, modular **Media:** earthenware **Techniques:** constructed, smoke fired **Size Range:** 12" × 12" and up **Price Range:** $250 to $25,000 for wall reliefs

## LAUREL NEFF

3180 23RD ST
SAN FRANCISCO, CA 94110
TEL 415-206-1394
Established: 1991
**Products:** mosaics **Media:** glass, mirror, ceramic tile **Techniques:** constructed **Size Range:** 1' × 1' to 12' × 12' or larger **Price Range:** $100 and up for portable pieces; $15 and up/sq. ft.

## NEWPORT TILE WORKS

MARK LEHRMAN
JODY GEORGE
215 NW 1ST
NEWPORT, OR 97365
TEL 541-265-3071
FAX 541-265-7086
Established: 1969
**Products:** tiles **Media:** stoneware, earthenware **Techniques:** hand pressed **Size Range:** 2" × 2" to 6" × 6" **Price Range:** $4 to $20 for tile

## SHEL NEYMARK

SHEL NEYMARK ARCHITECTURAL CERAMICS
PO BOX 25
EMBUDO, NM 87531-0025
TEL 505-579-4432
FAX 505-579-4432
Established: 1974
**Products:** tiles, wall reliefs, installations **Media:** frost free, raku, glazes **Techniques:** relief, flat, extruded **Size Range:** 4" × 6" to 15' × 40' **Price Range:** $25 to $100,000 for tiles to large installations; $130 to $200/sq. ft.

## LEON NIGROSH

LEON NIGROSH/CERAMIC DESIGNER
11 CHATANIKA AVE
WORCESTER, MA 01602-1109
TEL 508-757-0401
Established: 1963
**Products:** murals, wall reliefs custom designs **Media:** stoneware, porcelain, earthenware **Techniques:** constructed, molded, hand built **Size Range:** 4" × 6" to 5' × 20' **Price Range:** $100 to $300/sq. ft.

## SUSAN NOWOGRODZKI

TOUCHSTONE CERAMICS
261 ELLIOT RD
EAST GREENBUSH, NY 12061
TEL 518-477-7780
Established: 1974
**Products:** tiles, murals **Media:** stoneware, porcelain, earthenware **Techniques:** constructed **Size Range:** 8" × 12" to 4' × 6' **Price Range:** $125 to $2,500 per piece for tile mural

## ONE OFF STUDIO

CAROL SMERALDO
35 LAKEMIST CT
EAST PRESTON, NS B2Z 1G4
CANADA
TEL 902-434-1336
FAX 902-434-1336
Established: 1972
**Products:** murals, platters, wall reliefs **Media:** stoneware, porcelain **Techniques:** constructed, molded, wheel thrown **Size Range:** 12" × 30" to 5' × 10' **Price Range:** $150 to $6,000 for platters, murals, wall reliefs

## ★ ALENA ORT

4 WASHINGTON SQUARE VILLAGE
NEW YORK, NY 10012
TEL 212-254-6123
FAX 212-598-1020
Established: 1984
**Products:** tiles, platters, wall sculptures with neon **Media:** stoneware, neon **Techniques:** hand built **Size Range:** 8" × 8" × 10' × 36' **Price Range:** $40 to $10,000

See photograph page 142.

## ★ PHYLLIS PACIN

PHYLLIS PACIN CERAMIC DESIGN
4097 39TH AVE
OAKLAND, CA 94619
TEL 510-530-7059
Established: 1973
**Products:** tiles, murals, wall sculpture **Media:** raku, stoneware, earthenware, **Techniques:** raku fired, hand rolled textured **Size Range:** 4" × 4" to 9'6" × 27' **Price Range:** $350 and up for wall sculpture; $170/sq. ft.

See photograph page 143.

## ★ CAROLYN PAYNE

PAYNE CREATIONS TILE
4829 N ANTIOCH RD
KANSAS CITY, MO 64119
TEL 816-452-8660
FAX 816-452-0070
Established: 1972
**Products:** tiles, murals **Media:** hand-painted tile **Techniques:** re-glaze manufactured tiles **Size Range:** 6" × 6" to 10' × 26' **Price Range:** $10 to $25 for individual tiles; $75 to $250/sq. ft.

See page 132 for photographs and additional information.

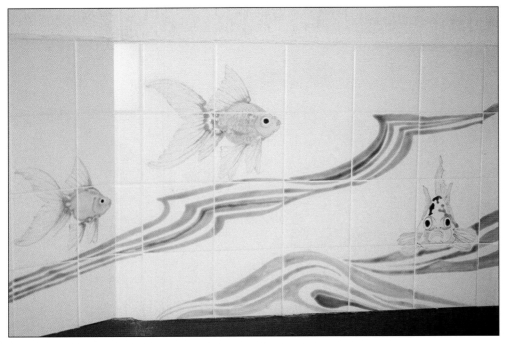

Phyllis Traynor Designs, Ltd., swimming pool surround (detail), custom glass glaze on matte commercial tile, 60' × 60'

## PEACE VALLEY TILE

64 BEULAH RD
NEW BRITAIN, PA 18901
TEL 215-340-0888
FAX 215-340-1536
Established: 1985
**Products:** tiles, mosaics, murals **Media:** stoneware, earthenware **Techniques:** constructed, molded, wheel thrown **Size Range:** 1" × 1" to unlimited **Price Range:** $100 and up for murals; $8 to $50/sq. ft.

## CHRISTINE PENDERGRASS

60610 BILLADEAU RD
BEND, OR 97702-9624
TEL 541-389-1823
Established: 1975
**Products:** tiles, murals, wall reliefs **Media:** stoneware, earthenware **Techniques:** constructed, wheel thrown **Size Range:** 1' × 1' to 6' × 5' **Price Range:** $400 to $2,000 for wall reliefs

## DONALD C. PENNY

DON'S POTTERY
2005 BAYTREE RD
VALDOSTA, GA 31602-3503
TEL 912-247-0289
FAX 912-244-1443
Established: 1960
**Products:** tiles, murals, waterfalls with pools **Media:** stoneware, porcelain, earthenware **Techniques:** constructed, molded, carved **Size Range:** 4" × 4" to 68" × 212" **Price Range:** $65 to $100/sq. ft.

## ★ PHYLLIS TRAYNOR DESIGNS LTD.

**PHYLLIS TRAYNOR**
**PO BOX 365**
**POUND RIDGE, NY 10576**
**TEL 914-764-8346**
**Established: 1979**
**Products:** tiles, murals, wall reliefs **Media:** stoneware, earthenware, glaze on commercial tile **Techniques:** numerous ceramic techniques **Size Range:** 1' × 1' and up **Price Range:** $125 and up/sq. ft.

See photograph page 144.

## PICTURE QUILTS AND MORE

PEGGY M. LARSON
31 S ASHLAND AVE
PALATINE, IL 60067-6301
TEL 847-705-5385
Established: 1984
**Products:** tiles, murals, switchplates **Media:** stoneware **Techniques:** hand painted tiles **Size Range:** 4¹/4" × 4¹/4" and up **Price Range:** $15 and up for murals

## ★ SARA AND TOM POST

**T.S. POST CERAMICS**
**604 BARBERA PL**
**DAVIS, CA 95616**
**TEL 916-758-9365**
**FAX 916-758-9365**
**E-Mail: tspost@davis.com**
**Established: 1976**
**Products:** tiles, tile collage **Media:** stoneware, earthenware **Techniques:** constructed, molded, majolica **Size Range:** 2" × 2" to 4' × 5' **Price Range:** $150 to $6,000 for tile collage; $44 to $200/sq. ft.

See photograph this page.

## POWNING DESIGNS LTD.

PETER W. POWNING
R.R. #5
SUSSEX, NB
CANADA
TEL 506-433-1188
FAX 506-433-6979
Established: 1972
**Products:** tiles, murals, fireplace surrounds **Media:** glass, raku **Techniques:** constructed, molded, wheel thrown **Size Range:** 18" × 24" to 10' × 20' **Price Range:** $150 to $250/sq. ft.

## PROJECTILE

DAVID ALAN CATRAMBONE
4630 SALOMA AVE
SHERMAN OAKS, CA 91403
TEL 818-501-3614
FAX 818-501-3614
Established: 1988
**Products:** tiles, mosaics, murals **Media:** glass, tile, marble **Techniques:** constructed, cut-broken **Size Range:** 8" × 8" to 4' × 12' **Price Range:** $1,500 to $3,000 for murals; $30 to $150/sq. ft.

## QUILT TILES

VERONIQUE BLANCHARD
PO BOX 334, 6732 SCHOOL LN
SOLEBURY, PA 18963
TEL 215-862-3734
FAX 215-862-3734
E-Mail: vero@quilttiles.com
Established: 1995
**Products:** tiles **Media:** earthenware **Techniques:** constructed, molded **Size Range:** 4" × 4" to 15" × 15" **Price Range:** $17.95 to $395 for decos and tile tables

## VEENA RAGHAVAN

VEENA RAGHAVAN CERAMICS
123-40 83RD AVE 7E
KEW GARDENS, NY 11415
TEL 718-544-2391
Established: 1970
**Products:** panels or screens, platters, planters, clocks **Media:** stoneware, porcelain, earthenware, mixed media **Techniques:** constructed, wheel thrown, raku fired **Size Range:** 10" × 10" to 24" × 24" **Price Range:** $45 to $200 for platters, clocks, panels, planters

## RED CLAY TILE

SHARON JOHNSON
1293 OXFORD RD NE
ATLANTA, GA 30306-2426
TEL 404-378-5312
FAX 404-378-3300
Established: 1984
**Products:** tiles, murals, wall reliefs **Media:** stoneware, earthenware, brick **Techniques:** constructed, molded **Size Range:** 4" × 4" to 12' × 12' **Price Range:** $2 to $30 for molded decorative tile; $100 to $150/sq. ft.

## MISSY REHFUSS

THE PAINTED REEF
53 STEINER AVE
NEPTUNE CITY, NJ 07753
TEL 908-776-7292
Established: 1985
**Products:** tiles, murals, sinks **Media:** porcelain, ceramic tiles/ware **Techniques:** detailed paintings **Size Range:** 4" × 4" to 4' × 18' **Price Range:** $500 to $5,000 for custom murals, matching accessories

## WILL RICHARDS

PO BOX 361
UNDERWOOD, WA 98651
TEL 509-493-3928
FAX 509-493-2732
Established: 1980
**Products:** platters, wall reliefs, lighting **Media:** stoneware **Techniques:** constructed **Size Range:** 11" × 11" to 3' × 12' **Price Range:** $120 to $2,500 for plates and panels

## EILEEN PENDERGAST RICHARDSON

409 E SOLA ST
SANTA BARBARA, CA 93101
TEL 805-899-4241
Established: 1959
**Products:** tiles, platters **Media:** porcelain **Techniques:** constructed, wheel thrown, underglaze paintings **Size Range:** 2" × 10" to 2" × 15" **Price Range:** $500 to $1,500 for platters; $250 to $350/sq. ft.

Sara and Tom Post, *Vase/Flowers*, 1995, tile collage, majolica tile cut, reconstructed, 22" × 28"

# CERAMIC ART FOR THE WALL

## ROSEBUD TILE

STEPHEN BERGER
235 5TH AVE 3L
BROOKLYN, NY 11215
TEL 718-857-3859
Established: 1985
**Products:** panels or screens, architectural tile **Media:** earthenware **Techniques:** molded **Size Range:** 3" × 3" to 12" × 12" **Price Range:** $500 to $3,500 for mounted tile panels; $95 to $135/sq. ft.

## ★ JAMIE SANTANIELLO

**WAVERLY TILES**
**TEL 619-722-6199**
**FAX 619-438-2456**
**Established: 1975**
**Products:** tiles, murals, borders; custom work **Media:** earthenware, handmade tile **Techniques:** majolica underglaze **Size Range:** 13" × 13" to unlimited **Price Range:** $5 to $45 for borders, tics, decos; $200 to $750/sq. ft.

**See photograph this page.**

Jamie Santaniello, blue and white installation (detail), 36" × 48"

## LOIS S. SATTLER

LOIS SATTLER CERAMICS
3620 PACIFIC AVE
VENICE, CA 90292-5724
TEL 310-821-7055
Established: 1974
**Products:** platters, wall reliefs **Media:** stoneware, porcelain **Techniques:** constructed, molded low-fired **Size Range:** 14" × 16" to 3' × 6' **Price Range:** $220 to $2,000 from platters to wall pieces

## SCARBOROUGH DAVIDSON

DAVID CALVIN HEAPS
CATIE MORRIS
PO BOX 184
LLOYD, FL 32337-0184
TEL 904-997-9606
FAX 904-997-9606
Established: 1985
**Products:** tiles, platters, hanging vases **Media:** earthenware, inlaid colored clays **Techniques:** cast, molded **Size Range:** 15" × 5" to 48" × 48" **Price Range:** $60 to $1,200 for vases, platters

## LOREN SCHERBAK

5718 WAINWRIGHT AVE
ROCKVILLE, MD 20851
TEL 301-468-0159
Established: 1985
**Products:** tiles, platters, wall reliefs **Media:** stoneware, earthenware **Techniques:** cast, constructed, molded **Size Range:** 6" × 6" to 16" × 35" **Price Range:** $75 for 12" × 12" platters; $300 for triptych wall reliefs

## SCHUMACHER ARCHITECTURAL CERAMICS

ROBERT SCHUMACHER
36530 RIVERVIEW DR, PO BOX 129
CLARKSBURG, CA 95612-0129
TEL 916-744-1062
FAX 916-744-1062
Established: 1985
**Products:** tiles, murals, wall reliefs **Media:** stoneware, porcelain, earthenware **Techniques:** constructed, wheel thrown, raku fired **Size Range:** 4' × 4' to 40' × 40' **Price Range:** $100 to $10,000 for murals; $9 to $50/sq. ft.

## SEBASTIAN STUDIOS

BARBARA SEBASTIAN
1777 YOSEMITE AVE #4B-1
SAN FRANCISCO, CA 94124
TEL 415-822-3243
Established: 1975
**Products:** panels or screens, murals, wall reliefs **Media:** low fired clay and canvas **Techniques:** constructed **Size Range:** 12" × 12" to 20' × 100' **Price Range:** $75 to $150/sq. ft.

## ERICKA CLARK SHAW

451 EUREKA ST
SAN FRANCISCO, CA 94114-2714
TEL 800-484-9955 X 8271
Established: 1974
**Products:** wall reliefs **Media:** earthenware **Techniques:** constructed, molded, airbrushed **Size Range:** 12" × 12" to 60' to 40' **Price Range:** $180 to $250/sq. ft.

## MICHAEL SHEBA

140 EVELYN AVE
TORONTO, ON M6P 2Z7
CANADA
TEL 416-766-9411
Established: 1974
**Products:** murals, platters, wall reliefs **Media:** earthenware, raku **Techniques:** constructed, molded, wheel thrown **Size Range:** 14" × 14" to 6' × 10' **Price Range:** $250 to $750 for platters, wall reliefs; $150 to $250/sq. ft.

## CHRISTINE SIBLEY

CHRISTINE SIBLEY POTTERY AT
    URBAN NIRVANA
15 WADDELL ST NE
ATLANTA, GA 30307
TEL 404-688-3329
FAX 404-688-0665
Established: 1973
**Products:** tiles, murals, columns **Media:** stoneware, earthenware, cement, gypsom **Techniques:** cast, constructed, molded, slab construction **Size Range:** 6" × 8" to 4' × 6' **Price Range:** $5 to $450 for wall reliefs; $50 to $200/sq. ft.

## J. PAUL SIRES

CENTER OF THE EARTH
3204 N DAVIDSON ST
CHARLOTTE, NC 28205-1034
TEL 704-375-5756
FAX 704-375-5756
Established: 1983
**Products:** murals, platters, wall reliefs **Media:** stoneware, earthenware, brick **Techniques:** constructed, molded, carved **Size Range:** 19" × 19" to 24' × 24' **Price Range:** $450 for large platters; $25 to $150/sq. ft.

## NAN SMITH

NAN SMITH STUDIO
2310 NW 142ND AVE
GAINESVILLE, FL 32609
TEL 904-485-2942
FAX 904-329-8453
Established: 1977
**Products:** tiles, murals, wall reliefs, commissioned works **Media:** earthenware, mounted on plexiglass **Techniques:** constructed, molded, airbrushed, glazed **Size Range:** 24" x 18" to 8' x 20' **Price Range:** $2,500 to $25,000 for airbrushed tile installations

## PAT SMITH

90 GREENE ST
NEW YORK, NY 10012-3855
TEL 212-219-8519
Established: 1975
**Products:** murals, wall reliefs **Media:** porcelain, slate, copper, steel **Techniques:** cast, constructed **Size Range:** 12" x 12" to 8' x 6' **Price Range:** $400 to $1,800 for wall works or sculpture; $250 to $300/sq. ft.

## ★ SPIRAL STUDIOS

**LAURA SHPRENTZ**
**168 IRVING AVE #400E**
**PORT CHESTER, NY 10573**
**TEL 914-939-6639**
**Products:** tiles, murals, wall reliefs **Media:** stoneware, earthenware **Techniques:** constructed, molded, carved relief **Size Range:** 2" x 2" and up **Price Range:** $5 and up for individual tiles; $175 to $300/sq. ft.

**See photograph this page.**

## STARBUCK GOLDNER TILE

BETH STARBUCK
STEVEN GOLDNER
315 W FOURTH ST
BETHLEHEM, PA 18015
TEL 610-866-6321
FAX 610-866-5279
Established: 1980
**Products:** tiles, mosaics, wall reliefs **Media:** porcelain, earthenware, inlaid colored clays **Techniques:** constructed, molded **Size Range:** 6" x 6" to full walls **Price Range:** $1,000 and up for wall installations; $10 to $300/sq. ft.

## STATUS INC. CUSTOM CERAMICS

RICHARD SCOTT
107 W DENNY WAY
SEATTLE, WA 98119
TEL 206-282-0181
FAX 206-282-0181
E-Mail: status@wolfenet.com
Established: 1982
**Products:** tiles, murals, wall reliefs **Media:** earthenware **Techniques:** cast, molded **Size Range:** 3" x 3" to 72" x 230" **Price Range:** $6 to $30 for reliefs; $100 to $165/sq. ft.

## ALAN STEINBERG

BRATTLEBORO CLAYWORKS
RD 5 BOX 250 PUTNEY RD
BRATTLEBORO, VT 05301-9190
TEL 802-254-9174
Established: 1976
**Products:** murals, wall reliefs **Media:** stoneware, porcelain, inlaid colored clays **Techniques:** constructed **Size Range:** 4" x 4" to 4' x 8' **Price Range:** $18 to $7,000 for murals; $100 to $200/sq. ft.

## SUSANNE G. STEPHENSON

STEPHENSON CERAMICS
4380 WATERS RD
ANN ARBOR, MI 48103
TEL 313-663-2679
Established: 1960
**Products:** platters, wall reliefs **Media:** earthenware **Techniques:** constructed, molded, wheel thrown, various finishes **Size Range:** 12" x 12" to 27" x 30" **Price Range:** $300 to $2,000 for platters, wall reliefs

## ★ STEWART SPECIALTY TILES

**DIANNE STEWART**
**2899 E. BIG BEAVER RD #238**
**TROY, MI 48084**
**TEL 810-680-8453**
**FAX 810-680-8787**
**Established: 1992**
**Products:** tiles, mosaics, murals, interlocking cobblestones **Media:** stoneware, hand-painted tiles **Techniques:** hand-shaped tiles **Size Range:** 4" x 4" to unlimted **Price Range:** $50 to $300/sq. ft.

**See page 133 for photographs and additional information.**

## RENÉE AND JAMES STONEBRAKER

RED FISH BLUE FISH DESIGNS
901 WASHINGTON ST
HOBOKEN, NJ 07030
TEL 201-656-4854
E-Mail: rfishb@mail.idt.net
Established: 1989
**Products:** tiles, wall reliefs **Media:** stoneware, earthenware **Techniques:** molded **Size Range:** 4" x 4" to 24" x 24" **Price Range:** $25 to $400 for hand made relief tiles

## LORA SUMMERVILLE

LORA SUMMERVILLE CERAMICS
RT 3 BOX 249
CASEY, IL 62420-9219
TEL 217-923-5594
Established: 1990
**Products:** wall reliefs, kaleidoscopes **Media:** stoneware **Techniques:** constructed **Size Range:** 5" x 10" to 23" x 24" **Price Range:** $14 to $300 for mugs, fountains, kaleidoscopes

## SUMMITVILLE TILES, INC.

PETER C. JOHNSON, JR.
PO BOX 73
SUMMITVILLE, OH 43962
TEL 216-223-1511
FAX 216-223-1414
**Products:** tiles, murals, wall reliefs **Media:** porcelain, ceramic tiles **Techniques:** constructed, molded **Size Range:** 2" x 2" to unlimited **Price Range:** $25 to $180 for 6" x 6" murals

## SURVING STUDIOS

NATALIE AND RICHARD SURVING
RD4 BOX 449
MIDDLETOWN, NY 10940
TEL 914-355-1430
TEL 800-768-4954
FAX 914-355-1517
Established: 1961
**Products:** tiles, murals, wall reliefs, accessories **Media:** porcelain **Techniques:** constructed, pressed **Size Range:** 2" x 2" to 5' x 10' **Price Range:** $18 to $72 for individual relief tiles; $54 to $1,000/sq. ft.

## SYZYGY TILEWORKS

PO BOX 2443, 109 S BULLARD
SILVER CITY, NM 88062-2443
TEL 505-388-5472
**Products:** tiles, mosaics, wall reliefs **Media:** stoneware **Techniques:** molded **Size Range:** 12" x 12" to 3' x 4' **Price Range:** $8 to $25 for tile; $72 to $300/sq. ft.

## TALISMAN

TED LOWITZ
1776 W WINNEMAC AVE
CHICAGO, IL 60640-2762
TEL 773-784-2628
E-Mail: tlowitz@aol.com
Established: 1978
**Products:** tiles, murals, wall reliefs **Media:** stoneware **Techniques:** cast, molded **Size Range:** 2" x 2" to 6" x 6" **Price Range:** $20 to $65 for lineal foot of tile; $65 to $180/sq. ft.

Spiral Studios, *Oval Garden*, unmounted mural, hand-carved high relief, low-fire clay, opalescent glaze, 24" x 18". photo: D. James Dee

# CERAMIC ART FOR THE WALL

## DENISE S. TENNEN

CLAY CONSTRUCTIONS
2905 MONTEREY AVE S
ST LOUIS PARK, MN 55416-5801
TEL 612-922-2356
TEL 612-623-0346
Established: 1988
**Products:** murals, wall reliefs, wall sculptures **Media:** sculpture clay **Techniques:** cast, constructed **Size Range:** 12" x 12" to 10' x 36' **Price Range:** $250 to $12,000 for wall sculptures

## TERRA DESIGNS

ANNA SALIBELLO
241 E BLACKWELL ST
DOVER, NJ 07801-4140
TEL 201-539-2999
FAX 201-328-3624
Established: 1969
**Products:** tiles, mosaics, ceramic murals **Media:** stoneware, porcelain, earthenware **Techniques:** constructed, molded, extruded **Size Range:** ¹/₂" x ¹/₂" to 12' x 35' **Price Range:** $14 to $500/sq. ft.

## TETKOWSKI STUDIO

NEIL TETKOWSKI
432 W 19TH ST
NEW YORK, NY 10011
TEL 212-255-1850
FAX 212-255-2608
Established: 1987
**Products:** wall reliefs, murals, sculpture **Media:** earthenware **Techniques:** constructed, wheel thrown, salt or sodium fired **Size Range:** 18" x 18" to 10' x 24' **Price Range:** $5,000 for 36" disk; $300 to $400/sq. ft.

## TILE BY DESIGN

NAN OWEN
24291 SUNNYBROOK CR
LAKE FOREST, CA 92630
TEL 714-855-7877
FAX 714-855-2200
Established: 1976
**Products:** tiles, panels or screens, murals **Media:** porcelain, earthenware, glass **Techniques:** cast, molded, majolica **Size Range:** 4" x 4" to 10' x 32' **Price Range:** $80 to $250/sq. ft.

## THE TILE PEOPLE

KAY HAUCK
6603 N GREENVIEW ST
CHICAGO, IL 60626
TEL 773-274-9103
E-Mail: tilepeople@aol.com
Established: 1985
**Products:** tiles, murals, wall reliefs **Media:** stoneware, earthenware **Techniques:** constructed, molded **Price Range:** $10 for $50 for tiles; $100 to $400/sq. ft.

## TILE RESTORATION CENTER, INC

MARIE GLASSE TAPP
3511 INTERLAKE N
SEATTLE, WA 98103
TEL 206-633-4866
FAX 206-633-3489
Established: 1970
**Products:** tiles, murals, fireplaces, floors **Media:** stoneware **Techniques:** cast, molded, carved relief **Size Range:** 6" x 6" to 9' x 6' **Price Range:** $200 to $400 for plaques; $50 to $200/sq. ft.

## TILEMAKERS

MACHIKO ICHIHARA
PO BOX 741
SMYRNA, GA 30081-0741
TEL 888-434-6100
TEL 770-434-6100
FAX 770-434-7324
E-Mail: tilemakers@aol.com
Established: 1981
**Products:** tiles, mosaics, wall reliefs **Media:** stoneware, porcelain, tile, cement **Techniques:** cast, constructed, molded **Size Range:** 1" x 1" to 4' x 8' **Price Range:** $3 to $60 for relief tile, trim; $25 to $350/sq. ft.

## ★ TIMELESS TILE

**TIM MURPHY**
**5445 HWY 9**
**FELTON, CA 95018**
**TEL 408-355-0771**
**FAX 408-335-0772**
**E-Mail: timeless@scruznet.com**
**Established: 1971**
**Products:** tiles **Media:** stoneware, earthenware **Techniques:** cast, molded, pressed **Size Range:** 2" x 2" to 6" x 9" **Price Range:** $6 to $50 for individual tile; $16 to $50/sq. ft.

**See photograph this page.**

## VINCENT AND CAROLYN LEE TOLPO

SHAWNEE MOUNTAIN POTTERY
55918 US HWY 285 PO BOX 134
SHAWNEE, CO 80475
TEL 303-670-1733
Established: 1975
**Products:** murals, platters, wall reliefs **Media:** stoneware **Techniques:** constructed, wheel thrown press mold **Size Range:** 4" x 5" to 8' x 16' **Price Range:** $260 to $600 for platters; $50 to $150/sq. ft.

## ANDREA TRIGUBA

PO BOX 85
CALAIS, VT 05648
TEL 802-223-5094
Established: 1992
**Products:** tiles, murals **Media:** earthenware, ceramic tile **Techniques:** molded, hand painted, glazed **Size Range:** 2" x 2" and up **Price Range:** $10 to $50 for hand painted tiles

Timeless Tile, *Large Seashells,* 1997, high-relief decorative installation, hand-painted and handmade tile, 4¹/₄" x 8¹/₄"

## TRIKEENAN TILEWORKS

KRISTIN AND STEPHEN POWERS
9 FOREST RD
HANCOCK, NH 03449
TEL 603-525-4245
FAX 603-525-4245
Established: 1984
**Products:** tiles, mosaics, murals **Media:** stoneware, earthenware **Techniques:** constructed, molded, carved **Size Range:** 4" × 6" to 10' × 25' **Price Range:** $25 to $4,000 for individual tiles, murals; $100 to $500/sq. ft.

## KATHY TRIPLETT

175 MCDARIS COVE RD
WEAVERVILLE, NC 28787
TEL 704-658-3207
Established: 1972
**Products:** tiles, lighted panels, wall reliefs **Media:** earthenware, glass **Techniques:** constucted **Size Range:** 6" × 6" to 10' × 12' **Price Range:** $150 to $500/sq. ft.

## SUSAN TUNICK

771 WEST END AVE #10E
NEW YORK, NY 10025
TEL 212-962-1750
TEL 212-962-1864
Established: 1968
**Products:** mosaics, murals, wall reliefs **Media:** stoneware, porcelain, earthenware **Techniques:** constructed, ceramic mosaic **Size Range:** 7" × 7" to 16'L × 1'W **Price Range:** $600 to $18,000 for murals, wall reliefs

## GAYLE L. TUSTIN

3842 EDGEWOOD RD
WILMINGTON, NC 28403
TEL 910-392-4408
Established: 1982
**Products:** tiles, murals, wall reliefs **Media:** stoneware, earthenware, brick **Techniques:** cast, constructed, molded **Size Range:** 1" × 1" to 22' × 13' **Price Range:** $400 to $3,000 for original wall relief panels; $100 to $400/sq. ft.

## TWIN DOLPHIN MOSAICS

ROBERT STOUT
STEPHANIE JURS
808 WELLESLEY DR NE
ALBUQUERQUE, NM 87106
TEL 505-266-2675
Established: 1980
**Products:** mosaics **Media:** porcelain, glass, marble **Techniques:** hand assembled **Size Range:** 12" × 12" to 8' × 8' **Price Range:** $200 to $400/sq. ft.

## VACCARO STUDIO

LOUIS VACCARO
531 SPRINGTOWN RD
NEW PALTZ, NY 12561-3028
914-658-9859
**Products:** wall reliefs **Media:** earthenware **Techniques:** constructed **Size Range:** 2' × 2' to 4' × 5' **Price Range:** $800 to $2,000 for wall reliefs

## ★ SHERYL VANDERPOL

**UNTAPPED RESOURCE**
4020 PILGRIM LN NORTH
MINNEAPOLIS, MN 55441
TEL 612-542-1116
FAX 612-542-1119
http://members.aol.com/muntapped
Established: 1990
**Products:** tiles, murals, porcelain sinks **Media:** porcelain, commercial ceramic tile **Techniques:** kiln-fired on commercial tiles **Size Range:** 4" × 4" to unlimited **Price Range:** $200 to $5,000 for murals and sinks; $50 to $500/sq. ft.

See photograph this page.

## HELEN WEBBER

HELEN WEBBER DESIGNS
555 PACIFIC AVE
SAN FRANCISCO, CA 94133-4609
TEL 415-989-5521
FAX 415-989-5746
Established: 1972
**Products:** mosaics, murals, wall reliefs **Media:** fired sculpted clay tile **Techniques:** cast kiln-fired sculpted clay **Size Range:** 15" × 18" to 9' × 27' **Price Range:** $100 to $200 and up/sq. ft.

Sheryl VanderPol, *Wildflowers, Berries: Pussywillow*, painted, fired on commercial tile, installation on backsplash, hood and island

# CERAMIC ART FOR THE WALL

| | | |
|---|---|---|
| **LISTED ARTISTS** work at a professional level in the area of ceramic art for the wall. | | |
| ESTABLISHED | The year the artist began working as a professional. | **CAN'T FIND A CERTAIN ARTIST?** |
| PRODUCTS | Types of ceramic art created by the artist for display on walls. | Check the Index of Artists and Companies for a comprehensive listing of every artist in *The Designer's Sourcebook 12*. |
| TECHNIQUES | Techniques typically used by the artist to create the work. | |
| SIZE RANGE | Range of sizes for the artist's typical art for the wall. | **NEED AN ARTIST FOR YOUR PROJECT?** |
| PRICE RANGE | From lowest to highest, typical retail prices for the artist's ceramic art for the wall. Prices are reported per piece and/or per square foot. | See the Commissions Clearinghouse on THE GUILD's Web site. List project specs. Artists respond directly. Try it! *http://www.guild.com* |

## HERSHL WEBERMAN

TILES BY HEW
450 WESTMINSTER RD
BROOKLYN, NY 11218-6036
TEL 718-287-2457
Established: 1976
**Products:** tiles, murals **Media:** earthenware **Size Range:** 2" × 2" to 24" × 40" **Price Range:** $150 to $2,000 for murals; $20 to $100/sq. ft.

## MAUREEN R. WEISS

WHITE ENTERPRISES
321 HIGH SCHOOL RD #224
BAINBRIDGE ISLAND, WA 98110
TEL 206-842-9777
FAX 206-842-4847
Established: 1980
**Products:** tiles, platters, wall reliefs **Media:** stoneware, earthenware, glass **Techniques:** cast, molded, wheel thrown **Size Range:** 1" × 1" to 7' × 7' **Price Range:** $10 to $10,000 for wall, floor sculptures

## ★ HELEN WEISZ

**ARCHITECTURAL CERAMICS**
**1775 HILLSIDE RD**
**SOUTHAMPTON, PA 18966**
**TEL 215-322-5128**
**FAX 215-322-5062**
**E-Mail:** hfweisz@aol.com
**Established: 1972**
**Products:** tiles, panels or screens, wall reliefs **Media:** stoneware, earthenware, inlaid colored clays **Techniques:** constructed, hand colored, hand made **Size Range:** 2' × 2' to 5' × 130' **Price Range:** $900 to $30,000 for tile installation; $250 to $300/sq. ft.

**See photograph this page.**

## SUSAN AND JIM WHALEN

PARADOX POTTERY
RT 2 BOX 81G, MAPLE SWAMP RD
HORSESHOE, NC 28742
TEL 704-890-0525
**Products:** platters, sculpture, fish, plants **Media:** stoneware, earthenware **Techniques:** constructed, wheel thrown, raku fired **Size Range:** 4" × 3" to 36" × 9" **Price Range:** $20 to $500 for small fish to organic sculpture

## FRED WIESENER

231 W MAIN ST
DANVILLE, KY 40422
TEL 606-236-3079
FAX 606-236-0304
Established: 1970
**Products:** panels or screens, murals, wall reliefs **Media:** stoneware, cast bronze, fiber **Techniques:** cast, constructed **Size Range:** 60" × 18" to 9' × 7' **Price Range:** $950 to $9,500 for wall hangings; $150 to $250/sq. ft.

## WILBURTON POTTERY

ROBERT AND IRIS JEWETT
PO BOX 40161
BELLEVUE, WA 98015
TEL 206-455-9203
Established: 1992
**Products:** tiles, murals, wall reliefs **Media:** stoneware, porcelain **Techniques:** molded, slab built **Size Range:** 5" × 3" to 1' × 5' **Price Range:** $16 to $50 for relief tiles; $40 to $200/sq. ft.

## WISEMAN•SPAULDING DESIGNS

BRADLEY WISEMAN
PAUL SPAULDING
12 SHAWHILL RD
HAMDEN, ME 04444
TEL 207-862-3513
FAX 207-862-4513
Established: 1980
**Products:** tiles, wall reliefs **Media:** stoneware, porcelain **Techniques:** constructed, molded, wood fired **Size Range:** 1" × 6" to 3' × 3' **Price Range:** $2 to $150 for field tiles, hand-sculpted relief; $22 to $200/sq. ft.

## JAMES WRAY

JAMES WRAY STUDIO
116 VAN WINKLE GROVE
BEREA, KY 40403
TEL 606-986-4377
**Products:** tiles, mosaics, tiled tables **Media:** stoneware, mixed media **Techniques:** constructed, molded **Size Range:** 2" × 2" to 36" × 48" **Price Range:** $400 to $1,500 for tiled tables; $50 to $200/sq. ft.

## C. KEEN ZERO

GONZO MOJO ENTERPRISES
128 ODD ST
ATHENS, GA 30601
TEL 706-613-6270
Established: 1991
**Products:** tiles, mosaics, wall reliefs **Media:** stoneware, mixed media **Techniques:** constructed, molded **Size Range:** 16" Dia to 48" Dia **Price Range:** $500 to $2,500 for relief mosaic mandalas

## DALE ZHEUTLIN

55 WEBSTER AVE
NEW ROCHELLE, NY 10801
TEL 914-576-0082
FAX 914-738-8373
**Products:** tiles, murals, wall reliefs **Media:** porcelain **Techniques:** constructed **Size Range:** 13" × 13" to 20' × 20' **Price Range:** $250 to $350/sq. ft.

## ARNOLD ZIMMERMAN

76 AINSLIE ST
BROOKLYN, NY 11211
TEL 718-388-4914
FAX 212-242-3703
Established: 1979
**Products:** tiles, platters, wall reliefs **Media:** stoneware, glass cast metal **Techniques:** cast, constructed, molded **Size Range:** 4¹/₂" × 4¹/₂" to 120" × 240" **Price Range:** $500 to $25,000 for platters, tiles, murals; $20 to $150/sq. ft.

Helen Weisz, *Tioa*, colored clay, tile panels, 34"H × 44"W

## ILLAHE TILEWORKS
## SUE WERSCHKUL
**See page 140.**

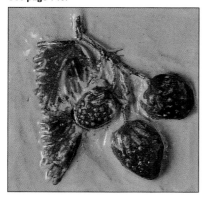

Garden Series: *Strawberries*, relief tile line, 4" x 4"

## ILLAHE TILEWORKS
## SUE WERSCHKUL
**See page 140.**

*Planting By The Moon*, mural including pieces from *Garden Series*, 28" x 34", each tile: 4" x 4"

## ILLAHE TILEWORKS
## SUE WERSCHKUL
**See page 140.**

*Garden Series: Frog in Ivy Frame*, available in a variety of designs and colors, 8" x 8"

## KŌP DESIGNS
## RODNEY AND LISA COOPER
**See page 141.**

Relief tiles as border accent, custom design

## FRESH FISH CERAMIC TILES
## NORMA HANLON AND KIRSTEN HANLON
**See page 139.**

*Carrot Tile*, sculptured vegetable tiles for kitchens, 4¹/₄" x 13"

## FRESH FISH CERAMIC TILES
## NORMA HANLON AND KIRSTEN HANLON
**See page 139.**

*Sea Turtle*, sculptured tile designs from nature, 9" x 9" x 3"

## PHILLIP HARRIS
## ASH WORKS
**See page 140.**

*Cycle*, 1997, porcelain tiles, 4" to 16"W

## PHILLIP HARRIS
## ASH WORKS
**See page 140.**

Composition with black and yellow, 1997, porcelain tiles 4" to 12"W

# CERAMIC ART FOR THE WALL

## *Elizabeth MacDonald*
**See page 143.**

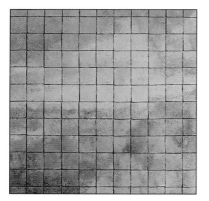

*Landscape*, 45" x 42¹/₂", layered pigment

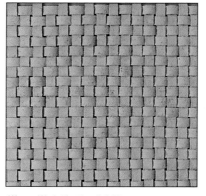

*Woven Work*, 3' x 3', relief: 2"

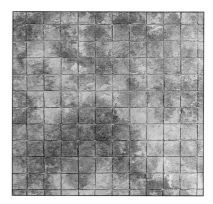

*Dance*, 45" x 42", tile size: 3"

Detail

Detail

Detail

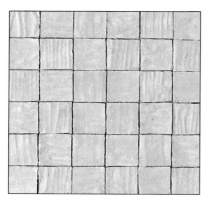

*Patterned Relief*, silver mica surface

*Pyramid*, from 8" to 18"

*Spiral Relief*, 34"

# ART QUILTS

# Collaborations Inc.

**Wendy Huhn**
**81763 Lost Creek Road**
**Dexter, OR 97431**
**FAX 541-937-8061**
**TEL  541-937-3147**
**E-Mail: WChuhn@aol.com**

**Melissa Holzinger**
**30516 SR 530 NE**
**Arlington, WA 98223**
**TEL  360-435-5060**

Huhn and Holzinger, professional artists since 1980, combine their expertise to embrace a wide range of surface design techniques. They are proficient in dying, painting, airbrush, photo transfer, silkscreen embellishment and all aspects of mixed media assemblage. Their work is included in national and international collections and exhibitions. Seriously but with a sense of humor, they work together to create a dynamic and talented art team.

Also see these GUILD publications:
*Designer's Edition: 10, 11*

A  *Balancing Act* (detail)

B  *Still Life/Balancing Act*, 1996, 60" x 47"

A

B

Photos: David Loveall

# Robin Cowley

**2451 Potomac Street**
**Oakland, CA 94602-3032**
**FAX 510-482-9465**
**TEL   510-530-1134**

Robin Cowley's original, one-of-a-kind art quilts are of a graphic nature with strong colors and an upbeat look. She works intuitively with fabric and thread, combining colors and textures with a sure hand and a keen understanding of the interaction between elements. Her work is generally machine pieced, quilted and appliquéd, using hand-dyed and commercial fabrics.

Robin has numerous works in private and corporate collections. Commissions are welcomed; slides and pricing are available upon request.

Also see this GUILD publication:
*Designer's Edition: 11*

A  *Nile Moon,* 47"H x 27"W

B  *Pink Jazz,* 48"H x 37"W

C  *Purple Jazz,* 48"H x 35"W

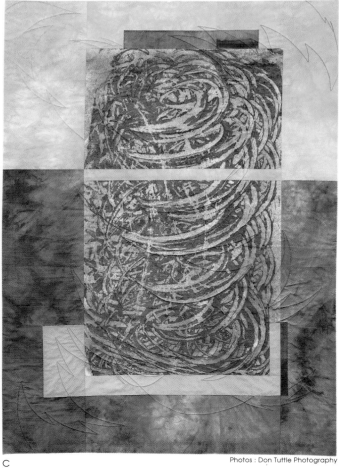

A

B

C

Photos : Don Tuttle Photography

# Marcia Hewitt Johnson

**71 Llanfair Circle**
**Ardmore, PA 19003**
**FAX 610-649-7282**
**TEL  610-649-7282**
**E-Mail: Marhewjohn@aol.com**

Marcia Johnson's contemporary art quilts for the wall are influenced by her photography, allowing her to create abstractions of specific places and scenes.

She creates her own colors in graduated palettes, bringing vibrant visual drama to each piece. Although her processes are unique, it is color that makes her work visually lasting. Quilts come with easy-to-install hardware, or can be framed, and bring color and texture to interiors.

Johnson's pieces are exhibited worldwide and are in residential and corporate collections, including Wilmington Trust, Owens Corning and Lehigh Hospital.

Please call for custom portfolio and price list.

Also see this GUILD publication:
*Designer's Edition: 11*

A  *Road 2 Santa Fe*, art quilt, 48" x 48"

B  *Colors 2 Dance 2*, art quilt, 33" x 61"

C  *Road to Taos*, art quilt, collection of
   Owens Corning, 48" x 62"

A

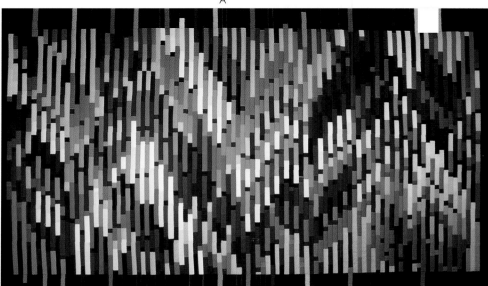

B

C

# Holley Junker

**4030 Greywell Way**
**Sacramento, CA 95864**
**TEL  916-488-5660**

Holley Junker originated the pointillist technique which characterizes her work. The overlapping pieces of fabric give tactile and visual depth to work which is an investigation of light and texture in the landscape.

Holley has exhibited internationally since 1980, and has work in corporate, private and public collections throughout the United States.

Commissions are tailored to color and space requirements. Prices and delivery time are based on size and intricacy. Prices begin at $150 per square foot.

A  *Ballyconry*, 1993, Alza Corporation, Palo Alto, CA, 56" x 58"

B  *Salt Meadow*, 1994, private collection in California, 84" x 114"

A

B

Photos: Sharon Risedorph

# Karen Laurence

531 Main Street #1002
Roosevelt Island, NY 10044
FAX 212-759-0511
TEL 212-751-8215

Karen Laurence has made hangings since the mid-1970s for private and corporate clients and for various spaces and uses.

Dyed, painted and found pieces are machine collaged on canvas backings, making the hangings sturdy, portable and easy to install. Sizes range from small to 7 by 10 feet. Prices start at $800.

Slides, prices and scheduling upon request. Some completed works are available.

A *Darkening of the Light*, 50" x 37"

B *River Road*, 31" x 26"

C *October*, 64" x 36"

A

B

C

# Therese May

651 North 4th Street
San Jose, CA 95112
FAX 408-292-5585
TEL 408-292-3247

Therese May's quilts are made up of playful fantasy animal and plant imagery, and are machine appliquéd using straight stitch and satin stitch. Threads are left uncut to form a network of texture across the surface. Acrylic paint is added as a finishing touch. Her work is widely published and exhibited throughout the U.S., Europe and Japan.

Prices for finished pieces range from $1,000 to $40,000. Commissions accepted; May will work with clients via drawings and samples.

More information available upon request.

Also see these GUILD publications:
*Designer's Edition: 6, 7, 8, 10, 11*

SHOWN: *K-Elephant*, 1996, fabric, paint, 48" x 48"

Photos: Superior Color

# Dottie Moore

**1134 Charlotte Avenue**
**Rock Hill, SC 29732**
**TEL   803 327-5088**

Dottie Moore has been producing art quilts for individual and corporate clients since 1980. She symbolically expresses the healing qualities and mystery found in earth, sky, trees and mountains. She hand paints the fabric and allows designs to evolve intuitively, without the use of sketches. Each piece is appliquéd, quilted and hand embroidered. She encourages commissions and enjoys collaborating with clients on co-created projects.

Dottie's work is collected, exhibited and published internationally.

Slides and prices are available upon request.

Also see these GUILD publications:
*Designer's Edition: 6, 7, 8, 9*

A  *Fire and Soul*, 30" x 33"

B  *Transitions*, 50" x 70"

A

B

Photos: Michael Harrison

Printed in Hong Kong ©1997 THE GUILD: The Designer's Sourcebook

# Sue H. Rodgers

**Instant Heirlooms**
**140 Laurel Road**
**Princeton, NJ 08540**
**FAX 609-921-7171**
**TEL  609-921-7171**

Quilts by Sue H. Rodgers have won top awards in major U.S. and international competitions, and have been placed in notable public and private collections.

Ms. Rodger's work is distinguished by trapunto, an ancient Italian technique that enriches the textural interest of the quilt surface with `embossed' areas of additional stuffing. Printed decorator fabrics are hand appliquéd to create complex layered images, accentuated by detailed hand quilting. These special techniques, brought together through outstanding craftsmanship, produce a compelling tactile work, sparkling with visual intensity.

Slide resumes are available, and commissions for special corporate or residential spaces are welcome.

*Chinoise*, hand-appliquéd, pieced, hand-quilted, decorator fabrics, 41" x 41"   Young Masters Studio

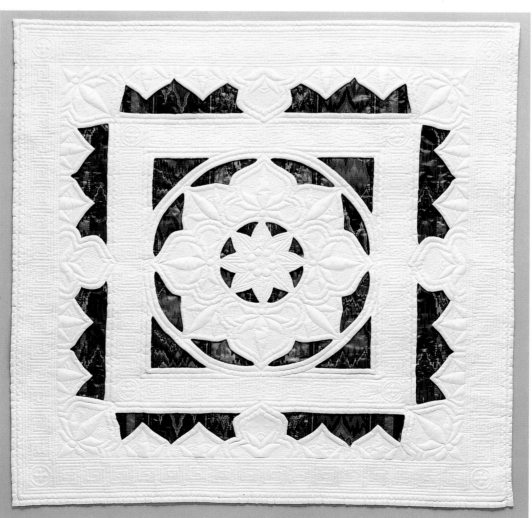

*Chinoise II, Lotus with Twisted Leaf*, hand-quilted cut-out trapunto, appliquéd over second quilt,   Photographic House
decorator fabrics, 45" x 45"

# Embassy Loan

THE GUILD can be an international passport for your art. At least that's how advertising in *The Designer's Sourcebook 10* worked out for Los Angeles artist Harriet Zeitlin, whose pieced fabric wall art caught the eye of no less than the U.S. Department of State.

Officials with the agency's Art in Embassies program — which places works by American artists in U.S. embassies around the world — were intrigued by the appliquéd wall quilt Zeitlin showed in THE GUILD REGISTER of Fiber Art for the Wall. They invited her to join the ranks of Robert Rauschenberg, Helen Frankenthaler, and other fine artists who have loaned pieces to the program.

"At first they wanted the kimono piece they saw in THE GUILD for the Taiwan Embassy," Zeitlin recalls. "Then they decided it wasn't a good idea to send a Japanese quilt to a Chinese country." Eventually, her colorful image of the Statue of Liberty was deemed more geopolitically appropriate. The work will hang in the Hong Kong Embassy for three years, exposing Zeitlin's work to an audience she never imagined.

"I'm very proud to show my work through this program," the artist says. "It's something I never would have expected. It's icing on the cake."

David I. Zeitlin

**Artist:** Harriet Zeitlin
**Liaison:** Art in Embassies Program,
U.S. Department of State
**Type of Work:** Appliquéd Wall Quilt
**Title:** *Statue of Liberty*
**Site:** U.S. Embassy, Hong Kong

# Joan Schulze

808 Piper Avenue
Sunnyvale, CA 94087
FAX 408-736-7833
TEL  408-736-7833

Joan Schulze has pioneered silk-and-paper layered constructions. These two-sided works function as traditional wall quilts or freestanding installations, or as screens in architectural and intimate spaces. Textures combine the elegance of painted silk with paper surfaces reminiscent of peeling frescoes. When back-lighted, they glow.

Lightfast, durable, easily installed.

Commissions accepted.

A  *Palimpsest*, quilt, 50"H x 59"W

B  *Memories of Tea*, quilt, 48" x 48"; and
*Drifting*, paper/silk construction, 48" x 48"

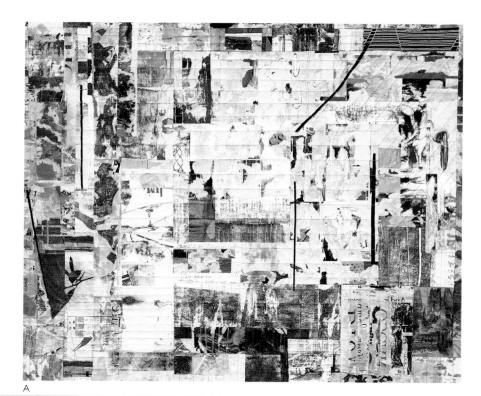

A

B

Photos: Sharon Risedorph

# Marge White

**Needling in the Pines**
**PO Box 4-3055 Fairway Drive**
**Arnold, CA 95223**
**FAX 209-795-0654**
**TEL   209-795-4240**
**E-Mail: MARJON@cdepot.net**

Marge White resides in the beautiful Sierra Mountains in California. Using an interesting layered technique to create depth and visual texture in her fabric collages, her heavily quilted landscapes bring warmth and beauty to their settings.

Mountains, trees, old barns, water and even birds and animals are subjects for her unusual creations. In each of these pieces, she uses cotton that can be washed or drycleaned.

She welcomes commissions. Call to request photos or slides.

Prices begin at $110 per square foot.

A  *Seasons Change*, 18" x 21"

B  *Solitary Contentment*, 25" x 32"

C  *Full Sail*, 44" x 55"

A

B

C

Photos: Tim Bottomley

Printed in Hong Kong ©1997 THE GUILD: The Designer's Sourcebook

PAPER

# Karen Adachi

702 Monarch Way
Santa Cruz, CA 95060
FAX 408-423-4431
TEL  408-429-6192

Karen Adachi creates three-dimensional hand-made paper pieces by using layers of irregularly shaped vacuumed-cast paper. Her work is shown nationally through major galleries and representatives.

The pieces are richly textured and embellished with dyes, acrylics, metallics. Painted bamboo and sticks are used to create a dramatic statement of pattern and line.

Collections include:
American Airlines
AT&T
Marriot Hotel
Stanford Hospital
Bally's Hotel
Bank of Reno
Saks Fifth Avenue
Bloomingdale's
International Paper

Custom work available in any size, shape and color. Call for slides and additional information.

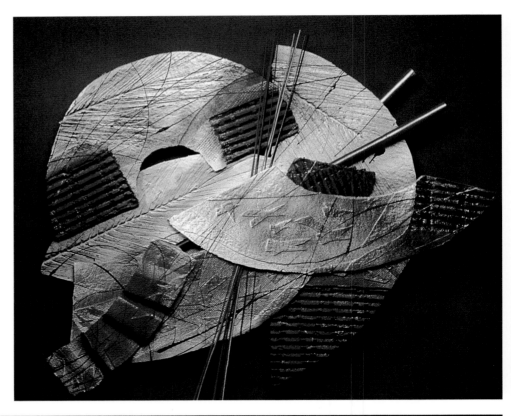

Printed in Hong Kong ©1997 THE GUILD: The Designer's Sourcebook

# John Babcock

4780 Soquel Creek Road
Soquel, CA 95073
FAX 408-462-5949
TEL   408-476-6302

John Babcock's medium is paper, and his work has been shown in major museums internationally. Works are included in many public and private collections, including the American Craft Museum.

John's art reflects a unique exploration of color relationships to evoke an emotional response. About his work he states, "I gravitate to earth forms for inspiration, perhaps because many of the colors that I use are earth-derived pigments. I draw upon images that come to me when I contemplate the pulsating or vibrating nature of waves, windblown sand, or Japanese rock gardens. I seek to capture the essence of these experiences and document them through the peculiarities of colored paper."

John uses paper of his own manufacture to build art works that are cast, inlaid and/or collaged. He manipulates various pigmented pulps of cotton, kozo and abaca fibers. Each type of fiber reflects light differently. One result of the fiber manipulation is the way the imagery changes focus; some images recede or appear as the viewer moves from side to side or as the light of day changes.

For large commissions, the artist will design maquettes for designers' proposals. Works range in size from 2 to 40 feet. Prices range from $800 to $20,000. The work is archival.

A  *Veiled Light*, 46" x 46"

B  *Pettit commision*, 48" x 40"

A

B

# Hye Sun Baik

4573 West 2nd Avenue
Vancouver, BC V6R 1K7
Canada
FAX 604-222-2076
TEL  604-222-2276
E-Mail: sga@mindlink.net

Award-winning fiber artist, Hye Sun Baik, is originally from Seoul, Korea. She has received Korea's National Contemporary Artist's Award and National Modern Art Award of Distinction. Since 1989, she has completed commissions for major corporations and public institutions, including the Samsung Corporation and the Banff Center for the Arts.

Hye Sun Baik makes her canvas out of hand-made paper, then creates her palette with paper pulp which she has dyed in various pastel shades. The highly textured work uses various mixed-media techniques. It is delicate looking, but sturdy, and conveys strong meditative and hypnotic impressions for the viewer.

Slides, pricing and scheduling upon request. Prices from $1,000 to $15,000.

A  *Dreams of Landscape II*, 1996, handmade paper, eight panel, each 4↑" x 29"

B  *Buddha's Calling III*, 1996, handmade paper, 92" x 38"

C  *Karma*, 1996, handmade paper, 92" x 38"

A

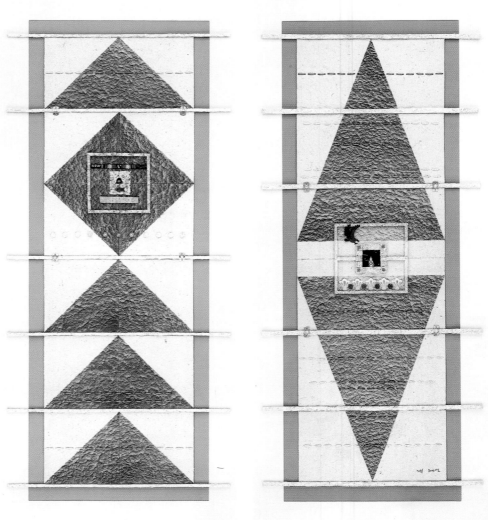

B

C

# Jocelyn Chateauvert

**123 First Avenue South**
**Mount Vernon, IA 52314**
**TEL   319-895-0195**

Jocelyn Chateauvert's interior panels create a textural atmosphere reminiscent of stone. They are suitable to hang on the wall or suspend from the ceiling. Lightweight, flexible and strong, her handmade paper panels can conform to a wall's angles and curves or can create a new contour.

Constructed in a grid pattern from flax paper, her panels start at $12.50 per square foot. Commissions accommodated up to 100 feet in length. Interior panels are lightfast, sound-absorbing and can be fire-retarded. Available in organic colors including charcoal (shown here), limestone and warm white. Samples available upon request.

In addition to her large panel pieces, she is recognized nationally for her sculptural paper jewelry.

David Puls

# Susan Gardels

**Sledrag Seed Productions**
**1316 Arthur Avenue**
**Des Moines, IA 50316**
**TEL   515-265-2361**

Susan Gardels creates artwork that is uncommonly site specific. Each commissioned piece interprets the history of the place where the work will be installed, as well as client needs for size, color and shape. Gardels researches the natural or human history of a place, transforms research into prose or poetry, then incorporates the words into an elegant visual statement.

Commissioned pieces include books, framed pages and ceremonial objects. Each piece is constructed from beautiful rag papers printed on an antique letterpress. Pieces can be clearly readable or the words and drawings can be cut into patterns and sewn into modern artifacts. Clients may request both: a beautiful handmade book and an abstract wall-sized piece for the corporate board room.

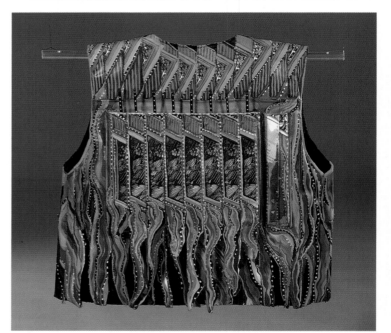

Photos: Jim Heemstra

# Fritzi Huber

134 Stoneybrook Road
Wilmington, NC 28405
FAX 910-686-4651
TEL 910-686-4651

Fritzi Huber has worked in handmade paper for over 20 years and is most recognized for her intense use of color and for her handsomely textured surfaces.

Fritzi Huber's works are in public and private collections across the United States and in Tokyo, Amsterdam, Mexico, Finland and Hungary.

Commissions include:
Duke Medical Center, Durham, NC
Dow Chemical, Houston, TX
IBM, Memphis, TN
Chamber of Commerce, La Jolla, CA
SAS Industries, Raleigh, NC

Please request slides, pricing and scheduling. All works can be treated to hang in an unframed format. Site specific installations welcomed. Completed works also available.

Also see this GUILD publication:
*THE GUILD: 1*

A  *Penelope's Pet Peeve #5*, 1996, 28" x 63"

B  *Penelope's Pet Peeve #1*, 1996, 37" x 43"

A

B

Photos: Arrow Ross

# Marlene Lenker

**Lenker Fine Arts**
**28 Northview Terrace**
**Cedar Grove, NJ 07009**
**FAX 201-239-8671 *51**
**TEL  201-239-8671**
**TEL  203-767-2098**

Marlene Lenker is an internationally recognized painter. For 28 years, she has been mastering her art. Marlene is listed in *Who's Who in American Art* and *American Women*. Her current series, *Mosaic Tile Fragments*, is created on 350-pound, 100% rag paper, incorporating innovative multi-media techniques that result in unique, iconic and elegant art. The tiles are adhered to board or canvas. Colors and patinas are lightfast, permanent and sealed with acrylic.

Inquires, studio visits, and commissions are welcomed.

Selected collections include: Arthur Young, Union Carbide, Warner-Lambert, Ortho, Merrill Lynch, Hewlett Packard, Pepsico, Prudential, Lever Bros., Johnson & Johnson, Sheraton, Kidder-Peabody.

A *Mosaic Fragment Series*, ©1996, 30" x 40"

B *Mosaic Fragment Series*, ©1996, 30" x 40"

A

B

Printed in Hong Kong ©1997 THE GUILD: The Designer's Sourcebook

# Nan Goss Studio

Nan Goss-Bilodeau
18801 SE 263rd Street
Kent, WA 98042
FAX 206-639-4898
TEL 206-639-9138
E-Mail: markb@halcyon.com

The artist's mixed-media assemblages are created by combining handmade papers, metallic leaf, and fabrics. These materials are pieced together with hand and machine stitching. The surfaces are further enhanced with traditional and nontraditional elements.

Wall pieces range in size from 16 inches square to 10 by 12 feet. The screens range in size from 12 x 24 inches to 2 x 5 feet, per panel.

Residential and commercial commission inquires welcomed. Completed works available.

A  *Autumn I & II*, 1996, mixed media,
   23"H x 36"W

B  *Screen with Twigs*, 1996, mixed media,
   48"H x 36"W

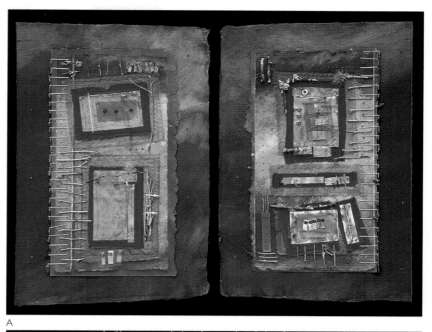

A

B

Photos: Ken Wagner

# Attention Getter

Sculptor Susan Venable likes a challenge. So when a Los Angeles-area designer came to her recently with an unusual request, she put her creativity to work. The designer needed a piece for the lobby of a corporate office, where a marble wall had been defaced. The work had to not only stand on its own, but draw attention from the marred surface.

"Most of my pieces are squares or rectangles," Venable explains, "but in this case we decided the piece should have a more complex shape, to take attention away from the blemished part of the marble."

Special design needs are nothing new for Venable, who has been creating intricate constructions of wire, encaustic and oil paint for several years. "With almost any commission, some kind of challenge comes up," the artist says. "That doesn't bother me; it just adds another element to the way I work."

In whatever context Venable's work appears, it's bound to intrigue the viewer. "There are a lot of paradoxes in my work," she says. "The pieces look like they'd be soft to the touch, but they're made of wire. And although they don't move, you get a sense of motion from the way they shimmer."

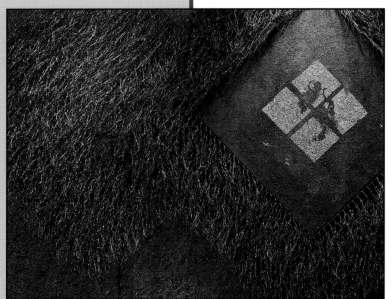

William Nettles

**Artist:** Susan Venable
**Liaison:** Fresh Paint, Culver City, CA
**Type of Work:** Construction of Steel and Copper Wire, Oil and Encaustic
**Title:** *Mistral* (detail)
**Site:** Oxford Properties, Torrance, CA

# Susan Singleton

AZO Inc.
1101 E. Pike Street
Seattle, WA 98122
FAX 206-322-5062
TEL  206-322-0390
TEL  800-344-0390
E-Mail: azo@azo.com

Singleton's *ZIGGURAT* works have been placed around the world, from the Tobu Sapporo Hotel in Japan to the U.S. Embassy in South Africa. The work ranges in size from 17 by 17 inches to 12 by 12 feet. Commissions, as well as available current work, can be further explained with a call to the AZO studio or by visiting the studio's Web site at http://www.azo.com.

These pieces reference ancient walls or objects from ancestral cultures. The work is made by stitching Asian papers together, forming a grid that is repeated in the patterns of metallic leafing and stenciling on the artwork surface. This work is a reflection of the artist's search for balance and spirit.

SHOWN: *ZIGGURAT*, installed for the 1996 Olympic Games, Atlanta Sheraton Hotel, 6'H x 8'W

Rick Semple

# Gloria Zmolek Smith

PO Box 1294
Cedar Rapids, IA 52406-1294
FAX 319-365-9611
TEL  319-365-9611
E-mail: zpaper@inav.net
http://soli.inav.net/~zpaper/

Gloria uses handmade paper to create quilts. She makes her paper using abaca and flax for durability. She creates the imagery by manipulating the wet pulp.

Pigments are used for coloring, making her papers much more resistant to fading than dyed fibers. The papers are stitched together on her sewing machine. Each piece can be displayed like a traditional quilt or can be framed.

Zmolek Smith's art is largely influenced by her children and concern for their world. *Vacuity of Vacuity,* seen below, asks the question, "Is there a limit to the number of people who can live together peaceably in our world?"

Her works are exhibited and collected nationally.

Slides, resumé and prices available upon request.

Also see these GUILD publications:
*Designer's Edition: 9, 11*

*Vacuity of Vacuity,* 1996, handmade paper, 38" x 38"

French Studios

# TAPESTRIES

# Anna Kocherovsky

6154 Quaker Hill Drive
West Bloomfield, MI 48322
TEL 810-661-0560

Anna Kocherovsky creates original works of art in tapestry for exhibition and commission. With their rich color and intriguing composition, Kocherovsky's *Woven Frescoes* can immediately transform an architectural space into an elegant environment.

The fine wool used to weave these tapestries is chemically moth-proofed and dyed with light-fast dyes. Installation can vary according to the wish of the client.

With ten years of experience in this field, Anna Kocherovsky has exhibited nationally, including a one-person show in Cleveland, OH. Her works are in collections in the United States, Canada, Russia and Japan.

Portfolio available upon request.

A *Four Seasons* (detail), 1996, tapestry

B *Treasure Island*, 1996, tapestry, 4' x 6'

A

B

# J.R. Koehler

**Koehler Studio**
**PO Box 279**
**Santa Fe, NM 87504**
**TEL  505-422-2201**

J.R. Koehler is one of the most sought-after weavers in the Southwest, with his vibrant tapestries attracting the attention of important collectors and museums. The tapestries combine bold designs and brilliant colors with superb craftsmanship. He lives in Santa Fe, where he maintains a studio full-time, finding inspiration for his work in the extraordinary landscape and the unique cultures of New Mexico.

Video, pricing and scheduling upon request.

*Oaxaca Stone III*, 1996, hand-dyed wool tapestry, 60" x 59¹/₂"

*Talus III*, 1996, hand-dyed wool tapestry, 48" x 96"

Photos: Pat Pollard, Ranchos de Taos, NM

# Jon Eric Riis
# Designs, Ltd.

Jon Eric Riis
875 Piedmont Avenue N.E.
Atlanta, GA 30309-4122
FAX 404-881-0322
TEL  404-881-9847

Jon Eric Riis has more than 25 years of professional experience in commissioned tapestries that are custom designed for the client. He has received two N.E.A. Fellowships, a Fullbright Grant and an American Institute of Architects Award.

Major commissions include: Shangri-La Portman Hotel, Shanghai, China; the Pavilion and Pan Pacific Hotels in Singapore; King Faisal Medical Center in Riyadh, Saudi Arabia.

Slides, pricing and scheduling upon request.

Also see this GUILD publication:
*THE GUILD: 4*

*Celestial Seas Tapestry* (detail), silk, metallic thread, gold-plated repoussé brass, and fresh-water pearls, 1996, Royal Caribbean Cruises Ltd., Splendour of the Seas, 27'H x 9'W

*Celestial Seas Tapestry*

Photos: Bart Kasten

# Klos Studios

**Nancy Smith Klos**
**2407 NE 9th Avenue**
**Portland, OR 97212**
**FAX 503-280-7985**
**TEL   503-282-7028**

For Nancy Smith Klos, weaving is a spiritual meditation and a way of living.

The trademark of her artistic work lies in the multiple fibers she chooses from hand-dyed and spun materials, mixed with commercial yarns. Her focus in pictorial tapestry is both sensual and organic. People are often drawn to her work because of its spiritual quality.

Nancy Smith Klos began weaving tapestries in 1990 and has been commissioned to weave residential, corporate and liturgical commissions for over eight years now. Her work *Ghost Dance* was profiled in the January 1997 edition of *Fiberarts* magazine. Ms Klos's work has also been published in *Handwoven, Surface Design Journal* and *Ornament*. Klos Studios offers workshops and lectures on the subjects of color and design, tapestry technique, and creative marketing for creative people. Ms. Klos shows her tapestries both nationally and internationally.

Nancy Smith Klos earned her B.A. in fine art from Connecticut College in New London. She also studied for five years in the Fiber Certificate Program at the Oregon College of Art and Craft in Portland.

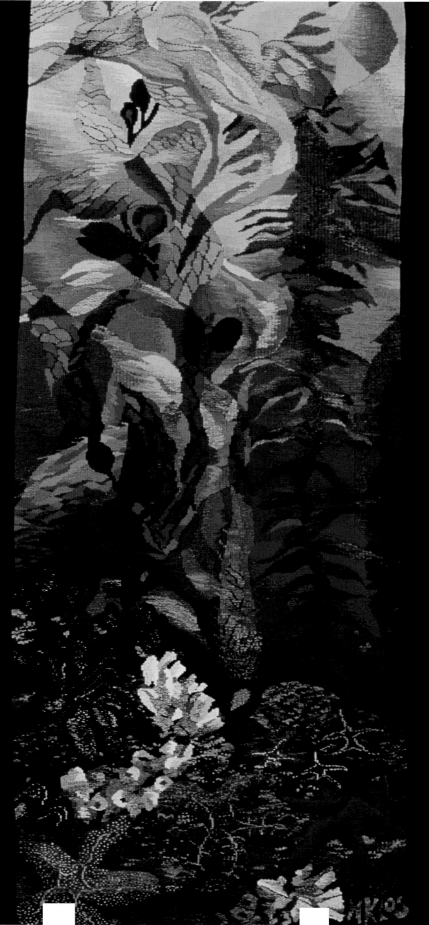

*Sculpture Garden,* (detail) pictorial tapestry, cotton wrap/ multi fiber weft, 3' x 8' © 1994

*Sculpture Garden,* installed at the Snapp residence in Coos Bay, OR

Photos: Charlie Kloppenberg

# Ann Schumacher

3743 Eaton Gate Lane
Auburn Hills, MI 48326
FAX 810-844-9240
TEL 810-844-9240

Ann Schumacher's hand-dyed tapestries, woven in wool, linen, silk and sisal, bring grace and beauty to private homes and public spaces. Well crafted and designed, these tapestries are rich in surface texture and vibrant color.

Among her awards as a professional artist and weaver for over 20 years, Schumacher has received a Michigan Arts Council grant, an American Tapestry Alliance award and a Fulbright Fellowship.

A *Circles of Infinity*, tapestry, 34" x 71"

B *The Blue Within*, tapestry, 31" x 52"

C *Sacred Protection*, tapestry, 42" x 53"

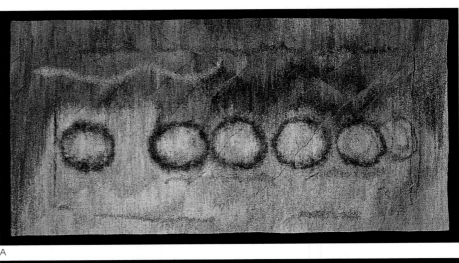

A

B

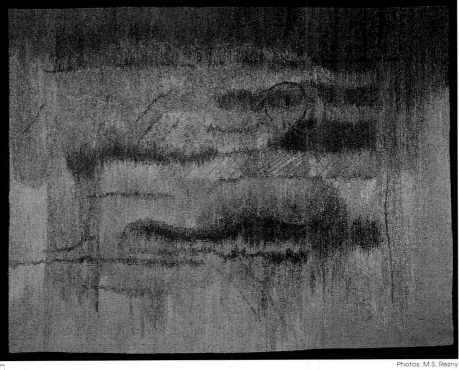

C

Photos: M.S. Rezny

Printed in Hong Kong ©1997 THE GUILD: The Designer's Sourcebook

# FIBER

# Banner Studio

**Ky Easton**
**6516 Bannockburn Drive**
**Bethesda, MD 20817**
**FAX 301-229-8822**
**TEL  301-229-8822**

Ky Easton uses a variety of materials (wool, linen, silk, nylon, Ultrasuede, metallics) and techniques (piecing, appliqué, stitching, embellishment) to produce banners, wall hangings, and atrium installations.

She has designed and fabricated many site-specific commissions, often incorporating words and/or images (such as logos) requested by the client.

Work may consist of multiple elements installed in a two- or three-dimensional format.

Budget, deadlines, installation, maintenance and code requirements are always given careful consideration.

Commissions welcomed.

A  *In Spirit Library*, 1996, 119" x 34"

B  *Fish Under the Moon*, 1996, 23¹/₂" x 108"

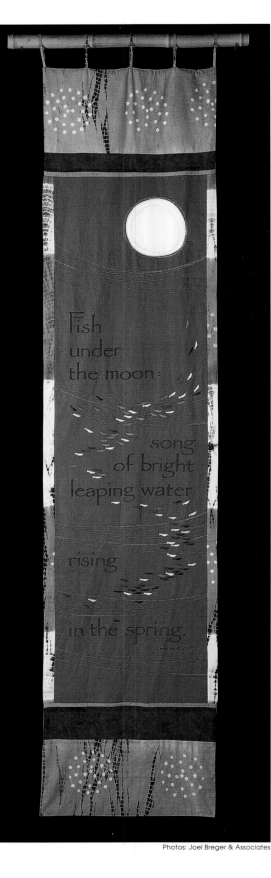

A

B

Printed in Hong Kong © 1997 THE GUILD: The Designer's Sourcebook

# Laura Militzer Bryant

2595 30th Avenue North
St. Petersburg, FL 33713
FAX 813-321-1905
TEL  813-327-3100

Exploring landscape through geometry, Laura Militzer Bryant's weavings evoke mysteriously ambiguous places. The richly colored, double-woven layers of wool, rayon and lurex shimmer and flicker, recede and advance, and tell a story of travelling through time and space.

Laura has created woven artworks for 19 years. She is included in many corporate and public collections such as Eli Lilly, Mobil Oil, Xerox Corporation, and the City of St. Petersburg. Her work is exhibited extensively in galleries and museums, and has been featured in *American Craft* and *Fiberarts* magazines. Laura has been awarded both National Endowment for the Arts and Florida State individual fellowships.

Also see these GUILD publications:
*Designer's Edition: 10, 11*

A *Welsh Wind,* 1996, weaving, 62" x 46"

B *Fall Leaves,* 1996, weaving on copper, 20" x 20"

C *Portcullis,* 1996, weaving on wood, with acrylic and metallic paint, 20" x 20"

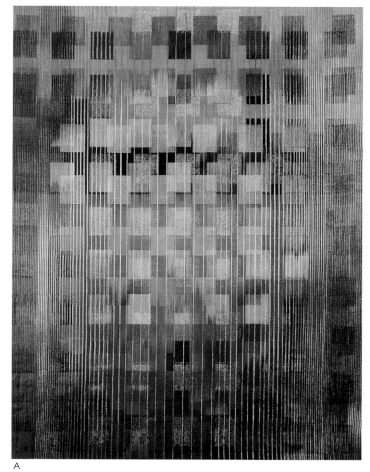

A

B

C

Photos: Thomas Bruce

# Beth Cunningham

**32 Sweetcake Mountain Road**
**New Fairfield, CT 06812**
**TEL  203-746-5160**

Through her use of rich textures, luscious colors, and meticulous craftsmanship, Beth Cunningham crosses the boundaries between fine art and fine craft.

These one-of-a-kind wall pieces are created by airbrushing an unprimed canvas with acrylic paints. Squares, strips or weavings of muslin, paint and silk are layered in precise square or rectangular formats. Paintings are commissioned by collectors, as well as corporate clients. Site-specific pieces may be large or small.

Completed works available. Gallery inquiries and exhibition opportunities welcomed.

Also see these previous GUILD editions:
*THE GUILD: 1, 2, 3, 4, 5*
*Designer's Edition: 6, 7, 8, 9, 10, 11*

A  *Petals,* 8" x 8"

B  *Flowing,* 17" x 20"

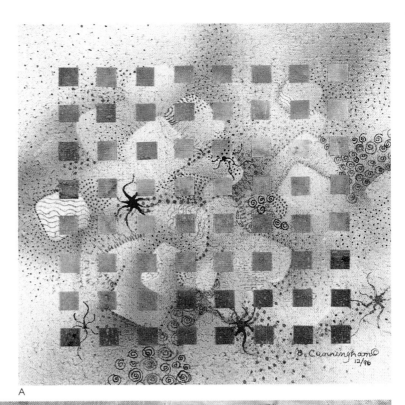

A

B

# Carl Erikson

**35 Morningside Commons**
**Brattleboro, VT 05301**
**TEL 802-254-9176**

Carl Erikson's textile constructions glow with color and unique design. The textiles in many are stretched over frameworks, building up bas-relief dimensions. In others, the textiles float freely from supporting rods. His designs range from pure abstractions to evocations of specific ideas and experiences.

Although much of Erikson's work is in the form of wall pieces, he has also created ceiling-mounted pieces — such as kites, magic carpets and totem poles — as well as bedcovers, window treatments and wall-substitutes. Site-specific work that incorporates the customer's fabric or design elements is particularly enticing to him.

Erikson has exhibited in galleries, public libraries, corporate spaces and restaurants.

Also see this GUILD publication:
*Designer's Edition: 11*

A  *Pansy*, mixed fabrics, textile construction, 33" x 28"

B  *Prism*, mixed fabrics, textile construction, 24" x 60"

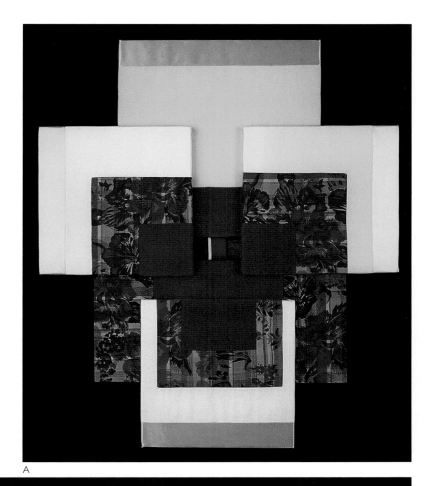

A

B

Photos: Jeff Baird

# Marilyn Forth

**416 David Drive**
**North Syracuse, NY 13212**
**FAX 315-458-0913**
**TEL   315-458-3786**

Marilyn Forth's batik paintings light up a room with nature's wonder. Add natural foliage to the mix and inside merges with outside.

Marilyn has exhibited for 20 years. She has created paintings for corporate and residential clients. Marilyn has taught fiber art at Syracuse University.

Satisfied clients are a must for this artist. Photos of completed commissions are sent to the client for final approval prior to shipping. The art is light-fast and guaranteed.

Also see these GUILD publications:
*Designer's Edition: 6, 7, 8, 10, 11*

*Garden Party*, batik, 45" x 45"

*Soir Jardin*, batik, 40" x 53"

Photos: Anthony Potter

*Soft Rock Symphony*, batik, 45" x 72", photo: Anthony Potter    Marilyn Forth, 416 David Drive, North Syracuse, NY 13212, FAX 315-458-0913, TEL 315-458-3786

# Suzanne Gernandt

18 Orange Street
Asheville, NC 28801
FAX 704-251-0521
TEL 704-281-0535
E-Mail: JGernandt@aol.com

Strongly influenced by ethnic traditions in textiles, Suzanne Gernandt utilizes a wide variety of surface design techniques. Through discharging and multiple dye baths, through shibori and warp painting, she layers color to create depth and intensity. With her hand-woven fabrics as a primary foundation, she uses stitchery and embellishments to enhance the exploration of primitive feelings evoked by symbols and marks.

Ms. Gernandt generally frames her pieces behind glass, often in groupings. Her award-winning work, featured in *Fiberarts* magazine, is in both private and corporate collections. Slides, resumé and prices are available upon request.

A *Artifacts of Childhood* (series), 18" x 72"

B *Beginnings*, 18" x 18"

C *A Peaceful Woman Lives Here*, 22" x 22"

A

B

C

Photos: Tim Barnwell

# Rebecca Gifford

Suncolors Studio
PO Box 16592
Saint Petersburg, FL 33733
TEL  813-323-5183

Rebecca creates site-specific designs for murals, wall panels, mobiles and banners. Her images are hand painted on fabrics or computer replicated.

Ms. Gifford has painted professionally since 1980 and is noted for a dramatic use of color. While in the Caribbean, her works recorded island life for private collections. Since 1990,

she has completed corporate and public commissions, and enhanced not only large spaces, but also residential environments.

Designs and pricing upon request.

A *Cranes & Cattails*, wall panel, 8'H x 3½'W

B *Plumage & Palms*, wall panel, 6'H x 3½'W

A

B

Photos: Jim Caulfield

# Marie-Laure Ilie

Marilor Art Studio
106 Via Sevilla
Redondo Beach, CA 90277
FAX 310-375-4977
TEL  310-375-4977

Ilie's large, abstract compositions achieve a sophisticated look and rich painterly effects by combining layers of organza with hand-painted silk or with cotton fabric coated with a special varnish. Her unusual appliqué technique allows for color fastness, easy maintenance and durability. These paintings can be hung like tapestries.

Since 1976, Ilie has exhibited extensively in the United States and in Europe. She has created innumerable successful commissions for residential and corporate collections.

Please call for prices, photos, slides, samples or proposal designs.

Also see these GUILD publications:
*THE GUILD: 4, 5*
*Designer's Edition: 7, 8, 9, 10, 11*

A *Kanaloa*, 7' x 9'

B *Summer Dance*, 51" x 49"

C *Travelogue*, 4' x 15'

A

B

C

Printed in Hong Kong ©1997 THE GUILD: The Designer's Sourcebook

# Gail Larned

Larned Marlow Studios
144 South Monroe Avenue
Columbus, OH 43205
FAX 614-258-7239
TEL 614-258-7239

Gail Larned creates an awareness of the natural world with her art which draws its inspiration from such organic forms as trees, plants and sea creatures. Her technique involves sewing coils together and combining them to create any image she desires. She is able to transform an ordinary image into extraordinary art. Gail welcomes inquiries about commissions and enjoys working closely with clients.

Larned has created fiber art for over 20 years and is represented in numerous corporate and private collections.

Collections include:
Pizzuti Development, Columbus, OH, Chicago, IL, Fairfield, CO, Houston, TX
Baton Rouge Chamber of Commerce, Baton Rouge, LA
Ohio Dept. of Agriculture, Reynoldsburg, OH
United Federal Bank, Clearwater, FL

Prices start at $1,000.

Also see these GUILD publications:
*THE GUILD: 1, 2, 3, 5*

A  *King Corn* (detail)

B  *King Corn*, 1996, Ohio Department of Agriculture, Reynoldsburg, OH, 18' x 5'

A

B

Photos: D.R. Goff, Quicksilver Photography

# Joyce P. Lopez

**Joyce Lopez Studio**
**1147 West Ohio Street #304**
**Chicago, IL 60622**
**FAX 312-243-5033**
**TEL  312-243-5033**

Joyce Lopez meticulously creates her sculpture out of metal poles and silk-like colored thread. With over 300 exquisite colors to choose from, color specifications are always met. These stunning works create significant pieces which enrich corporate, public and private interiors and collections.

Easily maintained, commissioned sculptures take two to four months to complete and cost $2,500 to $80,000. Call, fax or write for a brochure.

Collections include:
Sony Corporation
Bank of America
City of Chicago
Washington State
Michael Reese Hospital
Various private collections

Also see these GUILD publications:
*THE GUILD: 2, 3, 4, 5*
*Designer's Edition: 6, 7, 8, 9, 10, 11*
*Architect's Edition: 8*

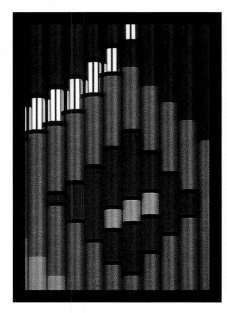

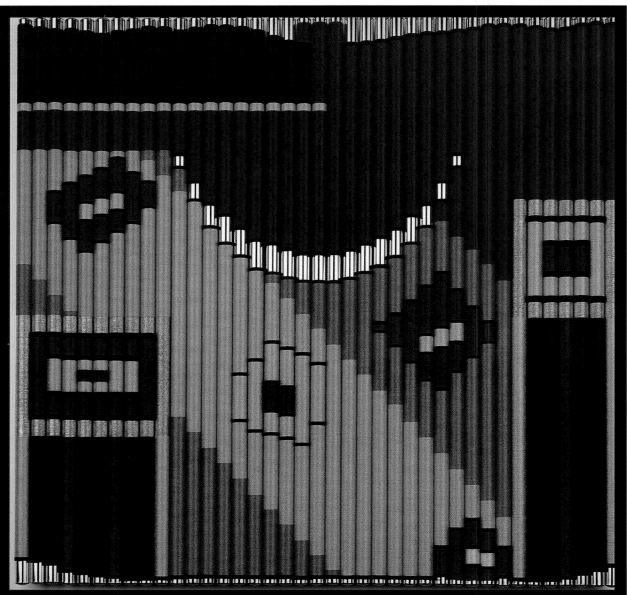

*Blue-Print Kimono*, chromed steel and thread sculpture, 32" x 32"

# Amanda Richardson

**An Vellan**
**Crean Bottoms**
**St. Buryan**
**Penzance**
**Cornwall TR19 6HD**
**U.K.**
**FAX 011-44-1736-810-485**
**TEL   011-44-1736-810-485**

Richardson's rich, light-reflective tapestries respond to their environment, varying with the angle and intensity of light. Fabrics are hand dyed, cut into intricate forms and bonded together to create a complex final image.

A professional artist for 19 years, Richardson has had numerous shows in America and Europe. Clients include BASF, Marriott Hotels, The Rouse Co., Hilton Hotels, The Oliver Carr Co., and the University of Alaska.

Pricing, scheduling and commission details are available upon request.

Also see these GUILD publications:
*Designer's Edition: 6, 7, 8, 9, 10*

*Sand Verbena*, Richardson Tapestry, 41" x 55"

*Sea and Rock*, Richardson Tapestry, Friday Harbor House, WA, 64" x 64"

# A Warm Welcome

**M**any artists use reprints of their GUILD pages as highly visual calling cards, relying on the detailed photographs to tell their story quickly and effectively. California sculptor Martin Sturman introduced himself to new neighbors through his reprints recently, when he moved to the Los Angeles suburb of Westlake Village. Sturman sent a sheaf of GUILD reprints to the editor of the community magazine.

"I sent them a packet, thinking they might do a little write-up," Sturman recalls. "But the editor liked my work so much that she wrote a whole feature on me, and then bought four of my pieces for her own collection."

Sturman's colorful steel sculpture has been featured in GUILD sourcebooks for many years. Although the self-taught artist has to confine his sculpting to weekends and evenings — devoting working hours to his thriving law practice — he's never treated his art as a hobby.

Barry Michlin

"It's always been serious for me," he says. "I'm getting to the age where I can think about retirement, and I'm really looking forward to devoting my full time to art. I'm very excited about that, knowing I've already established something of a reputation and found a market for what I do."

**Artist:** Martin Sturman
**Type of Work:** Stainless steel sculpture
**Title:** *Repose*
**Site:** Private residence, Westlake Village, CA

# Studio 5 Fiber Design

Vicki B. Schoenwald
JoAnn W. Bettinger
408 North Chestnut
North Platte, NE 69101
FAX 308-534-1289
TEL 800-386-2139
E-Mail: Studio5@nque.com

Vicki and her mother, JoAnn, believe strongly that you must do what you love most. That passion shows in each piece they create. They pay extraordinary attention to detail, neatness, color, fabrics and design.

Vicki and JoAnn customize each piece to suit the client's personality and the environment where the piece will be placed. Each piece is designed on the finest cotton or linen canvas.

Portfolio available upon request.

Commission work is encouraged.

A  *Warwycke Vase*, needlepoint, wool, 40"H x 26"W

B  *Four Seasons*, needlepoint, wool, 24"H x 30"W

A

B

Photos: Artistic Images by Yoaman L. Smith

# Harriet Zeitlin

**202 South Saltair Avenue
Los Angeles, CA 90049
TEL   310-472-0534**

Harriet Zeitlin has a love affair with found objects.
Feeling free to cut across the boundaries and
limitations of media in painting, printmaking,
sculpture and fiber, she continues to explore the
use of found objects and unconventional materials with richly ornamental patterns, textures and
sensuous brilliant colors.

Collections include:
Library of Congress, Washington, DC
Los Angles County Museum of Art
Grunwald Center for the Graphic Arts, UCLA
American Embassies, New Delhi and Hong Kong.

Prices upon request.

Also see this GUILD publication:
*Designer's Edition: 10*

A  *Two Masks*, 1996, plaster, acrylic, braided ties,
   each piece: 48" x 12"

B  *Ginger and Fred*, 1996, braided ties, feather
   boa, 93" x 48"

A

B

Printed in Hong Kong ©1997 THE GUILD: The Designer's Sourcebook

## A.R.T. TAPESTRIES BY VICTORIA STREET

VICTORIA STREET
5701 ANDREWS RD
MEDFORD, OR 97501
TEL 541-770-1141
FAX 541-770-2030
Established: 1980
**Products:** tapestries **Techniques:** weaving, beading, unique fiber combinations **Size Range:** no size limit **Price Range:** $150 to $350/sq. ft.

## DOUG ABBOTT

PULP CREEK
4905 14TH AVE S
MINNEAPOLIS, MN 55417
TEL 612-827-6853
Established: 1992
**Products:** paper **Techniques:** casting, laminating, embedding **Size Range:** 12" × 12" to 72" × 72" **Price Range:** $150 to $1,800/piece

## SOPHIE ACHESON

ACHESON STUDIOS
6 POST OFFICE LN PO BOX 372
GREENS FARMS, CT 06436
TEL 203-255-1349
Established: 1978
**Products:** paper
**Techniques:** painting, appliqué, embossing **Size Range:** 5" × 5" to 40" × 50"
**Price Range:** $300 to $3,000/sq. ft.

## ★ KAREN ADACHI

**702 MONARCH WAY**
**SANTA CRUZ, CA 95060-3091**
**TEL 408-429-6192**
**Established: 1972**
**Products:** paper **Techniques:** painting, dyeing, airbrush **Size Range:** 2' × 2' to 7' × 10' **Price Range:** $500 to $4,000/piece

See page 166 for photographs and additional information.

## SANDY ADAIR

FIBRE DESIGN
RR 3 BOX 912
BOONE, NC 28607-9544
TEL 704-264-0259
Established: 1978
**Products:** tapestries, macramé **Techniques:** weaving, embroidery, off-loom weaving **Size Range:** 1' × 3' to 6' × 10' **Price Range:** $100 to $125/sq. ft.

## ★ B.J. ADAMS

**ART IN FIBER**
**2821 ARIZONA TERRACE NW**
**WASHINGTON, DC 20016-2642**
**TEL 202-364-8404**
**FAX 202-686-1042**
**Established: 1970**
**Products:** fabric constructions **Techniques:** painting, appliqué, machine embroidery **Size Range:** 12" × 12" to unlimited (modular) **Price Range:** $150 to $500/sq. ft.

See photograph page 200.

## ELLYN AHMER

KALEIDOSCOPE SOLUTIONS
608 TOMBSTONE CYN, PO BOX 714
BISBEE, AZ 85603
TEL 520-432-8026
FAX 520-432-8026
Established: 1989
**Products:** fabric constructions
**Techniques:** weaving, dyeing
**Size Range:** 6" × 6" to 5' × 10'
**Price Range:** $90/sq. ft.

## ADELA AKERS

16200 RIO NIDO RD
GUERNEVILLE, CA 95446
TEL 707-869-9753
Established: 1963
**Products:** tapestries **Techniques:** weaving, dyeing **Size Range:** 3' × 3' to 8' × 30' **Price Range:** $300 to $600/sq. ft., trade discount available

## LEONORE ALANIZ

519 E 82ND ST #58
NEW YORK, NY 10028-7171
TEL 212-737-4416
**Products:** fabric constructions, transparent banners, hand printed **Techniques:** tree leaves imprinted on fabric, with text **Size Range:** any size **Price Range:** $80 and up/sq. ft.

## DONNA ALBERT

DONNA ALBERT STUDIO
15 OAK HILL DR
PARADISE, PA 17562
TEL 717-687-5114
FAX 717-687-5115
Established: 1969
**Products:** art quilts, pictorial quilts **Techniques:** embroidery, quilting, heat-fusion appliqué **Size Range:** 12" × 18" to 10' × 10' **Price Range:** $400 to $8,000/piece

## MARTA AMUNDSON

HC36-85 GOOSE KNOB DR
RIVERTON, WY 82501
TEL 307-856-3373
FAX 307-856-5176
Established: 1976
**Products:** art quilts **Techniques:** appliqué, embroidery, quilting **Size Range:** 2' × 2' to 12' × 12' **Price Range:** $500 to $18,000/piece

## ANANSA-PURUO DESIGNS

ROBYN DAUGHTRY
8 FILBERT COURT
GAITHERSBURG, MD 20879
TEL 301-258-8313
FAX 301-258-8920
Established: 1980
**Products:** paper **Techniques:** painting, dyeing, collage **Size Range:** 8" × 14" to 6' × 8' **Price Range:** $150 to $225/sq. ft.

## ★ SUSAN BEDFORD ANDRADE

**DRAGONFLIGHT FANTASY**
 **FIBER ART**
**945 POINT RD**
**MARION, MA 02738-1289**
**TEL 508-748-2907**
**Established: 1985**
**Products:** fabric constructions **Techniques:** appliqué, quilting, soft sculpture **Size Range:** 4" × 5" to 20' × 20' **Price Range:** $25 to $6,000/piece

See photograph page 201.

## DINA ANGEL-WING

1054 CRAGMONT AVE
BERKELEY, CA 94708
TEL 510-526-3006
FAX 510-559-9572
Established: 1981
**Products:** mixed media installations **Techniques:** paper casting with assamblage **Size Range:** 12" × 12" to 40" × 60" **Price Range:** $300 to $2,000/piece

## CAROL ARMSTRONG

CAROL ARMSTRONG QUILTS
STAR SIDING RD HC 01 BOX 125
SHINGLETON, MI 49884
TEL 906-452-6469
Established: 1980
**Products:** art quilts **Techniques:** appliqué, embroidery, quilting **Size Range:** 8" × 8" to 100" × 100" **Price Range:** $50 to $5,000/piece

## ART IN QUILTS

KAY KOEPER SORENSEN
24920 73RD ST
SALEM, WI 53168
TEL 414-843-2348
Established: 1977
**Products:** art quilts
**Techniques:** dyeing, quilting, piecing
**Size Range:** 12" × 12" to 120" × 120"
**Price Range:** $100 to $200/sq. ft.

## SANDY ASKEW

50951 EXPRESSWAY
BELLEVILLE, MI 48111
TEL 313-483-5529
Established: 1975
**Products:** fiber installations
**Techniques:** contemporary coil weaving
**Size Range:** 12" × 36" to 6' × 12' **Price Range:** $100 to $5,000/piece

## CATHY PHILLIPS ATEN

CATHY ATEN TEXTILES
RR 2 BOX 154
SANTA FE, NM 87505-8659
TEL 505-983-7753
Established: 1978
**Products:** painted wool tapestries **Techniques:** painting, stamping or printing **Size Range:** 4' × 6' to 10' × 20' **Price Range:** $1,800 to $8,000/piece

## ELLEN ATHENS

PO BOX 1386
MENDOCINO, CA 95460-1386
TEL 707-937-2642
Established: 1982
**Products:** tapestries **Techniques:** weaving **Size Range:** 2' × 2' to 5' × 15' **Price Range:** $400 to $18,000/piece

## CAROL ATLESON

FIBER ART STUDIO
465 RUSKIN RD
AMHERST, NY 14226-4235
TEL 716-834-9384
Established: 1979
**Products:** tapestries **Techniques:** weaving **Size Range:** 2' × 3' to 7' × 7' **Price Range:** $1,200 to $10,000/piece

# FIBER ART FOR THE WALL

## BAAS STUDIO

BARB MACLEOD
RR 1
THORNBURY, ON N0H 2P0
CANADA
TEL 519-599-2963
Established: 1974
**Products:** 2D, 3D fiber installations **Techniques:** weaving, airbrush, padde fabric construcions **Size Range:** 3' × 4' to unlimited **Price Range:** $50 to $250/sq. ft.

## ★ JOHN BABCOCK

**4780 SOQUEL CREEK RD**
**SOQUEL, CA 95073**
**TEL 408-476-6302**
**FAX 408-462-5949**
**Established: 1966**
**Products:** hand-formed paper **Techniques:** laminating, casting, pouring **Size Range:** 3' × 2' to 6' × 15' **Price Range:** $800 to $10,000/piece

See page 167 for photographs and additional information.

## JOANN BACHELDER

RIVERTOWN TEXTILES
1001 S HENRY ST
BAY CITY, MI 48706-5007
TEL 517-892-3013
Established: 1978
**Products:** wall hangings
**Techniques:** dyeing, weaving
**Size Range:** 20" × 20" to 9' × 12'
**Price Range:** $350 to $2,500/piece

## BADGER CREEK GALLERY

MICHAEL BERRY
LINDA FARRELL
380 HWY 92, PO BOX 344
CRAWFORD, CO 81415
TEL 970-921-7595
Established: 1977
**Products:** wood and fiber installations
**Techniques:** weaving, beading, laminating
**Size Range:** 8" × 12" to 6' to 8' **Price Range:** $50 to $4,000/piece

## ★ HYE SUN BAIK

**4573 W 2ND AVE**
**VANCOUVER, BC V6R 1K7**
**TEL 604-222-2276**
**FAX 604-222-2076**
**E-Mail:** sga@mindlink.net
**Established: 1989**
**Products:** paper **Techniques:** embroidery, airbrush, pulp painting **Size Range:** 30" × 40" to 30" × 339" **Price Range:** $1,000 to $15,000/piece

See page 168 for photographs and additional information.

## SALLY BAILEY

HOOKED ON ART
PO BOX 60204
SANTA BARBARA, CA 93160-0204
TEL 805-563-0227
Established: 1969
**Products:** hooked art hangings
**Techniques:** traditional hooking
**Size Range:** 12" × 18" to 36" × 72"
**Price Range:** $75 to $200/sq. ft.

## MARTIN K. BAKER

ARTESANOS TIPICOS/COYOTE
  DESIGNS
715 CLEVELAND ST
MISSOULA, MT 59801-3738
TEL 406-728-2789
FAX 406-728-3668
Established: 1974
**Products:** tapestries
**Techniques:** painting, silkscreen, weaving
**Size Range:** 24" × 24" to 22' × 36'
**Price Range:** $10 to $100/sq. ft.

## JUDY BALES

2154 125TH ST
FAIRFIELD, IA 52556
TEL 515-472-9585
Established: 1986
**Products:** mixed media installations
**Techniques:** weaving, painting, wrapping **Size Range:** 12" × 36" to 4' × 12'
**Price Range:** $200 to $3,000/piece; $10 to $100/sq. ft.

## ELAINE BALL

1227 ABBE HILL RD
MT VERNON, IA 52314
TEL 319-895-8279
Established: 1964
**Products:** mixed media installations
**Techniques:** weaving, dyeing, casting
**Size Range:** 20" × 20" to 8' × 8' **Price Range:** $350 to $3,500/piece

B.J. Adams, *Coherent Connections*, 1995, appliqué with machine embroidery (fabrics and threads), three panels, 5'H × 4½'W total size, commissioned by Jefferson Pilot Corporation, Greensboro, NC, photo: Breger & Associates

## DORIS BALLY

BALLY DESIGN, INC.
420 N CRAIG ST
PITTSBURGH, PA 15213-1105
TEL 412-621-3709
FAX 412-621-9030
Established: 1963
**Products:** tapestries **Techniques:** weaving **Size Range:** 20" × 20" to 94" × 20' **Price Range:** $155/sq. ft.

## ★ BANNER STUDIO

**KY EASTON**
**6516 BANNOCKBURN DR**
**BETHESDA, MD 20817**
**TEL 301-229-8822**
**FAX 301-229-8822**
**Established: 1985**
**Products:** fiber installations **Techniques:** embroidery, appliqué, quilting **Size Range:** 2' × 3' to 15' × 10' **Price Range:** $75 to $1,500/piece

See page 184 for photographs and additional information.

## BARBARA FARRELL ARTS

BARBARA FARRELL
PO BOX 2944
SANFORD, FL 32772-2944
TEL 407-321-0100
FAX 407-321-8666
Established: 1973
**Products:** mixed media installations **Techniques:** painting, stitchery, fresco **Size Range:** 4' × 5' to 10' × 12' **Price Range:** $100 minimum/sq. ft.

## ★ BARKER-SCHWARTZ DESIGNS

**JOYCE BARKER-SCHWARTZ**
**915 SPRING GARDEN ST,**
**STUDIO 315**
**PHILADELPHIA, PA 19123-2605**
**TEL 215-236-0745**
**Established: 1984**
**Products:** woven appliquéd hangings **Techniques:** weaving, painting, appliqué **Size Range:** 3' × 3' to 10' × 18' **Price Range:** $50 to $125/sq. ft.

See page 43 for photographs and additional information.

## TERESA BARKLEY

9 KENSINGTON TERR
MAPLEWOOD, NJ 07040
TEL 201-378-5815
Established: 1978
**Products:** art quilts **Techniques:** appliqué, painting, quilting **Size Range:** 16" × 20" to 103" × 110" **Price Range:** $500 to $20,000/piece

## SONYA LEE BARRINGTON

837 47TH AVE
SAN FRANCISCO, CA 94121-3207
TEL 415-221-6510
Established: 1972
**Products:** art quilts **Techniques:** dyeing, quilting, piecing, appliqué **Size Range:** 2' × 2' to 8' × 8' **Price Range:** $125 to $225/sq. ft.

## BARRON CUSTOM WALLHANG-INGS & WINDOW TREATMENTS

BARBARA, STEVE, RUTH BARRON
1943 NEW YORK AVE
HUNTINGTON STATION, NY 11768
TEL 516-549-4242
FAX 516-549-9122
Established: 1973
**Products:** fiber installations, window treatments **Techniques:** embroidery, weaving, wrapping **Size Range:** 2' × 1' to 24' × 24' **Price Range:** $150 to $175/sq. ft.

## CATHY BARTELS

1079 WYKOFF WAY
LAGUNA BEACH, CA 92651-3036
TEL 714-494-8942
FAX 714-497-0400
Established: 1982
**Products:** mixed media installations 'canvas reconstructions' **Techniques:** painting, photo techniques, machine-image transfers **Size Range:** 24" × 24" to 10' × 10' **Price Range:** $300 to $5,000/piece; $50 to $150/sq. ft.

## DOREEN BECK
## DINK SIEGEL

100 W 57TH ST #10G
NEW YORK, NY 10019-3327
TEL 212-246-9757
Established: 1974
**Products:** art quilts **Techniques:** appliqué, quilting **Size Range:** 2' × 3' to 4' × 5' **Price Range:** $1,500 to $10,000/piece

## JUDY BECKER

27 ALBION ST
NEWTON, MA 02159-2119
TEL 617-332-6778
Established: 1981
**Products:** art quilts **Techniques:** appliqué, dyeing, quilting **Size Range:** 3' × 3' to 10' × 15' **Price Range:** $900 to $8,000/piece; $50 to $100/sq. ft.

## PAMELA E. BECKER

5 HENDRICK RD
FLEMINGTON, NJ 08822-7155
TEL 908-806-4911
Established: 1978
**Products:** painted fabric constructions **Techniques:** appliqué, painting, piecing **Size Range:** 28" × 32" to 8' × 16' **Price Range:** $3,000 and up/piece

## NANCY BELFER

1217 DELAWARE AVE #805
BUFFALO, NY 14209
TEL 716-881-5920
**Products:** tapestries **Techniques:** weaving, painting, embroidery **Size Range:** 30" × 72" to 45" × 72" **Price Range:** $100 to $150/sq. ft.

## SUE BENNER

8517 SAN FERNANDO WAY
DALLAS, TX 75218-4306
TEL 214-324-3550
Established: 1980
**Products:** art quilts **Techniques:** dyeing, painting, quilting **Size Range:** 15" × 15" to 12' × 15' **Price Range:** $400 to $25,000/piece

## ASTRID HILGER BENNETT

909 WEBSTER ST
IOWA CITY, IA 52240-4738
TEL 319-338-9176
Established: 1978
**Products:** art quilts **Techniques:** dyeing, painting, screen printing **Size Range:** 18" × 24" to 8' × 10' **Price Range:** $250 to $8,000/piece

Susan Bedford Andrade, *Christmas Presence III*, 1996, cotton, lamé, silk, brocade, tinsel, plastic and paint, 58" × 58"

| | |
|---|---|
| **LISTED ARTISTS** work at a professional level in the area of fiber art for the wall. | |
| ESTABLISHED — The year the artist began working as a professional. | |
| PRODUCTS — Types of fiber art created by the artist for display on walls. | **CAN'T FIND A CERTAIN ARTIST?** Check the Index of Artists and Companies for a comprehensive listing of every artist in *The Designer's Sourcebook 12.* |
| TECHNIQUES — Techniques typically used by the artist to create the work. | |
| SIZE RANGE — Range of sizes for the artist's typical art for the wall. | **NEED AN ARTIST FOR YOUR PROJECT?** See the Commissions Clearinghouse on THE GUILD's Web site. List project specs. Artists respond directly. |
| PRICE RANGE — From lowest to highest, typical retail prices for the artist's fiber art for the wall. Prices are reported per piece and/or per square foot. | Try it! *http://www.guild.com* |

## CHRISTINA BENSON-VOS

15 GRAMERCY PARK
NEW YORK, NY 10003
TEL 212-982-5960
Established: 1986
**Products:** tapestries **Techniques:** weaving **Size Range:** 4' × 6' to 6' × 8'
**Price Range:** $5,000 to $15,000/piece

## LYNN BERKOWITZ

PO BOX 121
SLATEDALE, PA 18079-0121
TEL 610-767-8072
Established: 1978
**Products:** fabric constructions
**Techniques:** dyeing, weaving
**Size Range:** 10" × 10" to 8' × 8'
**Price Range:** $400 to $5,000/piece

## JANNA BERNSTEIN

CREATIONS
319 FERNWAY COVE
MEMPHIS, TN 38117-2012
TEL 901-680-0812
Established: 1974
**Products:** tapestries, fiber installations, rugs **Techniques:** weaving, screen printing, wrapping **Size Range:** 1' × 1' and up **Price Range:** $100 to $400/sq. ft.

## HELGA BERRY

FIBER COMPOSITION
PO BOX 112230
ANCHORAGE, AK 99511-2230
TEL 907-346-2392
FAX 907-346-2216
E-Mail: fibercom@alaska.net
Established: 1972
**Products:** tapestries **Techniques:** weaving **Size Range:** 8" × 8" to 4' × 7'
**Price Range:** up to $15,000/piece

## LOUISE LEMIEUX BÉRUBÉ

CENTRE DES METIERS D'ART
1751 RUE RICHARDSON, BUREAU 5530
MONTREAL, QC H3K 1G6
CANADA
TEL 514-933-3728
FAX 514-933-6305
Established: 1979
**Products:** fabric constructions
**Techniques:** weaving with metal wires
**Size Range:** 8" × 8" to 6' × 6' **Price Range:** $300 to $15,000/piece

## LAURIE R. BIEZE

BIEZES CITY CENTER
GALLERY & STUDIO
216 S BARSTOW
EAU CLAIRE, WI 54701
TEL 715-833-0007
Established: 1964
**Products:** paper
**Techniques:** painting, dyeing, casting
**Size Range:** 18" × 18" to 4' × 6'
**Price Range:** $200 to $4,000/piece; $100 to $200/sq. ft.

## BIG SUR HANDWOVENS

LAVERNE MCLEOD
HC67 BOX 1145
BIG SUR, CA 93920
TEL 408-667-2788
Established: 1986
**Products:** fiber installations
**Techniques:** weaving, quilting, beading
**Size Range:** 8½" × 14" to 5' × 5'
**Price Range:** $500 to $9,000/piece

## ELIZABETH BILLINGS

E.P. BILLINGS, WEAVER
ONE PHILLIPS COVE
CAPE NEDDICK, ME 03902
TEL 207-361-2777
Established: 1987
**Products:** tapestries
**Techniques:** weaving, natural-dyed ikat
**Size Range:** 24" × 24" to 20' × 30'
**Price Range:** $100 to $350/sq. ft.

## BINGO PAJAMA WALLWORKS

SHANNON SCHERING
MATTHEW SCHERING
PO BOX 165
6 WASHINGTON ST #C
TRUMANSBURG, NY 14886
TEL 607-387-4924
Established: 1993
**Products:** fiber/wood wallworks
**Techniques:** dyeing, airbrushing, wood sculpting **Size Range:** 12" × 12" to 40" × 60" **Price Range:** $100 to $800/piece

## ★ CECILIA BLOMBERG

**3613 44TH ST CT NW**
**GIG HARBOR, WA 98335**
**TEL 253-858-8210**
**FAX 253-858-7447**
**E-Mail: cblomberg@worldnet.att.net**
**Established: 1976**
**Products:** tapestries **Techniques:** weaving **Size Range:** 12" × 12" to 8' × 20' **Price Range:** $300 to $50,000/piece

**See photograph this page.**

## REBECCA BLUESTONE

PO BOX 1704
SANTA FE, NM 87504-1704
TEL 505-989-9599
FAX 505-986-3412
E-Mail: 103327.3312@compuserve.com
Established: 1984
**Products:** tapestries
**Techniques:** weaving, dyeing, embroidery **Size Range:** 60" × 36" to 20' × 6'
**Price Range:** $110 to $225/sq. ft.

## NANCY BONEY

97 KING ST
FANWOOD, NJ 07023-1517
TEL 908-889-8219
Established: 1973
**Products:** fabric constructions
**Techniques:** appliqué, fabric sculpture
**Size Range:** 24" × 36" to 5' × 8' **Price Range:** $73 to $100/sq. ft.

Cecilia Blomberg, *Gentle Intrusion*, 1991, tapestry, 39" × 57"

## DANA BOUSSARD

2 HEART CREEK RRT #1
ARLEE, MT 59821
TEL 406-726-3357
FAX 406-726-4136
Established: 1966
**Products:** fiber installations
**Techniques:** airbush, appliqué, painting
**Size Range:** 3' × 4' to 10' × 100'
**Price Range:** $150 to $300/sq. ft.

## KAREN BOVARD

SPECTRUM QUILTS
259 FARM HILL RD
MIDDLETOWN, CT 06457-4224
TEL 203-346-1116
Established: 1986
**Products:** art quilts
**Techniques:** painting, beading, quilting
**Size Range:** 2' × 2' to 100" × 120"
**Price Range:** $80 to $150/sq. ft.

## GEORGE-ANN BOWERS

1199 CORNELL AVE
BERKELEY, CA 94706-2305
TEL 510-524-3611
Established: 1983
**Products:** tapestries
**Techniques:** weaving, painting, dyeing
**Size Range:** 15" × 15" to 48" × 108"
**Price Range:** $200 to $300/sq. ft.

## ODETTE BRABEC

1107 GOLF AVE
HIGHLAND PARK, IL 60035-3637
TEL 847-432-2704
Established: 1977
**Products:** tapestries **Techniques:** weaving **Size Range:** 24" × 24" to 5' × 10' **Price Range:** $1,000 to $13,000/piece

## DAVID BRACKETT

404 PENN ST
NEW BETHLEHEM, PA 16242
TEL 814-275-1846
**Products:** fabric constructions
**Techniques:** weaving, dyeing, screen printing **Size Range:** 73" × 57" to 96" × 120" **Price Range:** $2,000 to $6,000/piece

## JEANNE BRAEN

14 LEVESQUE LN
MONT VERNON, NH 03057-1420
TEL 603-672-7822
Established: 1975
**Products:** tapestries **Techniques:** weaving **Size Range:** 3' × 5' to 9' × 12' **Price Range:** $80 to $100/sq. ft.

## LAURENCE BRANSCU

ART/DESIGN
6527 N NORTHWEST HWY
CHICAGO, IL 60631
TEL 312-631-1682
FAX 312-631-1682
Established: 1980
**Products:** hand-painted silk **Techniques:** painting, airbrushing, resist dyeing **Size Range:** 15" × 15" to 4' × 8' **Price Range:** $150 to $4,000/piece

## ANN BRAUER

2 CONWAY ST
SHELBURNE FALLS, MA 01370
TEL 413-625-8605
Established: 1981
**Products:** art quilts **Techniques:** quilting **Size Range:** 8" × 10" to 8' × 9' **Price Range:** $45 to $5,000/piece; $45 to $150/sq. ft.

## LYNDA BROTHERS

4255 HITCH BLVD
MOORPARK, CA 93021-9731
TEL 805-523-3101
Established: 1969
**Products:** tapestries **Techniques:** painting, weaving, marbling **Size Range:** unlimited **Price Range:** $35 to $400/sq. ft.

## TAFI BROWN

TY BRYN DESIGN STUDIOS
PO BOX 319
ALSTEAD, NH 03602-0319
TEL 603-756-3412
Established: 1975
**Products:** art quilts
**Techniques:** quilting, cyanotype **Size Range:** 12" × 12" to 96" × 96" **Price Range:** $250 to $18,000/piece

## KATE BROWNING-WARE

KATE BROWNING ORIGINALS
PO BOX 767
INGRAM, TX 78025-0767
TEL 210-238-3311
FAX 210-238-3323
Established: 1979
**Products:** fiber installations
**Techniques:** weaving, painting, dyeing
**Size Range:** 24" × 24" and up **Price Range:** $800 to $12,000/piece; up to $200/sq. ft.

## RACHEL BRUMER

1112 HARVARD AVE E
SEATTLE, WA 98102
TEL 206-328-7007
Established: 1990
**Products:** art quilts
**Techniques:** dyeing, appliqué, quilting
**Size Range:** 50" × 40" to 80" × 80" **Price Range:** $2,000 to $3,500/piece

## ★ LAURA MILITZER BRYANT

**2595 30TH AVE N**
**ST PETERSBURG, FL 33713**
**TEL 813-327-3100**
**FAX 813-321-1905**
**Established: 1980**
**Products:** tapestries
**Techniques:** weaving, painting, dyeing
**Size Range:** 20" × 20" to 54" × 100"
**Price Range:** $900 to $10,000/piece

**See page 185 for photographs and additional information.**

## LOIS BRYANT

503 S 8TH ST
LINDENHURST, NY 11757-4616
TEL 516-226-7819
Established: 1979
**Products:** fiber installations **Techniques:** weaving **Size Range:** 1' × 1' to 8' × 17' **Price Range:** $175 to $250/sq. ft.

## ELIZABETH J. BUCKLEY

HERITAGE TAPESTRIES
13418 MOUNTIAN VIEW AVE NE
ALBUQUERQUE, NM 87123
TEL 505-291-9635
Established: 1982
**Products:** tapestries **Techniques:** weaving **Size Range:** 8" × 12" to 30" × 48" **Price Range:** $500 to $10,000/piece

Barbara Cade, *Pansies*, 1996, handmade felt, 8'W × 38"H × 6"D, photo: Cindy Momchilov

# FIBER ART FOR THE WALL

## PATTI J. BULLARD

SOUTHWEST TAPESTRIES
103 CHAMBERLAIN AVE
COLORADO SPRINGS, CO 80906
TEL 719-579-0597
FAX 719-576-4196
Established: 1990
**Products:** fabric constructions **Techniques:** painting, quilting, machine embroidery **Size Range:** 15" x 36" to 48" x 60" **Price Range:** $100 to $1,000/piece

## MYRA BURG

2913 3RD ST #201
SANTA MONICA, CA 90405
TEL 310-399-5040
FAX 310-399-0623
Established: 1977
**Products:** mixed media installations, rare wood, metals **Techniques:** wrapping, assemblies **Size Range:** 1' x 1' to 100' x 200' **Price Range:** $150 to $100,000/piece; $150 to $450/sq. ft.

## TRICIA BURLING

WILLOWWEAVE
37 WELLS RD
MONROE, CT 06468
TEL 203-268-4794
Established: 1979
**Products:** wall hangings
**Techniques:** dyeing, weaving, wrapping
**Size Range:** panels up to any size
**Price Range:** $45 to $50/sq. ft.

## SUSAN EILEEN BURNES

3137 IRA RD
AKRON, OH 44333-1245
TEL 330-668-4760
FAX 216-526-0874
Established: 1993
**Products:** fiber installations **Techniques:** embroidery, appliqué, beading
**Size Range:** 6" x 6" to 5' x 6' **Price Range:** $200 to $10,000/piece

## ELIZABETH A. BUSCH

RR 1 BOX 365
BANGOR, ME 04401-9705
TEL 207-942-7820
FAX 207-942-7820
Established: 1987
**Products:** art quilts
**Techniques:** airbush, painting, quilting
**Size Range:** 12" x 12" to 10' x 25'
**Price Range:** $200 to $12,000/piece; $200 to $300/sq. ft.

## MARY BALZER BUSKIRK

BUSKIRK STUDIOS
53 VIA VENTURA
MONTEREY, CA 93940-4340
TEL 408-375-6165
Established: 1956
**Products:** tapestries **Techniques:** painting, weaving, gold and silver leaf
**Size Range:** 1' x 1' to 20' x 20' **Price Range:** $100 to $175/sq. ft.

## ★ BARBARA CADE

**262 HIDEAWAY HILLS DR**
**HOT SPRINGS, AR 71901-8841**
**TEL 501-262-4065**
**FAX 501-262-4065 (Call first)**
**Established: 1968**
**Products:** sculpture
**Techniques:** weaving, felting, mixed media **Size Range:** 2' x 2' to 8' x 10'
**Price Range:** $500 to $10,000/piece

**See photograph page 203.**

## MONECA CALVERT

3858 BALTIC CIR
ROCKLIN, CA 95677
TEL 916-632-3306
Established: 1983
**Products:** art quilts **Techniques:** appliqué, embroidery, quilting, piecing **Size Range:** 2' x 2' to 8' x 8' and larger **Price Range:** $1,800 to $20,000/piece

## SUZY CAMÉLEON

5422 CONSTANCE
NEW ORLEANS, LA 70115-2034
TEL 504-899-9044
Established: 1977
**Products:** silk wallhangings
**Techniques:** painting dyeing quilting
**Size Range:** 2' x 3' to 4' x 6' **Price Range:** $100 to $1,000/piece; $25 to $100/sq. ft.

## LAUREN MUKAMAL CAMP

25 THERESA LN
SANTA FE, NM 87505
TEL 505-474-7943
Established: 1996
**Products:** art quilts
**Techniques:** appliqué, quilting, embellishment **Size Range:** 12" x 12" to 72" x 72" **Price Range:** $150 to $200/sq. ft.

## SUSAN CARLSON

FABRIC IMAGES
272 CRANBERRY MEADOW RD
BERWICK, ME 03901
TEL 207-698-5358
FAX 207-698-5416
Established: 1983
**Products:** art quilts
**Techniques:** appliqué, quilting, piecing
**Size Range:** 12" x 12" to 4' x 6' **Price Range:** $400 to $6,000/piece

## LUCINDA CARLSTROM

LUCINDA CARLSTROM STUDIO
1075 STANDARD DR NE
ATLANTA, GA 30319-3357
TEL 404-231-0227
Established: 1974
**Products:** mixed media installations
**Techniques:** quilting, gold leaf piece work with paper, silk **Size Range:** 20" x 20" to 80" x 120" **Price Range:** $160 to $250/sq. ft.

## ERIKA CARTER

2440 KILLARNEY WAY SE
BELLEVUE, WA 98004-7038
TEL 206-451-9712
Established: 1984
**Products:** art quilts
**Techniques:** appliqué, painting, quilting
**Size Range:** 26" x 36" to 60" x 66"
**Price Range:** $125 to $175/sq. ft.

## BETH CASSIDY

2416 NW 60TH ST
SEATTLE, WA 98107
TEL 206-783-6226
FAX 206-706-0406
Established: 1980
**Products:** fabric constructions **Techniques:** quilting, laminating, beading
**Size Range:** 12" x 12" to any size
**Price Range:** $300 to $8,000/piece; $10 to $75/sq. ft.

Martha Chatelain, *Earthprint*, 1996, handmade paper wall sculpture with copper, 56" x 37" x 3"

## MARY ALLEN CHAISSON

ALLEN POINT STUDIO
ALLEN POINT RD RR1 BOX 285
S HARPSWELL, ME 04079
TEL 207-833-6842
FAX 207-833-6820
Established: 1972
**Products:** art quilts
**Techniques:** appliqué, painting, quilting
**Size Range:** 2' × 2' to 7' × 7' **Price Range:** $100/sq. ft.

## CLAUDIA A. CHASE

MIRRIX TAPESTRY STUDIO
N1465 NORTH RD
GREENVILLE, WI 54942
TEL 414-757-0457
Established: 1990
**Products:** tapestries **Techniques:** weaving **Size Range:** 1' × 1' to 5' × 8' **Price Range:** $150 to $300/sq. ft.

## ★ JOCELYN CHATEAUVERT

**JOCELYN CHATEAUVERT DESIGN**
**123 1ST AVE S**
**MT VERNON, IA 52314**
**TEL 319-895-0195**
**Established: 1991**
**Products:** paper **Techniques:** hand papermaking **Size Range:** 4' × 4' to 28' × 100' **Price Range:** $12.50 to $15/sq. ft.

See page 169 for photographs and additional information.

## ★ MARTHA CHATELAIN

**ARTFOCUS, LTD.**
**PO BOX 9855**
**SAN DIEGO, CA 92169-0855**
**TEL 619-581-6410**
**FAX 619-581-6536**
**E-Mail:** artfocus@aol.com
**Established: 1981**
**Products:** paper **Techniques:** casting **Size Range:** 1' × 1' to 6' × 12' **Price Range:** $300 to $9,000/piece; $10 to $175/sq. ft.

See photograph page 204.

## JILL NORDFORS CLARK

JILL NORDFORS CLARK FIBER ART &
   INTERIOR DESIGN
3419 N ADAMS ST
TACOMA, WA 98407-6038
TEL 206-759-6158
Established: 1974
**Products:** mixed media installations **Techniques:** appliqué, embroidery, painting **Size Range:** 16" × 20" to 30" × 40" **Price Range:** $750 to $1,200/piece

## ★ SUSANNE CLAWSON

**5093 VELDA DAIRY RD**
**TALLAHASSEE, FL 32308-6801**
**TEL 904-893-5656**
**Established: 1984**
**Products:** mixed media installations
**Techniques:** painting, casting, resist
**Size Range:** 15" × 15" to 8' × 12' **Price Range:** $300 to $10,000/piece

See photograph this page.

## JANE BURCH COCHRAN

6830 RABBIT HASH HILL RD
RABBIT HASH, KY 41005
TEL 606-586-9169
Established: 1970
**Products:** art quilts **Techniques:** quilting, beading **Size Range:** 20" × 20" to 6' × 6' **Price Range:** $500 to $10,000/piece

## ANTONIO COCILOVO

LIFEFORMS
2600 PINE DR
PRESCOTT, AZ 86301-4098
TEL 602-445-1643
Established: 1974
**Products:** paint on custom fabrics **Techniques:** painting, airbrush **Size Range:** 2' × 2' and up **Price Range:** $200 to $5,000/piece; $30 to $50/sq. ft.

## ELAINE ALBERS COHEN

32106 LAKE RD
AVON LAKE, OH 44012-1808
TEL 216-933-5979
Established: 1965
**Products:** cast paper reliefs **Techniques:** casting, dyeing, painting **Size Range:** 18" × 24" to 6' × 6' **Price Range:** $100 to $150/sq. ft.

## LAURA F. COHN

INDONESIAN CONNECTIONS
431 MARY WATERSFORD RD
BALA CYNWYD, PA 19004
TEL 610-667-5071
FAX 610-667-7932
Established: 1989
**Products:** batik paintings **Techniques:** painting, dyeing, wax resist (batik) **Size Range:** 15" × 12" to 556" × 56" **Price Range:** $300 to $2,000/piece

## JUDITH CONTENT

JUDITH CONTENT TEXTILES
   AND DESIGNS
827 MATADERO AVE
PALO ALTO, CA 94306-2606
TEL 415-857-0289
Established: 1979
**Products:** fabric constructions **Techniques:** dyeing, appliqué, quilting **Size Range:** 5' × 12" to 16' × 12' **Price Range:** $400 to $10,000/piece

## BRIGITTE SEKIRKA COOPER

BSC DESIGN
PO BOX 871840
WASILLA, AK 99687-1840
TEL 907-373-6067
Established: 1979
**Products:** art quilts
**Techniques:** painting, appliqué, quilting **Size Range:** 24" × 24" to 10' × 10' **Price Range:** $70 to $200/sq. ft.

## STEPHANIE RANDALL COOPER

2911 YORK RD
EVERETT, WA 98204-5407
TEL 206-745-2115
FAX 205-745-2115
Established: 1987
**Products:** art quilts **Techniques:** painting, dyeing, rip and tear assembly **Size Range:** 12" × 12" to 108" × 144" **Price Range:** $200 to $8,000/piece

## BARBARA CORNETT

FIBERSTRUCTIONS
1101 JEFFERSON ST
LYNCHBURG, VA 24504-1709
TEL 804-528-3136
Established: 1976
**Products:** mixed media installations **Techniques:** painting, felting, fiber sculpture **Size Range:** 2' × 3' to 12' × 20' **Price Range:** $500 to $50,000/piece

## JOANNE M. COTTELL

461 GREENWOOD AVE
AKRON, OH 44320
TEL 330-864-0821
E-Mail: lsrr85a@prodigy.com
Established: 1985
**Products:** art quilts **Techniques:** painting, dyeing, photo transfer **Size Range:** 2' × 2' to 8' × 8' **Price Range:** $300 to $2,800/piece; $30 to $60/sq. ft.

## COVERINGS BY RIFFI

RIFFI KAUFMAN
RD #2 MOUNTAINVIEW RD
PATTERSON, NY 12563
TEL 914-878-6642
Established: 1980
**Products:** art quilts **Techniques:** quilting **Size Range:** 24" × 24" to 64" × 54" **Price Range:** $300 to $1,200/piece

## ★ ROBIN COWLEY

**2451 POTOMAC ST**
**OAKLAND, CA 94602-3032**
**TEL 510-530-1134**
**FAX 510-482-9465**
**Established: 1990**
**Products:** art quilts
**Techniques:** dyeing, appliqué, quilting **Size Range:** 16" × 16" to 90" × 84" **Price Range:** $150 to $250/sq. ft.

See page 155 for photographs and additional information.

Susanne Clawson, *Africa Africa*, 1994, mixed media, 32" × 23" × 4"

# FIBER ART FOR THE WALL

## JOYCE CRAIN

2901 BENTON BLVD
MINNEAPOLIS, MN 55416-4328
TEL 612-920-1704
Established: 1970
**Products:** mixed media installations
**Techniques:** interlacing **Size Range:** 12" × 12" to 9' × 15' **Price Range:** $500 to $40,000/piece

## BARBARA LYDECKER CRANE

18 HILL ST
LEXINGTON, MA 02173-4318
TEL 617-862-1579
Established: 1985
**Products:** art quilts **Techniques:** dyeing, painting, quilting **Size Range:** 2' × 2' to 6' × 6' **Price Range:** $200 to $8,000/piece

## CREATIVE VISIONS

NANCY M. EHA
3898 DELLVIEW AVE
SAINT PAUL, MN 55112
TEL 612-633-3668
FAX 612-633-2107
Established: 1990
**Products:** contemporary beadwork
**Techniques:** embroidery, appliqué, beading **Size Range:** 2" × 2" to 3' × 2' **Price Range:** $50 to $5,000/piece

## ★ GLORIA E. CROUSE

**FIBER ARTS**
**4325 JOHN LUHR RD NE**
**OLYMPIA, WA 98516-2320**
**TEL 206-491-1980**
**Established: 1970**
**Products:** fabric installations **Techniques:** beading, embroidery, rug hooking **Size Range:** 5" × 5" to 20' × 20' **Price Range:** $50 to $150/sq. ft.

See page 44 for photographs and additional information.

## MELODY CRUST

26530 LK FENWICK RD S
KENT, WA 98032
TEL 206-859-0446
Established: 1991
**Products:** art quilts
**Techniques:** quilting, embroidery, beading **Size Range:** 10" × 10" to 60" × 80"
**Price Range:** $125 to $250/sq. ft.

## BETH CUNNINGHAM

32 SWEETCAKE MOUNTAIN RD
NEW FAIRFIELD, CT 06812-4107
TEL 203-746-5160
Established: 1976
**Products:** mixed media installations
**Techniques:** airbrush, painting, layering
**Size Range:** 1' × 1' to 6' × 12' **Price Range:** $100 to $150/sq. ft.

## MARGARET CUSACK

124 HOYT ST
BROOKLYN, NY 11217-2215
TEL 718-237-0145
FAX 718-237-2430
Established: 1972
**Products:** fiber installations, wall hangings **Techniques:** appliqué, airbrush, dyeing **Size Range:** 18" × 24" to 72" × 144" **Price Range:** $180 to $500/sq. ft.

## JUDY B. DALES

JUDY DALES, QUILTMAKER
6107 PALM RIDGE CT
KINGWOOD, TX 77345
TEL 713-360-0861
Established: 1980
**Products:** art quilts
**Techniques:** quilting, curved piecing
**Size Range:** 30" × 40" to 90" × 90"
**Price Range:** $500 to $10,000/piece

## SUZANNE DALTON

DALTON & FOLES DESIGN
12387 SCOTT RD
ELLSWORTH, MI 49729
TEL 616-599-2496
FAX 616-599-2496
E-Mail: suzdalton@aol.com
Established: 1977
**Products:** fiber installations **Techniques:** weaving **Size Range:** 2' × 6' to 30' × 40' **Price Range:** $1,200 to $40,000/piece

## DARYL DANCER-WADE

DARYL DANCER-WADE
 TEXTILE STUDIO
241 LANARK ST
WINNIPEG, MB R3N 1L3
CANADA
TEL 204-487-1893
FAX 204-487-3710
Established: 1988
**Products:** tapestries **Techniques:** weaving **Size Range:** 10" × 8" to 5' × 15' **Price Range:** $75 to $4,000/piece; $75 to $125/sq. ft.

## KAY HENNING DANLEY

MULTNOMAH STUDIO
8675 SW ALYSSA LN
PORTLAND, OR 97225
TEL 503-297-7404
Established: 1978
**Products:** paintings on silk
**Techniques:** dyeing, painting, stamping
**Size Range:** 24" × 15" to 72" × 36"
**Price Range:** $150 to $2,500/piece

## NATALIE DARMOHRAJ

NATALKA DESIGNS
PO BOX 40309
PROVIDENCE, RI 02940-0309
TEL 401-351-8841
FAX 401-351-2685
**Products:** woven wall pieces
**Techniques:** dyeing, weaving **Size Range:** 40" × 40" to 60" × 90" **Price Range:** $500 to $5,000/piece

## HEIDI DARR-HOPE

3718 TOMAKA RD
COLUMBIA, SC 29205-1558
TEL 803-782-5341
FAX 803-771-4140
Established: 1982
**Products:** one-of-a-kind accent pillows **Techniques:** embroidery, painting, collage **Size Range:** 10" × 14" to 6' × 12' **Price Range:** $300 to $8,000/piece

## KAREN DAVIDSON

PO BOX 637
HANA, HI 96713-0637
TEL 808-248-7094
Established: 1980
**Products:** paper
**Techniques:** casting, dyeing, painting
**Size Range:** 24" × 24" to 8' × 15'
**Price Range:** $300 to $10,000/piece

## D. JOYCE DAVIES

185 ROBINSON ST PH2
OAKVILLE, ON L6J 7N9
CANADA
TEL 905-845-6823
FAX 905-845-6823
Established: 1980
**Products:** art quilts **Techniques:** appliqué, quilting, embellishments **Size Range:** 36" × 36" to 70" × 70"
**Price Range:** $800 to $3,500/piece

## ALONZO DAVIS

PO BOX 12248
MEMPHIS, TN 38182-0248
TEL 901-276-9070
FAX 901-276-0660
Established: 1973
**Products:** paper **Techniques:** painting, weaving **Size Range:** 30" × 22" to 8' × 10' **Price Range:** $1,500 to $15,000/piece

## ARDYTH DAVIS

11436 HOLLOW TIMBER CT
RESTON, VA 22094-1980
TEL 703-904-8027
Established: 1975
**Products:** fabric constructions
**Techniques:** dyeing, painting, pleating
**Size Range:** 12" × 12" to 80" × 80"
**Price Range:** $150 to $10,000/piece

## JAMIE DAVIS

JAMIE DAVIS SCULPTURE
1239 MILE CREEK RD
PICKENS, SC 29671
TEL 864-868-3302
FAX 864-868-4250
Established: 1973
**Products:** mixed media installations, fiber, metal collage **Techniques:** painting, embossing, cutting metal **Size Range:** 22" × 24" to 48" × 6' and up
**Price Range:** $175/sq. ft.

## MICHAEL DAVIS

SHIBORI WEST
172 HIGH ST
ELKINS, WV 26241
TEL 304-636-1557
Established: 1969
**Products:** art quilts
**Techniques:** dyeing, quilting, piecing
**Size Range:** 1' × 1' to 30' × 30' **Price Range:** $30 to $55/sq. ft.

## NANCY STANFORD DAVIS

26 AUSTIN RD
WILMINGTON, DE 19810-2203
TEL 302-478-7529
Established: 1992
**Products:** art quilts
**Techniques:** dyeing, quilting, weaving
**Size Range:** 2' × 2' to 8' × 8' **Price Range:** $75 to $125/sq. ft.

## NANETTE DAVIS-SHAKLHO

16818 SE POWELL #202
PORTLAND, OR 97236
TEL 503-665-2444
Established: 1986
**Products:** mixed media installations
**Techniques:** dyeing, painting, laminating, pleating **Size Range:** 2' × 2' to 6' × 12' **Price Range:** $1,100 to $21,600/piece; $185 to $300/sq. ft.

## JANICE PAINE DAWES

RR 3 BOX 237
SULLIVAN, IL 61951
TEL 217-797-5506
Established: 1981
**Products:** traditional quilts **Techniques:** embroidery, appliqué, quilting
**Size Range:** 12" × 12" to 7' × 7' **Price Range:** $40 to $100/sq. ft.

## BERTHA DAY

BOX 304
SAINT ANDREWS, NB E0G 2X0
CANADA
TEL 506-529-8837
FAX 506-529-3375
Established: 1994
**Products:** fabric constructions **Techniques:** painting, embroidery, appliqué
**Size Range:** 15" × 15" to 72" × 72" **Price Range:** $200 to $7,000/piece

## JEAN DEEMER

1537 BRIARWOOD CIR
CUYAHOGA FALLS, OH 44221-3623
TEL 216-929-1995
Established: 1975
**Products:** paper constructions **Techniques:** painting, collage **Size Range:** 18" × 24" to 5' × 6' **Price Range:** $375 to $3,500/piece

## ANDREA DEIMEL

82 E HILLCREST AVE
CHALFONT, PA 18914
TEL 215-997-7964
Established: 1977
**Products:** mixed media installations
**Techniques:** embroidery, sculptural wood frames **Size Range:** 12" × 10" to 24" × 30" **Price Range:** $400 to $1,000/piece

## E. DELZOPPO

GREY SEAL WEAVING STUDIO
#3886 POINT MICHAUD
CAPE BRETON ISLAND, NS
B0E 1W0
CANADA
TEL 902-587-2494
Established: 1984
**Products:** damask compositions **Techniques:** weaving, drawloom damask
**Size Range:** 6" × 6" to 45" × 72" **Price Range:** $150 to $3,000/piece

## LINDA DENIER

DENIER TAPESTRY STUDIO
745 EDENWOOD DR
ROSELLE, IL 60172-2824
TEL 708-893-5854
Established: 1990
**Products:** tapestries **Techniques:** weaving **Size Range:** 3" × 5" to 5' × 6' **Price Range:** $150 to $175/sq. ft.

## LAURA DILL-KOCHER

70 LAFAYETTE PKWY
ROCHESTER, NY 14625
TEL 716-381-0669
Established: 1979
**Products:** tapestries
**Techniques:** weaving, dyeing, felting
**Size Range:** 12" × 12" to 30' × 8'
**Price Range:** $55 to $150/sq. ft.

## SALLY DILLON

7123 DALEWOOD LN
DALLAS, TX 75214-1812
TEL 214-821-1018
Established: 1970
**Products:** art quilts **Techniques:** dyeing, painting, quilting **Size Range:** 12" × 12" to 72" × 96" **Price Range:** $100 to $10,000/piece; $75 to $200/sq. ft.

## JUDITH DINGLE

JUDITH DINGLE DESIGN
140 EVELYN AVE
TORONTO, ON M6P 2Z7
CANADA
TEL 416-766-9411
Established: 1978
**Products:** fabric constructions, textile, mixed media constructions **Techniques:** laminating, quilting, pieced and constructed **Size Range:** 48" × 48" to 20' × 40' **Price Range:** $125 to $250/sq. ft.

## JUDY DIOSZEGI

JUDY DIOSZEGI, DESIGNER
2628 ROSLYN CIR
HIGHLAND PARK, IL 60035-1910
TEL 708-433-2585
Established: 1976
**Products:** tapestries **Techniques:** appliqué, embroidery, quilting **Size Range:** 18" × 36" to 12' × 24' **Price Range:** $200 to $30,000/piece

## SEENA DONNESON

SEENA DONNESON STUDIO
4349 10TH ST
LONG ISLAND CITY, NY 11101-6926
TEL 718-706-1342
Established: 1968
**Products:** tapestries, mixed media installations, paper **Techniques:** painting, molding **Size Range:** 20" × 20" to 60" × 60" **Price Range:** $1,000 to $15,000/piece

## MORRIS DAVID DORENFELD

PO BOX 126 ISLAND AVE
SPRUCE HEAD, ME 14859
TEL 207-594-5142
Established: 1979
**Products:** tapestries **Techniques:** weaving **Size Range:** 60" × 36" to 72" × 46" **Price Range:** $1,200 to $3,000/piece

## ARNELLE A. DOW

THE BATIK LADY
448 MILTON ST
CINCINNATI, OH 45210-1428
TEL 606-261-4523
Established: 1973
**Products:** fiber installations **Techniques:** appliqué, painting, batik, oriental rug restoration **Size Range:** 2" × 2" to 10' × 65' **Price Range:** $65 to $15,000/piece

## PAT DOZIER

LOWER ARROYO HONDO RD
ARROYO HONDO, NM 87513
TEL 505-776-8576
Established: 1992
**Products:** tapestries **Techniques:** weaving **Size Range:** 24" × 24" to 80" × 32" **Price Range:** $95 to $125/sq. ft.

## SUSAN DUNSHEE

986 ACEQUIA MADRE ST
SANTA FE, NM 87501-2819
TEL 505-982-0988
**Products:** fiber constructions **Techniques:** dyeing, laminating, machine stitching **Size Range:** 10" × 18" to 12' × 12' **Price Range:** $95 to $210/sq. ft.

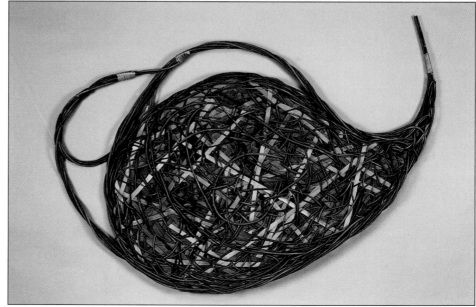

Carla and Greg Filippelli, *Dharma Works*, woven wall sculpture in hand-dyed and painted rattan, metallic leather, 48"H × 78"W, photo: Tim Barnwell

# FIBER ART FOR THE WALL

## DONNA DURBIN

4034 WOODCRAFT ST
HOUSTON, TX 77025-5709
TEL 713-664-4764
Established: 1987
**Products:** mixed media tapestries
**Techniques:** weaving, painting, collage
**Size Range:** 8" × 8" to 8' × 20' **Price Range:** $150 to $200/sq. ft.

## MARGIT ECHOLS

ROWHOUSE PRESS
170 WESTERVELT RD
WASHINGTON, NJ 02882
TEL 908-689-6231
FAX 908-689-2197
Established: 1976
**Products:** art quilts **Techniques:** quilting **Size Range:** 24" × 24" to 12' × 12' **Price Range:** $1,000 to $10,000/piece

## ELLEN ANNE EDDY

THREAD MAGIC
6257 N LAKEWOOD AVE #2
CHICAGO, IL 60660
TEL 312-262-2751
Established: 1988
**Products:** art quilts
**Techniques:** dyeing, embroidery, appliqué **Size Range:** 18" × 18" to 52" × 71" **Price Range:** $150 to $4,000/piece

## LORE EDZARD

507 SUNBERRY CT
BRENTWOOD, TN 37027
TEL 615-661-7571
Established: 1967
**Products:** tapestries **Techniques:** dyeing, embroidery, weaving, knotting
**Size Range:** 2' × 3' to 8' × 10' **Price Range:** $100 to $150/sq. ft.

## EFREM WEITZMAN ART WORKS

EFREM WEITZMAN
PO BOX 1092
SOUTH FALLSBURG, NY 12779-1092
TEL 914-434-2408
FAX 914-434-2408
Established: 1960
**Products:** tapestries **Techniques:** appliqué, weaving, quilting, arraiolos, hand-tufting **Size Range:** 4' × 7' to 90' × 20'
**Price Range:** $175 to $400/sq. ft.

## SU EGEN

SU EGEN, HANDWEAVER/DESIGNER
2233 E HAWTHORNE ST
TUCSON, AZ 85719-4941
TEL 520-325-0009
FAX 520-325-0009
E-Mail: suavian@azstarnet.com
Established: 1970
**Products:** tapestries **Techniques:** weaving **Size Range:** unlimited **Price Range:** $125 and up/piece; $100 to $300/sq. ft.

## SYLVIA H. EINSTEIN

11 OAK AVE
BELMONT, MA 02178-2751
TEL 617-484-9541
Established: 1980
**Products:** art quilts **Techniques:** quilting **Size Range:** 8" × 8" to 60" × 90" **Price Range:** $150 to $6,000/piece

## ARLYN ENDE

ARLYN ENDE TEXTILES
464 WILDWOOD LN
SEWANEE, TN 37375-3016
TEL 615-598-0660
Established: 1972
**Products:** tapestries rugs, fiber installations **Techniques:** hooking variations, collage **Size Range:** 40" × 50" to 20' × 60' **Price Range:** $65 to $200/sq. ft.

## NANCY N. ERICKSON

DANCING RABBIT STUDIOS
3250 PATTEE CANYON RD
MISSOULA, MT 59803-1703
TEL 406-549-4671
Established: 1963
**Products:** art quilts, oil paintstick works
**Techniques:** appliqué, painting, quilting
**Size Range:** 16" × 24" to 9' × 10' **Price Range:** $400 to $8,200/piece

## ★ CARL ERIKSON

**35 MORNINGSIDE COMMONS**
**BRATTLEBORO, VT 05301**
**TEL 802-254-9176**
**Established: 1992**
**Products:** fabric constructions, stretched-fabric shapes **Techniques:** appliqué, stitching, piecing **Size Range:** 18" × 18" to 60" × 60" **Price Range:** $400 to $2,000/piece

**See page 187 for photographs and additional information.**

## JOHANNA ERICKSON

GLAD RAGS
48 CHESTER ST
WATERTOWN, MA 02172
TEL 617-926-1737
Established: 1970
**Products:** tapestries, fiber installations
**Techniques:** weaving **Size Range:** 3' × 2' to 10' × 5' **Price Range:** $50 to $500/piece

## KAREN EUBEL

150 1ST AVE #404
NEW YORK, NY 10009-5704
TEL 212-995-9624
Established: 1970
**Products:** paper **Techniques:** painting, weaving, stenciling **Size Range:** 1' × 1' to 4' × 5' **Price Range:** $400 to $2,200/piece

## EURO ARTS

BEATA PIES
543 PACIFIC ST
BROOKLYN, NY 11217-1902
TEL 212-229-2854
FAX 212-229-2854
Established: 1983
**Products:** mixed media installations
**Techniques:** weaving, painting, stamping **Size Range:** 18" × 18" to 72" × 96"
**Price Range:** $1,000 to $10,000/sq. ft.

## PHYLLIS 'CERATTO' EVANS

6969 ISLAND CENTER RD NE
BAINBRIDGE ISLAND, WA 98110
TEL 206-842-5042
Established: 1987
**Products:** fiber collage **Techniques:** laminating **Size Range:** unlimited **Price Range:** $400 to $10,000/piece

## JUDITH POXSON FAWKES

LAURA RUSSO GALLERY
805 NW 21ST AVE
PORTLAND, OR 97209-1408
TEL 503-226-2754
Established: 1970
**Products:** tapestries **Techniques:** weaving **Size Range:** 3' × 3' to 8' × 20' **Price Range:** $150 minimum/sq. ft.

## MARTHA FERRIS

9433 FISHER FERRY RD
VICKSBURG, MS 39180
TEL 601-636-4066
FAX 601-634-1007
Established: 1990
**Products:** mixed media installations
**Techniques:** painting, dyeing, stamping
**Size Range:** 16" × 20" to 6' × 12'
**Price Range:** $400 to $7,000/piece

## FIBER ART STUDIO

KAIJA RAUTIAINEN
1610 JOHNSTON ST GRANVILLE ISLAND
VANCOUVER, BC V6H 3LS2
CANADA
TEL 604-688-3047
FAX 604-528-9978
Established: 1974
**Products:** tapestries **Techniques:** weaving **Size Range:** 16" × 16" to 7' × 5' **Price Range:** $300 to $350/sq. ft.

## ★ CARLA AND GREG FILIPPELLI

**CRANBERRY CREEK**
**423 BOB BARNWELL RD**
**ASHEVILLE, NC 28803**
**TEL 704-628-2177**
**FAX 704-628-2177**
**Established: 1980**
**Products:** wall sculptures and installations **Techniques:** weaving, dyeing, random weave **Size Range:** 3' × 3' and up **Price Range:** $250 to $15,000/piece

**See photograph page 207.**

## DORIS FINCH

DORIS FINCH FABRIC ART
2144 CRESCENT DR
ALTADENA, CA 91001-2112
TEL 818-797-6172
Established: 1987
**Products:** fabric constructions
**Techniques:** dyeing, appliqué, stuffing
**Size Range:** 30" × 20" to 90" × 48"
**Price Range:** $1,000 to $7,000/piece

## FIRST WEAVERS OF THE AMERICAS

MARTINA MASAQUIZA
825 LOCUST ST
LAWRENCE, KS 66044
TEL 800-571-0156
FAX 913-838-4486
Established: 1986
**Products:** tapestries **Techniques:** weaving **Size Range:** 20" × 20" to 46" × 27" **Price Range:** $75 to $500/piece; $27 to $50/sq. ft.

## PAMELA FLANDERS

FLANDERS FINE ART
6820 ROYALWOOD WAY
SAN JOSE, CA 95120-2228
TEL 408-997-8438
Established: 1983
**Products:** paper **Techniques:** laminating, painting, collage **Size Range:** 8" × 8" to 40" × 60" **Price Range:** $200 to $500/piece

## MARTI FLEISCHER

128 MONTICELLO RD
OAK RIDGE, TN 37830-8258
TEL 423-483-0772
Established: 1990
**Products:** tapestries **Techniques:** weaving **Size Range:** 4" × 3" to 4' × 7' **Price Range:** $200 to $2,000/piece; $60 to $100/sq. ft.

## MARI MARKS FLEMING

1431 GLENDALE AVE
BERKELEY, CA 94708-2027
TEL 510-548-3121
FAX 510-548-3121
Established: 1989
**Products:** mixed media installations **Techniques:** laminating, painting, fiber constructions **Size Range:** 18" × 12" to 10' × 15' **Price Range:** $500 to $15,000/piece

## BARBARA FLETCHER

88 BEALS ST
BROOKLINE, MA 02146-3011
TEL 617-277-3019
Established: 1987
**Products:** paper **Techniques:** airbush, casting, dyeing **Size Range:** 3" × 4" to 30" × 40" **Price Range:** $25 to $1,000/piece

## ★ DOROTHY FLYNN

**356 S BROADLEIGH RD**
**COLUMBUS, OH 43209-1908**
**TEL 614-237-8358**
**FAX 614-488-2826**
**Established: 1979**
**Products:** art quilts **Techniques:** embroidery, appliqué, quilting **Size Range:** 36" × 36" to 75" × 45" **Price Range:** $250 to $1,250/piece

See photograph this page.

## THE FOOTHILLS COMPANY

PAMELA JOHNSON-BRICKELL
PO BOX 962
APEX, NC 27502
TEL 919-363-0334
FAX 919-363-0334
Established: 1985
**Products:** mixed media installations **Techniques:** weaving, painting, elements from nature **Size Range:** 18" × 25" to 45" × 50" **Price Range:** $450 to $4,000/piece

## PAULA FORESMAN

QUILT ESSENTIAL
2 WOODLAND WAY
MANSFIELD, MA 02048
TEL 508-339-2292
FAX 508-339-6761
E-Mail: pkf@ici.net
Established: 1988
**Products:** art quilts **Techniques:** painting, appliqué, quilting **Size Range:** 6" × 8" to 6' × 8' **Price Range:** $20 to $75/sq. ft.

## ROBERT FORMAN

412 GRAND ST
HOBOKEN, NJ 07030-2703
TEL 201-659-7069
Established: 1975
**Products:** yarn painting **Techniques:** yarn glued to board **Size Range:** 24" × 30" to 60" × 96" **Price Range:** $1,500 and up/piece

## ★ MARILYN FORTH

**416 DAVID DR**
**N SYRACUSE, NY 13212-1929**
**TEL 315-458-3786**
**FAX 315-458-0913**
**Established: 1974**
**Products:** framed batiks **Techniques:** painting, wax drawn line **Size Range:** 1' × 1' to 4' × 6' **Price Range:** $180 to $2,500/piece

See pages 188-189 for photographs and additional information.

## FOWLER AND THELEN STUDIO

201 FAIRBROOK ST
NORTHVILLE, MI 48167-1503
TEL 313-348-6654
Established: 1972
**Products:** mixed media installations **Techniques:** weaving **Size Range:** 2' × 3' to 50' × 50' **Price Range:** $500 to $5,000/piece

## MARY EDNA FRASER

PO BOX 12250
CHARLESTON, SC 29422
TEL 803-762-2594
Established: 1974
**Products:** fiber installations **Techniques:** dyeing, batik on silk **Size Range:** 5' × 3' to 3' × 74 yds. **Price Range:** $150 to $125/sq. ft.

## CHRISTINE FRENCH

101 SEMINARY ST
BEREA, OH 44017
TEL 216-826-0169
Established: 1986
**Products:** mixed media installations **Techniques:** painting, dyeing, casting **Size Range:** 7" × 5' to 6' × 12' **Price Range:** $100 to $1,000/piece

## LIZ FREY

LIZ FREY HANDWOVENS
W 2390 SATSOP-CLOQUALLUM RD
ELMA, WA 98541
TEL 360-482-1291
Established: 1986
**Products:** fiber installations, fiber constructions **Techniques:** dyeing, painting, weaving, warp painting **Size Range:** 1' × 1' to no limit **Price Range:** $40 to $400/sq. ft.

## SUZAN FRIEDLAND

444 CABRILLO
SAN FRANCISCO, CA 94121
TEL 415-750-9463
Established: 1990
**Products:** fiber installations **Techniques:** painting, dyeing **Price Range:** $500 to $5,000/piece; $180/sq. ft.

## ALEXANDRA FRIEDMAN

45 GLASTONBURY BLVD
GLASTONBURY, CT 06033-4411
TEL 860-633-9999
Established: 1972
**Products:** tapestries **Techniques:** weaving, embroidery **Size Range:** open and flexible **Price Range:** $150 to $250/sq. ft.

## ★ JAN FRIEDMAN

**1409 E DAVENPORT ST**
**IOWA CITY, IA 52245-3021**
**TEL 319-338-1934**
**Established: 1979**
**Products:** tapestries **Techniques:** weaving, dyeing, collage **Size Range:** 24" × 20" to 15' × 10' **Price Range:** $110 to $120/sq. ft.

See photograph page 211.

## GAIL CAMPBELL

PO BOX 927
BISBEE, AZ 85603-0927
TEL 520-432-1205
Established: 1992
**Products:** mixed media installations **Techniques:** weaving, assemblage **Size Range:** 16" × 12" to 60" × 45" **Price Range:** $125 to $2,000/piece

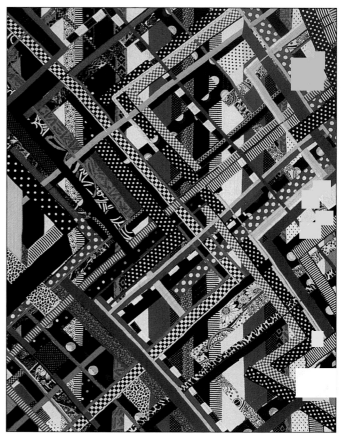

Dorothy Flynn, *Check the Plumb Line*, assorted fabric strips layered on base, embellished with ribbon and threads, 45" × 72".

# FIBER ART FOR THE WALL

## DEB GALL

ONE STITCH AT A TIME
6102 NORTHERN DANCER DR
AUSTIN, TX 78746-2108
TEL 512-329-8189
Established: 1987
**Products:** art quilts
**Techniques:** quilting, embellishing
**Size Range:** 2' x 2' to 10' x 10' **Price Range:** $100 to $2,000/piece

## JUDITH GEIGER

JUDITH GEIGER GALLERY
1921 DE LA VINA ST #B
SANTA BARBARA, CA 93101-2816
TEL 805-687-8868
FAX 805-687-8868
Established: 1982
**Products:** hand-painted silk **Techniques:** dyeing, painting, gutta resist
**Size Range:** 4" x 6" to 33" x 44" **Price Range:** $20 to $450/piece

## ★ SUZANNE GERNANDT

18 ORANGE ST
ASHEVILLE, NC 28801
TEL 704-281-0535
FAX 704-251-0521
E-Mail: jgernand@aol.com
Established: 1991
**Products:** fiber installations **Techniques:** weaving, painting, dyeing, screen printing, embroidery **Size Range:** 10" x 10" to 72" x 72" **Price Range:** $75 to $150/sq. ft.

See page 190 for photographs and additional information.

## CAROL H. GERSEN

STUDIO ART QUILTS
18839 MANOR CHURCH RD
BOONSBORO, MD 21713-2511
TEL 301-432-6484
Established: 1981
**Products:** art quilts **Techniques:** dyeing, quilting **Size Range:** 3' x 3' to 5' x 8' **Price Range:** $900 to $6,000/piece

## ★ REBECCA GIFFORD

SUNCOLORS STUDIO
PO BOX 16592
ST PETERSBURG, FL 33733
TEL 813-323-5183
Established: 1980
**Products:** fiber installations **Techniques:** painting, dyeing **Size Range:** 3' x 2' to 34' x 42' **Price Range:** $150 to $3,000/piece; $25 to $50/sq. ft.

See page 191 for photographs and additional information.

## JAMES R. GILBERT

WOVEN STRUCTURES
PO BOX 474
BLOOMFIELD HILLS, MI 48303-0474
TEL 810-772-7087
Established: 1970
**Products:** fiber installations **Techniques:** weaving, screen printing, color dyeing **Size Range:** 3' x 3' to 6' x 90' **Price Range:** $350 to $7,000/piece

## ★ JOAN GIORDANO

JOAN GIORDANO STUDIOS
136 GRAND ST
NEW YORK, NY 10013
TEL 212-431-6244
FAX 212-431-6244
Established: 1975
**Products:** mixed media installations **Techniques:** painting, welding, metal fabricating **Size Range:** 30" x 24" to 16' x 8' **Price Range:** $1,600 to $12,000/piece

See page 95 for photographs and additional information.

## DEANNA GLAD

PO BOX 1962
SAN PEDRO, CA 90733
TEL 310-831-6274
Established: 1970
**Products:** fabric constructions, bas-relief wall hangings **Techniques:** embroidery, appliqué, quilting, stamping **Size Range:** 24" x 30" to 7' x 5½' **Price Range:** $1,100 to $8,000/piece

## ROBERTA GLIDDEN

TEXTILE ARTS STUDIO
1009 23RD ST
OGDEN, UT 84401
TEL 801-394-5688
Established: 1980
**Products:** painting on silk
**Techniques:** painting, dyeing
**Size Range:** 20" x 20" to 36" x 48"
**Price Range:** $150 to $1,000/piece

## SANDRA GOLBERT

PO BOX 193
PIERMONT, NY 10968
TEL 914-365-6093
FAX 914-356-6093
Established: 1980
**Products:** fiber installations **Techniques:** dyeing, wrapping, paper making **Size Range:** 10" x 10" to 6' x 20' **Price Range:** $200 to $50,000/ piece

## JON GOLDMAN

GOLDMAN ARTS
107 SOUTH ST #403
BOSTON, MA 02111-2811
TEL 617-423-6606
FAX 617-423-6601
E-Mail: zoozles@aol.com
Established: 1980
**Products:** inflatable sculptures
**Techniques:** airbrush, appliqué, quilting
**Size Range:** 1' x 1' to 100' x 100'
**Price Range:** $5 to $40,000/piece

## LAYNE GOLDSMITH

PO BOX 563
SNOHOMISH, WA 98291-0563
TEL 206-334-5569
FAX 206-334-5569
Established: 1972
**Products:** felted wall constructions
**Techniques:** dyeing, felting, mixed textile media **Size Range:** 4' x 5' to 12' x 60' **Price Range:** $500 to $45,000/piece; $100 to $300/sq. ft.

## INA GOLUB

366 ROLLING ROCK RD
MOUNTAINSIDE, NJ 07092-2120
TEL 908-232-5376
FAX 908-232-7981
Established: 1963
**Products:** tapestries
**Techniques:** appliqué, beading, weaving
**Size Range:** 2' x 2' to 10' x 12' **Price Range:** $2,000 to $25,000/piece

## RUTH GOWELL

7010 ARONOW DR
FALLS CHURCH, VA 22042-1805
TEL 703-532-8645
Established: 1978
**Products:** wall hangings **Techniques:** dyeing, weaving **Size Range:** 16" x 16" to 5' x 10' **Price Range:** $250 to $4,000/piece

## ★ CHARLES GRAY

14425 N 42ND PL
PHOENIX, AZ 85032
TEL 602-996-2319
FAX 602-493-7304
E-Mail: artistgray@aol.com
Established: 1976
**Products:** Kinetic Canvas™
**Techniques:** weaving **Size Range:** 1' x 1' to 40' x 60' **Price Range:** $147 to $278/sq. ft.

See page 117 for photographs and additional information.

## LAURA ELIZABETH GREEN

5523 HIGHLAND ST S
ST PETERSBURG, FL 33705-5135
TEL 813-867-1204
Established: 1973
**Products:** art quilts
**Techniques:** appliqué, dyeing, quilting
**Size Range:** 4" x 4" to 8' x 8' **Price Range:** $250 to $2,500/piece

## BARBARA GRENELL

1132 HALLS CHAPPEL RD
BURNSVILLE, NC 28714-9760
TEL 704-675-4073
Established: 1972
**Products:** fiber installations
**Techniques:** dyeing, weaving **Size Range:** all sizes **Price Range:** $100 to $175/sq. ft.

## DON GRIFFIN

3306 KENJAC RD
BALTIMORE, MD 21244-1322
TEL 410-655-8755
Established: 1973
**Products:** mixed media installations
**Techniques:** painting, collage **Size Range:** 36" x 30" to 6' x 10' **Price Range:** $500 to $3,500/piece

## JOAN GRIFFIN

FIBER DESIGN STUDIO
1800 YORKTOWN DR
CHARLOTTESVILLE, VA 22901-3037
TEL 804-979-4402
FAX 804-979-4402
Established: 1980
**Products:** tapestries **Techniques:** weaving **Size Range:** 12" x 12" to 5' x 10' **Price Range:** $180 to $9,500/piece

## MARILYN GRISHAM

315 POST RD
EL DORADO, KS 67042-4059
Established: 1970
**Products:** tapestries **Techniques:** weaving, embroidery, weft-face brocade **Size Range:** 3' x 5' to 12' x 24' **Price Range:** $2,500 to $55,000/piece

### ISAELLE GUENAT

641 HOWARD AVE #310
MONTEBELLO, CA 90640
TEL 213-724-9544
**Products:** tapestries **Techniques:**
weaving **Size Range:** 15" × 15" to 50"
× 50" **Price Range:** $300 to
$3,00/piece

### CLAIRE FAY HABERFELD

QUILTVISION
10751 W 107TH CIR
WESTMINSTER, CO 80021
TEL 303-469-1403
Established: 1981
**Products:** art quilts
**Techniques:** appliqué, beading, quilting
**Size Range:** 1' × 1' to 10' × 10' **Price
Range:** $85 to $100/sq. ft.

### LINDA BANKS HANSEE

1959 OLSON RD
CORNING, NY 14830
TEL 607-937-8226
E-Mail: lhansee@aol.com
Established: 1980
**Products:** tapestries
**Techniques:** weaving, hand sewn yarns
**Size Range:** 12" × 14" and up **Price
Range:** $85 to $135/sq. ft.

### HARRIET HANSON

THE STUDIOSPACE
1732 W HUBBARD ST
CHICAGO, IL 60622-6271
TEL 312-243-4144
Established: 1970
**Products:** handmade paper
**Techniques:** dimensional sculpture
**Size Range:** 18" × 24" to 36" to 48"
**Price Range:** $600 to $3,000/piece

### TIM HARDING

HARDING DESIGN STUDIO
402 N MAIN ST
STILLWATER, MN 55082-5051
TEL 612-351-0383
Established: 1974
**Products:** fiber installations **Techniques:** dyeing, quilting, slashing and
fraying **Size Range:** 50" × 70" to 10' ×
18' **Price Range:** $75 to $175/sq. ft.

### CAROLE HARRIS

667 W BETHUNE
DETROIT, MI 48202
TEL 313-871-4155
FAX 313-964-0170
Established: 1976
**Products:** art quilts
**Techniques:** quilting, mixed media
**Size Range:** 37" × 16" to 75" × 60"
**Price Range:** $900 to $6,000/piece

### PETER HARRIS

TAPESTRY AND DESIGN
RR 2
AYTON, ON N0G 1C0
CANADA
TEL 519-665-2245
Established: 1973
**Products:** tapestries **Techniques:**
weaving **Size Range:** 36" × 48" to 60"
× 96" **Price Range:** $2,500 to
$10,000/piece

### RENEE HARRIS

RENEE HARRIS STUDIO
642 CLEMMER AVE
CINCINNATI, OH 45219-1038
TEL 513-241-5909
Established: 1985
**Products:** fiber installations
**Techniques:** embroidery, felting
**Size Range:** 16" × 20" to 3' × 4'
**Price Range:** $300 to $1,200/piece

### ANN L. HARTLEY

TREE HOUSE STUDIO
13515 SEA ISLAND DR
HOUSTON, TX 77069-2436
TEL 713-444-1118
Established: 1975
**Products:** mixed media collage
**Techniques:** painting, stamping/ printing,
wrapping **Price Range:** $300 to
$1,500/piece

### MARGE HAYES

FIBER STUDIO
1423 N 3RD ST
ABERDEEN, SD 57401
TEL 605-225-1352
Established: 1985
**Products:** fiber installations
**Techniques:** dyeing, felting, knitting
**Size Range:** 6" × 6" to 6' × 6' **Price
Range:** $80 to $10,000/piece

### SHARON HEIDINGSFELDER

8010 DAN THOMAS RD
LITTLE ROCK, AR 72206-4148
TEL 501-490-0405
FAX 501-671-2251
Established: 1973
**Products:** art quilts
**Techniques:** dyeing, quilting, screen
printing **Size Range:** 72" × 72" to
78" × 84" **Price Range:** $2,000 to
$6,500/piece

### MARTHA HEINE

7 HAGGIS CT
DURHAM, NC 27705-2166
TEL 919-479-3270
Established: 1980
**Products:** tapestries **Techniques:**
weaving **Size Range:** 48" × 36" to 60"
× 72" **Price Range:** $2,200 to
$7,600/piece; $175 to $250/sq. ft.

### SHEILA A. HELD

2762 MAYFAIR CT
WAUWATOSA, WI 53222-4105
TEL 414-475-6479
Established: 1975
**Products:** tapestries **Techniques:**
weaving **Size Range:** 36" × 36" to 80"
× 50" **Price Range:** $1,000 to
$6,000/piece; $200 to $300/sq. ft.

### HELIO GRAPHICS

DAWN WILKINS
PO BOX 6213
KEY WEST, FL 33041-6213
TEL 305-294-7901
Established: 1980
**Products:** mixed media installations,
painted canvas and nature prints **Tech-
niques:** painting, screen printing,
pressed images **Size Range:** 20" × 20"
to 50" × 60" **Price Range:** $100 to
$2,000/piece

### BARBARA HELLER

FIBRE ARTS STUDIO
4796 W SEVENTH AVE
VANCOUVER, BC V6T 1C6
CANADA
TEL 604-224-3047
Established: 1975
**Products:** tapestries **Techniques:**
weaving **Size Range:** 12" × 12" to 4' ×
6' **Price Range:** $350 to
$10,000/piece; $350 to $450/sq. ft.

### SUSAN HART HENEGAR

5449 BELLEVUE AVE
LA JOLLA, CA 92037-7625
TEL 619-459-5681
FAX 619-459-5693
Established: 1978
**Products:** tapestries
**Techniques:** weaving, Aubusson
tapestry **Size Range:** 8" × 8" to 8' × 24'
**Price Range:** $150 to $400/sq. ft.

Jan Friedman, *Oriental Scroll: Daybreak*, 1995, woven tapestry with wool
yarn and dyed silk fabric, 26"W × 40"H

# FIBER ART FOR THE WALL

## MARILYN HENRION

505 LAGUARDIA PL #23D
NEW YORK, NY 10012-2005
TEL 212-982-8949
Established: 1978
**Products:** art quilts **Techniques:** hand quilting **Size Range:** 24" x 24" to 80" x 80" **Price Range:** $500 to $7,500/piece

## HELENA HERNMARCK

HELENA HERNMARCK TAPESTRIES
879 N SALEM RD
RIDGEFIELD, CT 06877-1714
TEL 203-438-9220
FAX 203-431-9570
Established: 1964
**Products:** tapestries **Techniques:** weaving **Size Range:** 10 sq. ft. to 400 sq. ft. **Price Range:** $600 to $1,200/sq. ft.

## JANE HERRICK

4219 MEADOW LN
EAU CLAIRE, WI 54701-7487
TEL 715-833-9745
Established: 1982
**Products:** fabric constructions **Techniques:** laminating, painting, drawing, heat transfer **Size Range:** 18" x 24" to 6' x 8' **Price Range:** $600 to $4,000/ piece

## SUSAN HERSEY

105 DANVERS ST
SAN FRANCISCO, CA 94114
TEL 415-621-4125
FAX 415-436-9871
Established: 1960
**Products:** paper **Techniques:** painting, dyeing, spraying **Size Range:** 17" x 13" to 6' x 10' **Price Range:** $200 to $5,000/piece

## PAMELA HILL

PO BOX 800
8500 LAFAYETTE
MOKELUMNE HILL, CA 95245-0800
TEL 209-286-1217
FAX 209-286-1001
Established: 1975
**Products:** art quilts **Techniques:** quilting, piecing **Size Range:** 40" x 40" to 10' x 24' **Price Range:** $600 to $5,000/piece

## ★ BILL HIO

**34 CYPRESS DR**
**SCOTIA, NY 12302-4325**
**TEL 518-399-7404**
**Established: 1995**
**Products:** tapestries **Techniques:** needle stitch **Size Range:** 2' x 2' to 4'10" x 8' **Price Range:** $70 to $100/sq. ft.

See photograph this page.

## M. HOLSENROTT HOCKHAUSER

1409 LAS CANOAS LN
SANT BARBARA, CA 93104
TEL 805-966-2921
Established: 1967
**Products:** hand made paper art **Techniques:** painting, casting, hand made paper **Size Range:** 14" x 18" to 48" x 96" **Price Range:** $750 to $25,000/piece

## JANE HOFFMAN

BLUE RIVER STUDIO
PO BOX 529
ALPINE, AZ 85920
TEL 520-333-5956
Established: 1974
**Products:** tapestries **Techniques:** weaving, dyeing **Size Range:** 10" x 10" to 71" x 48" **Price Range:** $200 to $10,000/piece; $200 to $400/sq. ft.

## MIDGE HOFFMAN

PO BOX 1239
91239 N HARRISON ST
COBURG, OR 97408
TEL 541-485-0047
Established: 1981
**Products:** art quilts
**Techniques:** painting, appliqué, fusing **Size Range:** 2'6" to 2' to 11' x 28' **Price Range:** $100 to $150/sq. ft.

## DOROTHY HOLDEN

301 KENT RD
CHARLOTTESVILLE, VA 22903-2409
TEL 804-971-5803
Established: 1977
**Products:** art quilts **Techniques:** quilting **Size Range:** 2' x 2' to 6' x 7' **Price Range:** $850 to $6,500/piece

## ELIZABETH HOLSTER

PAPER BY HOLSTER
727 E A ST
IRON MOUNTAIN, MI 49801-3505
TEL 906-779-2592
Established: 1974
**Products:** paper **Techniques:** casting, painting, drawing/collagraph **Size Range:** 24" x 24" to 60" x 60" **Price Range:** $500 to $5,000/piece

## ★ MELISSA HOLZINGER

**COLLABORATIONS INC.**
**30516 SR 530 NE**
**ARLINGTON, WA 98223**
**TEL 360-435-5060**
**Established: 1980**
**Products:** art quilts **Techniques:** painting, screen printing, airbrush, photo transfer **Size Range:** 24" x 24" to 72" x 72" **Price Range:** $1,000 to $5,000/piece; $150 to $200/sq. ft.

See page 154 for photographs and additional information.

## ★ KATHERINE HOLZKNECHT

**22828 57TH AVE SE**
**WOODINVILLE, WA 98072-8660**
**TEL 206-481-7788**
**Established: 1976**
**Products:** mixed media installations **Techniques:** dyeing, laminating, lashing **Size Range:** 2' x 2' to 20' x 60' **Price Range:** $150 to $300/sq. ft.

See page 97 for photographs and additional information.

Bill Hio, *Red Wood Magnified*, 1997, gros point stitch, 62" x 57"

## DORA HSIUNG

HSIUNG DESIGN
95 WARREN ST
NEWTON, MA 02159-2334
TEL 617-969-4630
Established: 1978
**Products:** wall hangings **Techniques:**
wrapping, original off-loom weaving
**Size Range:** 12" × 12" to 16' × 21'
**Price Range:** $200 to $30,000/piece

## JOHN D. HUBBARD

1420 W LITTLE SHAG RD
GWINN, MI 49841
TEL 906-227-2194
Established: 1968
**Products:** paper **Techniques:** casting, airbrush, paper assemblage **Size Range:** 18" × 20" to 48" × 60" **Price Range:** $500 to $4,500/piece

## ★ FRITZI HUBER

**134 STONYBROOK RD**
**WILMINGTON, NC 28405**
**TEL 910-686-4651**
**FAX 910-686-4651**
**Established: 1980**
**Products:** paper **Techniques:** painting, casting, collage **Size Range:** 8¹/₂" × 11¹/₂" to 60" × 360" **Price Range:** $110 to $250/sq. ft.

See page 171 for photographs and additional information.

## DOROTHY HUGHES

DOROTHY HUGHES STUDIO
850 N MILWAUKEE AVE
CHICAGO, IL 60622-4143
TEL 312-421-7045
FAX 312-563-1456
Established: 1970
**Products:** fiber sculpture **Techniques:** dyeing, weaving **Size Range:** 12" × 12" to 22' × 33' **Price Range:** $300 to $90,000/piece; $150 to $500/sq. ft.

## ★ WENDY HUHN

**COLLABORATIONS INC.**
**81763 LOST CREEK RD**
**DEXTER, OR 97431-9735**
**TEL 541-937-3147**
**FAX 541-937-8061**
**E-Mail:** wchuhn@aol.com
**Established: 1980**
**Products:** art quilts **Techniques:** painting, screen printing, airbrush, photo transfer **Size Range:** 24" × 24" to 72" × 72" **Price Range:** $1,000 to $5,000/piece; $150 to $200/sq. ft.

See page 154 for photographs and additional information.

## CONSTANCE HUNT

1270 SANCHEZ ST
SAN FRANCISCO, CA 94114-3833
TEL 415-282-5170
Established: 1980
**Products:** tapestries **Techniques:** weaving **Size Range:** 6" × 9" to 72" × 80" **Price Range:** $400 to $20,000/piece

## JANET M. HUTCHINSON

ISLAND SILK
LAUREL RUN FARM HC-82 BOX 253A
MARLINTON, WV 24954
TEL 304-799-7158
FAX 304-799-7158
Established: 1986
**Products:** fiber installations **Techniques:** painting, dyeing **Size Range:** 30" × 20" to 8' × 4' **Price Range:** $250 to $3,000/piece

## ★ MARIE-LAURE ILIE

**MARILOR ART STUDIO**
**106 VIA SEVILLA**
**REDONDO BEACH, CA 90277**
**TEL 310-375-4977**
**FAX 310-375-4977**
**Established: 1975**
**Products:** fiber wall hangings **Techniques:** painting, appliqué, layering **Size Range:** 2' × 3' to 8' × 15' **Price Range:** $60 to $130/sq. ft.

See below and page 192 for photographs and additional information.

## IRA ONO DESIGNS

PO BOX 112
VOLCANO, HI 96785
TEL 808-967-7261
**Products:** fabric constructions, Japanese-paste paper screens **Techniques:** painting, Japanese-paste paper **Size Range:** 16" × 24" to 7' × 15' **Price Range:** $400 to $4,000/piece

## ELAINE IRELAND

711 HAMPSHIRE ST
SAN FRANCISCO, CA 94110-2129
TEL 415-648-8813
Established: 1972
**Products:** tapestries **Techniques:** weaving combined w/mixed mediums **Size Range:** miniatures to unlimited **Price Range:** $500 to $1,000/sq. ft.

## PEG IRISH

114 METOXIT RD
WAQUOIT, MA 02536-7723
TEL 508-548-3230
Established: 1988
**Products:** fiber installations **Techniques:** dyeing, embroidery, rug hooking **Size Range:** 8" × 8" to 4' × 8' **Price Range:** $150 to $300/sq. ft.

## CAROL KASMER IRVING

THE WEAVER'S WEB
1204 8TH AVE S
ESCANABA, MI 49829-3217
TEL 906-786-0331
Established: 1977
**Products:** wall or floor rugs **Techniques:** weaving **Size Range:** 2' × 3' to 6' × 12' **Price Range:** $35 to $50/sq. ft.

## SUSAN IVERSON

SUSAN IVERSON - TAPESTRIES
904 BUFORD OAKS CIR
RICHMOND, VA 23235-4680
TEL 804-272-0225
Established: 1975
**Products:** tapestries **Techniques:** dyeing, weaving **Size Range:** 3' × 7' to 8' × 12' **Price Range:** $125 to $200/sq. ft.

## JK DESIGN

JOYCE KLIMAN
34 LASALLE PKWY
VICTOR, NY 14564
TEL 716-381-3259
Established: 1980
**Products:** art quilts **Techniques:** stamping, painting, quilting, appliqué, photo transfer **Size Range:** 2' × 2' to 10' × 10' **Price Range:** $125 to $4,000/piece

## JACKLYN JURAS ARTIQUITIES

JACKLYN JURAS
627 CAROL VILLA DR
MONTGOMERY, AL 36109
TEL 334-273-0420
FAX 334-832-4449
Established: 1971
**Products:** fabric constructions **Techniques:** painting, dyeing, quilting **Size Range:** 4' × 2' to 8¹/₂' × 10' **Price Range:** $55 to $1,750/piece; $30 to $100/sq. ft.

Marie-Laure Ilie, *Dutch Lillies Triptych*, hand-painted silk, 48"H × 60"W

# FIBER ART FOR THE WALL

## NANCY JACKSON

TIMSHEL TAPESTRY STUDIO
10 BUENA VISTA AVE
VALLEJO, CA 94590
TEL 707-554-4128
Established: 1983
**Products:** tapestries
**Techniques:** weaving, dyeing, painting
**Size Range:** 2' × 3' to 8' × 10' **Price Range:** $1,200 to $16,000/piece; $200 to $350/sq. ft.

## CARRIE JACOBSON-MAY

504 PACHECO AVE
SANTA CRUZ, CA 95062
TEL 408-459-9559
Established: 1974
**Products:** tufted wall hangings
**Techniques:** dyeing, wrapping, tufting
**Size Range:** 30" × 30" to 10' × 12'
**Price Range:** $65 to $100/sq. ft.

## VICTOR JACOBY

1086 17TH ST
EUREKA, CA 95501-2623
TEL 707-442-3809
Established: 1975
**Products:** tapestries **Techniques:** weaving **Size Range:** 2' × 2' to 8' × 24'
**Price Range:** $400 to $48,000/piece

## MARY E. JAEGER

MARY E. JAEGER LTD.
404 E 55TH ST #4D
NEW YORK, NY 10022
TEL 212-755-3814
FAX 212-755-3814
Established: 1980
**Products:** fabric constructions **Techniques:** dyeing, painting, appliqué **Size Range:** 10" × 10" to 15' × 4' **Price Range:** $50 to $75/sq. ft.

## LUCY A. JAHNS

1702 BELMONT DR
GREEN OAKS, IL 60048
TEL 847-362-2144
Established: 1982
**Products:** fabric constructions **Techniques:** appliqué, embroidery, painting **Size Range:** 24" × 36" to 6' × 10' **Price Range:** $600 to $5,800/piece

## MICHAEL JAMES

STUDIO QUILTS
258 OLD COLONY AVE
SOMERSET, MA 02726-5930
TEL 508-672-1370
FAX 508-672-1370
Established: 1973
**Products:** art quilts **Techniques:** quilting, piecing **Size Range:** 39" × 39" to 72" × 144" **Price Range:** $3,500 to $16,000/piece

## JANICE JANAS

PO BOX 461
ARVADA, CO 80001-0461
TEL 303-467-2007
Established: 1980
**Products:** mixed media constructions **Techniques:** painting, dyeing, stamping **Size Range:** 18" × 24" to 2½' × 3½' **Price Range:** $400 to $8,000/piece

## CATHERINE JANSEN

152 HEACOCK LN
WYNCOTE, PA 19095-1517
TEL 215-884-3174
Established: 1976
**Products:** art quilts
**Techniques:** photo process on cloth
**Size Range:** 8" × 10" to room sized
**Price Range:** $225 to $20,000/piece

## JOCELYN STUDIO

JOCELYN GOLDMAN
39 OLD TOWN RD
EAST HADDAM, CT 06423-1453
TEL 203-526-1581
FAX 203-526-2205
Established: 1988
**Products:** art quilts
**Techniques:** weaving, appliqué, embroidery **Size Range:** 12" × 12" to 36" × 48" **Price Range:** $200 to $1,000/piece

## JOELL MILEO, PAPERMAKER

JOELL MILEO
PO BOX 8
MENDON, NY 14506-0008
TEL 716-624-9152
Established: 1988
**Products:** paper **Techniques:** airbush, casting, dyeing **Size Range:** 11" × 14" to 2' × 3' **Price Range:** $125 to $1,500/piece

## ROSITA JOHANSON

657 WOODBINE AVE
TORONTO, ON M4E 2J3
CANADA
TEL 416-699-4881
Established: 1984
**Products:** miniature fiber art
**Techniques:** appliqué, embroidery
**Size Range:** 6" × 6" to 8" × 9" **Price Range:** $900 to $10,000/piece

## ★ MARCIA HEWITT JOHNSON

71 LLANFAIR CIR
ARMORE, PA 19003
TEL 610-649-7282
E-Mail: marhewjohn@aol.com
Established: 1988
**Products:** art quilts
**Techniques:** painting, dyeing, quilting
**Size Range:** 3' × 3' to 6' × 6' **Price Range:** $500 to $5,000/piece

See page 156 for photographs and additional information.

## VICKI L. JOHNSON

V & T GRAPHICS
225 MUIR DR
SOQUEL, CA 95073-9523
TEL 408-476-7567
FAX 408-476-7567
Established: 1970
**Products:** art quilts
**Techniques:** appliqué, painting, quilting
**Size Range:** 2' × 2' to 6' × 8' **Price Range:** $400 to $10,000/piece

## ANN JOHNSTON

910 YORK RD
LAKE OSWEGO, OR 97034-1742
TEL 503-635-1173
Established: 1981
**Products:** art quilts
**Techniques:** dyeing, quilting, painting
**Size Range:** 8" × 8" to 9' × 9' **Price Range:** $400 to $10,000/piece

## ★ JON ERIC RIIS DESIGNS, LTD.

JON ERIC RIIS
875 PIEDMONT AVE NE
ATLANTA, GA 30309
TEL 404-881-9847
FAX 404-881-0322
Established: 1971
**Products:** tapestries **Techniques:** weaving, embroidery, beading, repousse metal **Size Range:** 24" × 24" to 65' × 10' **Price Range:** $2,000 to $65,000/piece

See page 180 for photographs and additional information.

## JOYCE HULBERT TAPESTRY & TEXTILE RESTORATION

JOYCE HULBERT
2339 3RD ST STE 31
SAN FRANCISCO, CA 94107-3137
TEL 415-255-4560
Established: 1988
**Products:** textile restorations
**Techniques:** dyeing, weaving, sewing
**Size Range:** miniature to 10' × 12'
**Price Range:** project estimate based on hourly fee/piece

## ★ HOLLEY JUNKER

4030 GREYWELL WAY
SACRAMENTO, CA 95864-6051
TEL 916-488-5660
Established: 1980
**Products:** mixed media art quilts
**Techniques:** quilting, painting, embroidery **Size Range:** 4' × 6' to 8' × 9'
**Price Range:** $150 and up/sq. ft.

See page 157 for photographs and additional information.

## JUNO SKY STUDIO

BETTY FULMER
844 S MAIN ST
FINDLAY, OH 45840
TEL 419-423-9591
FAX 419-423-9907
Established: 1971
**Products:** paper **Techniques:** painting, dyeing, casting **Size Range:** 10" × 14" to 68" × 160" **Price Range:** $300 to $10,000/piece

## DEBRA KAM

136 DRINKWATER RD
HAMPTON FALLS, NH 03844
TEL 603-772-8580
Established: 1993
**Products:** art quilts
**Techniques:** painting, quilting, piecing
**Size Range:** 1' × 1' to 6' × 4' **Price Range:** $500 to $3,000/piece

## HENDRIKA KAMSTRA

GINKGO STUDIO
1825 W COTTAGE ST
STEVENS POINT, WI 54481-3414
TEL 715-341-3599
Established: 1984
**Products:** mixed media installations
paper **Techniques:** dyeing, casting, airbrushing **Size Range:** 15" × 12" to 30"
× 40" **Price Range:** $195 to
$1,350/piece

## JANIS KANTER

1923 W DICKENS AVE
CHICAGO, IL 60614-3935
TEL 312-252-2119
FAX 312-862-0440
Established: 1988
**Products:** tapestries with neon **Tech-
niques:** weaving **Size Range:** 4' × 4'
to 5' × 8' **Price Range:** $5,000 to
$10,000/piece

## ANNA KARESH

ART STUDIO WEST
PO BOX 900528
SAN DIEGO, CA 92190-0528
TEL 619-258-0766
FAX 619-565-1161
Established: 1970
**Products:** mixed media installations
**Techniques:** casting, painting **Size
Range:** 2' × 3' to 8' × 12' **Price
Range:** $60 to $120/sq. ft.

## MARCIA KARLIN

45 KINGS CROSS DR
LINCOLNSHIRE, IL 60069-3342
TEL 708-940-4930
Established: 1985
**Products:** art quilts **Techniques:**
dyeing, painting, embroidery **Size
Range:** 15" × 20" to 7' × 8' **Price
Range:** $500 to $10,000/piece

## KATHLEEN O'CONNOR, QUILTS

KATHLEEN O'CONNOR
RR 3 BOX 735
PUTNEY, VT 05346
TEL 802-387-4172
Established: 1988
**Products:** art quilts
**Techniques:** painting, dyeing, quilting
**Size Range:** 42" × 42" to 13' × 27'
**Price Range:** $500 to $6,000/piece

## DENISE KATZ

ART FRAMES
2336 14TH ST
BOULDER, CO 80304
TEL 303-444-8046
Established: 1975
**Products:** paper **Techniques:** paint-
ing, dyeing, casting **Size Range:** 24" ×
30" to 40" × 40" **Price Range:** $250 to
$600/piece

## ANNE MARIE KENNY

INDUSTRIAL QUILT STUDIO
1465 HOOKSETT RD #109
HOOKSETT, NH 03106-1862
TEL 603-268-0336
Established: 1982
**Products:** industrial quilts **Tech-
niques:** painting, stitching, wire-cloth
**Size Range:** 3' × 3' to 12' × 12' **Price
Range:** $1,500 to $25,000/piece

## BETTY KERSHNER

PO BOX 3266
SEWANEE, TN 37375-3266
TEL 615-598-5723
Established: 1970
**Products:** fiber installations
**Techniques:** painting, dyeing, stamping
**Size Range:** 4' × 2' to 20' × 6' **Price
Range:** $30 to $100/sq. ft.

## SUSAN KIMBER

61 WARREN ST
NEW YORK, NY 10007-1016
TEL 212-766-3714
Established: 1973
**Products:** mixed media tapestries
**Techniques:** weaving, painting, photog-
raphy **Size Range:** 12" × 12" to
4' × 16' **Price Range:** $350 to
$20,000/piece

## CHRIS KING

RR 1
BADDECK, NS B0E 1B0
CANADA
TEL 902-295-3141
FAX 902-295-3141
Established: 1989
**Products:** art quilts **Techniques:**
dyeing, piecing ("dyed and pieced")
**Size Range:** 9" × 12" to 10' × 10'
**Price Range:** $150 to $2,000/piece

## SARA NEWBERG KING

KING'S KREATIONS
6950 100TH ST NW
PINE ISLAND, MN 55963-9659
TEL 507-356-8839
Established: 1984
**Products:** art quilts **Techniques:**
quilting, embroidery, discharge shibori
**Size Range:** 6" × 6" to 9' × 12' **Price
Range:** $50 to $2,500/piece

## LINDA KISCELLUS

LIFE QUILTS
6744 N OCONTO AVE
CHICAGO, IL 60631-3914
TEL 773-763-5669
FAX 773-763-5504
Established: 1993
**Products:** art quilts
**Techniques:** appliqué, hand made
papers **Size Range:** 13" × 15" to
30" × 40" **Price Range:** $150 to
$1,000/piece; $90 to $120/sq. ft.

## KIMBERLY HALDEMAN KLEIN

K.H. KLEIN
925 GRANDVIEW BLVD
LANCASTER, PA 17601-5105
TEL 717-293-9453
Established: 1976
**Products:** art quilts **Techniques:**
quilting, piecing **Size Range:** 40" × 40"
to 60" × 60" **Price Range:** $400 to
$1,200/piece

Nancy Koenigsberg, *November*, 1996, polynylon-coated copper wire, copper screen backing, 30" × 30" × 3",
photo: D. James Dee

# FIBER ART FOR THE WALL

## M.A. KLEIN

M.A. KLEIN DESIGN
PO BOX 2443
FAIR OAKS BLVD #344
SACRAMENTO, CA 95825
TEL 800-700-7815
Established: 1962
**Products:** mixed media installations **Techniques:** painting, embroidery, collage **Size Range:** 10" x 12" to 9' x 12' **Price Range:** $225 to $25,000/piece

## ★ NANCY SMITH KLOS

KLOS STUDIOS
2407 NE 9TH AVE
PORTLAND, OR 97212
TEL 503-282-7028
FAX 503-282-7985
**Established: 1985**
**Products:** tapestries
**Techniques:** weaving, painting, dyeing
**Size Range:** 12" x 12" and up **Price Range:** $100 to $10,000/piece; $300 to $350/sq. ft.

See page 181 for photographs and additional information.

## SALLY KNIGHT

SALLY KNIGHT, FIBER ART
38 S CREST DR
BURLINGTON, VT 05401
TEL 802-865-9100
E-Mail: whitekni@together.net
Established: 1989
**Products:** art quilts
**Techniques:** appliqué, quilting, beading
**Size Range:** 6" x 6" to 40" x 40"
**Price Range:** $400 to $4,500/piece

## ELLEN KOCHANSKY

EKO
1237 MILE CREEK RD
PICKENS, SC 29671-8703
TEL 864-868-9749
FAX 864-868-4250
Established: 1978
**Products:** fiber installations
**Techniques:** quilting, wrapping
**Size Range:** 6" x 6" to 6' x 20'
**Price Range:** $150 to $400/sq. ft.

## ★ ANNA KOCHEROVSKY

**WOVEN FRESCOES**
6154 QUAKER HILL DR
WEST BLOOMFIELD, MI 48322
TEL 810-661-0560
**Established: 1987**
**Products:** tapestries **Techniques:** weaving **Size Range:** 12" x 12" to 5' x 20' **Price Range:** $150 to $500/sq. ft.

See page 178 for photographs and additional information.

## ★ JEREMY KOEHLER

KOEHLER STUDIO
PO BOX 279
SANTA FE, NM 87504-0279
TEL 505-422-2201
**Established: 1977**
**Products:** tapestries **Techniques:** weaving, dyeing **Size Range:** 36" x 36" to 120" x 96" **Price Range:** $125 to $200/sq. ft.

See page 179 for photographs and additional information.

## ★ NANCY KOENIGSBERG

435 E 57TH ST
NEW YORK, NY 10022-3062
TEL 212-644-2398
FAX 212-980-6642
**Established: 1964**
**Products:** fiber installations woven-wire constructions **Techniques:** weaving, knotting **Size Range:** 1' x 1' to 10' x 12' **Price Range:** $150 to $300/sq. ft.

See photograph page 215.

## JOAN KOPCHIK

1335 STEPHEN WAY
SOUTHAMPTON, PA 18966-4349
TEL 215-322-1862
Established: 1976
**Products:** paper **Techniques:** casting, painting, weaving **Size Range:** all sizes **Price Range:** $125 to $200/sq. ft.

## LIBBY KOWALSKI

32 UNION SQUARE E #216
NEW YORK, NY 10003
TEL 212-254-7551
FAX 212-254-7434
Established: 1981
**Products:** tapestries
**Techniques:** weaving **Size Range:** 14" x 27" to 96" x 120" **Price Range:** $500 to $6,000/piece

## WILFRED KOZUB

ZÖNIK
BOX 246
EDMONTON, AB T5J 2J1
CANADA
TEL 403-432-0430
FAX 403-433-1115
Established: 1990
**Products:** floor cloths
**Techniques:** painting acrylic on heavy canvas **Size Range:** 18" x 24" to 44" x 66" **Price Range:** $100 to $150/sq. ft.

## GRACE KRAFT

STONE SCHOOL HOUSE
MADRID, NM 87010
TEL 505-471-8062
Established: 1970
**Products:** fabric installations
**Techniques:** screen printing screened on silk, engraved aluminum frames
**Size Range:** 32" x 32" to 45' x 45'
**Price Range:** $600 to $36,000/piece

## DOROTHY SIMPSON KRAUSE

32 NATHANIEL WAY PO BOX 421
MARSHFIELD HILLS, MA 02051
TEL 617-837-1682
Established: 1968
**Products:** mixed media installations
**Techniques:** painting, laminating, digital imaging on fabric **Size Range:** 24" x 36" to 10' x 30' **Price Range:** $66 to $110/sq. ft.

## CANDACE KREITLOW

PO BOX 113
MAZOMANIE, WI 53560-0113
TEL 608-795-4680
Established: 1976
**Products:** woven wall constructions
**Techniques:** weaving, painting, sculpted over frame **Size Range:** 36" x 24" to 48" x 76" and larger **Price Range:** $600 to $6,000/piece

## TRACY KRUMM

12011 RED OAK CT N
BURNSVILLE, MN 55337
TEL 612-890-2605
Established: 1987
**Products:** paper **Techniques:** weaving, drawing, crochetimg **Size Range:** 7" x 7" to 60" x 60" **Price Range:** $300 to $5,000/piece

## LIALIA KUCHMA

2423 W SUPERIOR ST
CHICAGO, IL 60612-1213
TEL 312-227-5445
Established: 1973
**Products:** tapestries **Techniques:** weaving **Size Range:** 36" x 48" to 96" x 240" **Price Range:** $2,000 to $32,000/piece; $150 to $350/sq. ft.

## ★ SILJA LAHTINEN

**SILJA'S FINE ART STUDIO**
5220 SUNSET TRL
MARIETTA, GA 30068-4740
TEL 770-992-8380
FAX 770-992-0350
**Established: 1978**
**Products:** prints on chamois **Techniques:** beading, painting, screen printing, photo etching **Size Range:** 19" x 23" to 72" x 65" **Price Range:** $250 to $29,000 per group/piece; $3.03 to $292.50/sq. ft.

See page 98 for photographs and additional information.

## COLETTE LAICO

968C HERITAGE HILLS DR
SOMERS, NY 10589-1913
TEL 914-276-2591
Established: 1976
**Products:** mixed media installations
**Techniques:** painting **Size Range:** 9" x 12" to 4' x 6' **Price Range:** $300 to $2,000/piece

## MARY LANE

703 N FOOTE ST
OLYMPIA, WA 98502
TEL 360-754-1105
Established: 1982
**Products:** tapestries **Techniques:** weaving **Size Range:** 4" x 4" to 5' x 10' **Price Range:** $100 to $5,000/piece

## RAGNHILD LANGLET

PO BOX 508
SAUSALITO, CA 94966-0508
TEL 415-332-5007
Established: 1965
**Products:** mixed media **Techniques:** painting, dyeing, embroidery **Size Range:** 18" x 24" to 4'x 8' or 8' x 4' **Price Range:** $1,500 to $10,000/piece; $350 to $500/sq. ft.

## ITALA LANGMAR

604 EXMOOR RD
KENILWORTH, IL 60043-1021
TEL 708-251-0427
Established: 1984
**Products:** fiber installations, papier mache vessels **Techniques:** painting, casting, crocheting **Size Range:** 15" x 25" to 5' x 7' **Price Range:** $150 to $4,000/piece; $15 to $45/sq. ft.

### ★ GAIL LARNED

**LARNED MARLOW STUDIOS**
**144 S MONROE AVE**
**COLUMBUS, OH 43205-1084**
**TEL 614-258-7239**
**Established: 1974**
**Products:** fiber installations **Techniques:** dyeing, wrapping, knotting **Size Range:** 2' × 4' to 5' × 15' **Price Range:** $1,000 to $45,000/piece; $35 to $200/sq. ft.

**See page 193 for photographs and additional information.**

### KAREN LARSEN

CACOPHONY
7 AUSTIN PARK
CAMBRIDGE, MA 02139-2509
TEL 617-491-4025
Established: 1975
**Products:** art quilts
**Techniques:** appliqué, quilting, weaving **Size Range:** 22" × 22" to 10' × 15' **Price Range:** $60 to $100/sq. ft.

### JUDITH LARZELERE

CORPORATE FIBER ART
226 BEECH ST
BELMONT, MA 02178-1945
TEL 617-484-6091
Established: 1974
**Products:** art quilts
**Techniques:** quilting, strip piecing **Size Range:** 20" × 20" to 112" × 144" **Price Range:** $125 to $375/sq. ft.

### ★ KAREN LAURENCE

**531 MAIN ST #1002**
**ROOSEVELT ISLAND, NY 10044**
**TEL 212-751-8215**
**FAX 212-759-0511**
**Established: 1965**
**Products:** art quilts **Techniques:** dyeing, appliqué, laminating **Size Range:** 18" × 18" to 10' × 10' **Price Range:** $100 to $175/sq. ft.

**See page 158 for photographs and additional information.**

### ULRIKA LEANDER

CONTEMPORARY TAPESTRY
  WEAVING
107 WESTOVERLOOK DR
OAK RIDGE, TN 37830-3825
TEL 423-482-6849
FAX 423-483-7911
Established: 1971
**Products:** tapestries **Techniques:** weaving **Size Range:** 4' × 4' to 12' × 30' **Price Range:** $150 to $500/sq. ft.

### SUSAN WEBB LEE

963 WOODS LOOP
WEDDINGTON, NC 28173-9376
TEL 704-843-1323
Established: 1979
**Products:** art quilts **Techniques:** appliqué, painting, dyeing **Size Range:** 25" × 25" to 6' × 8' **Price Range:** $300 to $8,000/piece

### ★ LENKER FINE ARTS

**MARLENE LENKER**
**28 NORTHVIEW TER**
**CEDAR GROVE, NJ 07009**
**TEL 201-239-8671**
**TEL 860-767-2098**
**FAX 201-239-8671**
**Established: 1996**
**Products:** paper **Techniques:** painting, collage **Size Range:** 10" × 10" to 60" × 90" **Price Range:** $400 to $10,000/piece

**See page 172 for photographs and additional information.**

### MICHELLE LESTER

MICHELLE LESTER STUDIO
15 W 17TH ST FL 9
NEW YORK, NY 10011-5506
TEL 212-989-1411
FAX 212-627-8553
Established: 1967
**Products:** tapestries, children's rugs **Techniques:** weaving **Size Range:** unlimited **Price Range:** $250 to $550/sq. ft.

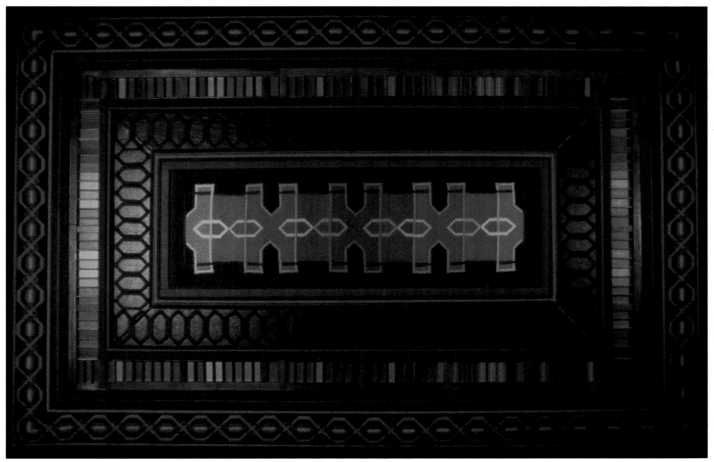

Dorothy Taylor Lindner, *The Eastern Gate*, fiber construction of needlepoint, wood, leather and paper, 45" × 69"

# FIBER ART FOR THE WALL

## ARLENE LEVEY

336 S HARDING RD
COLUMBUS, OH 43209-1946
TEL 614-231-8601
Established: 1982
**Products:** mixed media installations
**Techniques:** dyeing, embroidery, laminating **Size Range:** 24" × 24" to 144" × 144" **Price Range:** $250 to $10,000/piece; $25 to $100/sq. ft.

## JUDY ZOELZER LEVINE

9415 N FAIRWAY DR
MILWAUKEE, WI 53217-1322
TEL 414-351-2631
Established: 1991
**Products:** art quilts
**Techniques:** appliqué, beading, quilting
**Size Range:** 15" × 15" to 60" × 80"
**Price Range:** $200 to $4,000/piece

## VERENA LEVINE

VERENA LEVINE PICTORIAL AND
NARRATIVE QUILTS
4305 37TH ST NW
WASHINGTON, DC 20008
TEL 202-537-0916
Established: 1978
**Products:** art quilts
**Techniques:** appliqué, quilting, piecing
**Size Range:** 20" × 20" to 5' × 20'
**Price Range:** $150 minimum/sq. ft.

## ★ LINDA LHERMITE

**LES INSOLITES**
**3111 CLINT MOORE RD #205**
**BOCA RATON, FL 33496**
**TEL 561-989-0361**
**FAX 561-241-9860**
**Established: 1996**
**Products:** suede mosaics
**Techniques:** gluing and stitching
**Size Range:** 4' × 3' × 8'6" × 6' **Price Range:** $900 to $27,000/piece

See page 99 for photographs and additional information.

## BONNY LHOTKA

5658 CASCADE PL
BOULDER, CO 80303-2950
TEL 303-494-5631
FAX 303-494-3472
Established: 1972
**Products:** tapestries
**Techniques:** laminating, painting, stamping/printing digital imaging on fabric
**Size Range:** 24" × 36" to 10' × 30'
**Price Range:** $66 to $110/sq. ft.

## WENDY LILIENTHAL

740 BUTTERFIELD RD
SAN ANSELMO, CA 94960-1105
TEL 415-453-1019
Established: 1978
**Products:** hand-cast paper
**Techniques:** dyeing, casting, collage
**Size Range:** 18" × 24" to 4' × 9' **Price Range:** $500 to $5,000/piece

## LIN LACY LIMITED EDITIONS

LIN LACY
1021 FAIRMOUNT
SAINT PAUL, MN 55105
TEL 612-291-0587
Established: 1990
**Products:** art quilts **Techniques:** embroidery, appliqué, beading **Size Range:** 1' × 1' to 8' × 8' **Price Range:** $100 to $10,000/piece; $100 to $150/sq. ft.

## ★ DOROTHY TAYLOR LINDNER

**144 WITHEROW RD**
**SEWICKLEY, PA 15143-8315**
**TEL 412-741-6405**
**Established: 1967**
**Products:** fiber constructions **Techniques:** quilting, wrapping, needlepoint
**Size Range:** 12" × 12" to 60" × 120"
**Price Range:** $1,000 to $2,500/sq. ft.

See photograph page 217.

## RACHEL LINDSTROM

24231 N 41ST AVE
GLENDALE, AZ 85310-3235
TEL 602-780-0861
**Products:** mixed fiber collages **Techniques:** painting, dyeing, laminating **Size Range:** 20" × 20" to 72" × 72"
**Price Range:** $200 to $500/sq. ft.

## CAL LING

CAL LING PAPERWORKS
441 CHERRY ST
CHICO, CA 95928-5114
TEL 916-893-0882
FAX 916-893-1319
Established: 1983
**Products:** paper **Techniques:** painting, dyeing, casting **Size Range:** 11½" × 16" to 20' × 20' **Price Range:** $300 to $40,000/piece; $100 to $250/sq. ft.

## M. JOAN LINTAULT

306 N SPRINGER ST
CARBONDALE, IL 62901-1428
TEL 618-457-7815
Established: 1965
**Products:** art quilts
**Techniques:** dyeing, quilting, silkscreen
**Size Range:** 14" × 15" to 12' × 24'
**Price Range:** $1,000 to $30,000/piece; $200/sq. ft.

## ROSLYN LOGSDON

MONTPELIER ART CENTER
12826 LAUREL BOWIE RD
LAUREL, MD 20708
TEL 301-490-1136
Established: 1970
**Products:** hooked wall hangings
**Techniques:** rug hooking **Size Range:** 18" × 12" to 48" × 60" **Price Range:** $350 to $6,000/piece

## ★ GINNY LOHR

**GREEDY FOR COLOR - DESIGNS**
**BY GINNY LOHR**
**52 WOODSHIRE N**
**GETZVILLE, NY 14068**
**TEL 716-689-4752**
**Established: 1990**
**Products:** fabric constructions **Techniques:** painting, dyeing, screen printing
**Size Range:** 20" × 20" to 40" × 40"
**Price Range:** $200 to $1,000/piece

See page 65 for photographs and additional information.

## NATALIE LOMBARD

CELEBRATION BANNERS
137 E WASHINGTON ST
WEST CHICAGO, IL 60185
TEL 630-653-4477
FAX 630-462-7076
Established: 1990
**Products:** fabric constructions
**Techniques:** sculpted fabric
**Size Range:** 18" × 12" to 20' × 40'
**Price Range:** $200 to $15,000/piece

## KIT LONEY

PO BOX 857
FOLLY BEACH, SC 29439
TEL 803-588-6222
Established: 1980
**Products:** tapestries
**Techniques:** weaving, dyeing, painting
**Size Range:** 8" × 5" to 84" × 25"
**Price Range:** $175 to $2,000/piece

## PHYLLIS HARPER LONEY

10 GRASSHOPPER LN
ACTON, MA 01720
TEL 508-263-3715
Established: 1975
**Products:** dye-painted fabric **Techniques:** painting, quilting, sewn construction **Size Range:** 12" × 9" to 90" × 45" **Price Range:** $150 to $2,500/piece

## ★ JOYCE P. LOPEZ

**JOYCE LOPEZ STUDIO**
**1147 W OHIO ST #304**
**CHICAGO, IL 60622-5874**
**TEL 312-243-5033**
**FAX 312-243-5033**
**Established: 1979**
**Products:** sculpture/fiber **Techniques:** wrapping **Size Range:** 24" × 24" to 20' × 30' **Price Range:** $2,800 to $75,000/piece

See page 194 for photographs and additional information.

## ANTONIA LOWDEN

ANTONIA LOWDEN DESIGN
155 S ARLINGTON AVE
RENO, NV 89501-1701
TEL 702-826-3655
Established: 1970
**Products:** tapestries
**Techniques:** weaving, mixed media
**Size Range:** 2' × 2' to 6' × 12' **Price Range:** $500 to $20,000/piece

## PEGGY CLARK LUMPKINS

RR 1 BOX 4650
BROWNVILLE, ME 04414-9720
TEL 207-965-8526
Established: 1979
**Products:** transparent tapestry **Techniques:** weaving **Size Range:** 2' × 1'6" to 8' × 14' **Price Range:** $90 to $250/sq. ft.

## YAEL LURIE
## JEAN PIERRE LAROCHETTE

LURIE-LAROCHETTE
2216 GRANT ST
BERKELEY, CA 94703-1714
TEL 510-548-5744
Established: 1960
**Products:** tapestries **Techniques:** weaving **Size Range:** 8" × 12" to 6' × 16' **Price Range:** $600 to $35,000/piece

## NANCY LYON
102 SHAKER RD
NEW LONDON, NH 03257-5014
TEL 603-526-6754
Established: 1971
**Products:** hand-painted wall pieces
**Techniques:** painting, stamping or printing **Size Range:** 24" x 24" to unlimited **Price Range:** $30 to $50/sq. ft.

## MARGO MACDONALD
5814 CRESCENT BEACH RD
VAUGHN, WA 98394
TEL 206-884-2955
Established: 1980
**Products:** tapestries **Techniques:** weaving **Size Range:** 13" x 20" to 4'6" to 4'6" **Price Range:** $500 to $2,000/piece

## ANN MACEACHERN
MACEACHERN HANDWEAVING & BASKETRY
PO BOX 80
ACTON, ME 04001-0080
TEL 207-636-2539
Established: 1970
**Products:** fiber installations **Techniques:** embroidery, weaving, wrapping, knotting, twining **Size Range:** 8" x 12" to 2' x 8' **Price Range:** $50 to $500/piece

## ★ PATRICIA MACGILLIS
**12984 VIA GRIMALDI**
**DEL MAR, CA 92014**
**TEL 619-259-0589**
**Products:** mixed media installations
**Techniques:** weaving, painting, paper
**Size Range:** 45" x 45" to 12' x 10' **Price Range:** $500 to $5,000/piece

**See photograph this page.**

## JACKIE MACKAY
HANDWOVEN COUNTRY INTERIORS
RR 5
BERWICK, NS B0P 1E0
CANADA
TEL 902-538-3315
Established: 1984
**Products:** tapestries **Techniques:** dyeing, weaving **Size Range:** 3' x 5' to 5' x 5' **Price Range:** $300 to $2,000/piece

## ★ JENNIFER MACKEY
**CHIA JEN STUDIO**
**PO BOX 469**
**SCOTIA, CA 95565**
**TEL 707-764-5877**
**FAX 707-764-2505**
**Established: 1981**
**Products:** fabric constructions **Techniques:** painting, screen printing, appliqué
**Size Range:** 24" x 24" to 24' x 68"
**Price Range:** $11 to $25/sq. ft.

**See page 42 for photographs and additional information.**

## IRENE MAGINNISS
770 ANDOVER RD S
MANSFIELD, OH 44907-1511
TEL 419-756-2841
Established: 1970
**Products:** mixed media installations
**Techniques:** collage, embedding **Size Range:** 12" x 12" to 6' x 8' **Price Range:** $125 to $175/sq. ft.

## JULIANNA S. MAHLEY
404 COUNCIL DR NE
VIENNA, VA 22180-4740
TEL 703-281-9106
FAX 703-281-0368
Established: 1989
**Products:** fiber installations **Techniques:** painting, embroidery, dyeing
**Size Range:** 5" x 5" to 25" x 25"
**Price Range:** $400 to $2,000/piece

## PATRICIA MALARCHER
93 IVY LN
ENGLEWOOD, NJ 07631
TEL 201-568-1084
FAX 201-567-3709
Established: 1963
**Products:** fabric constructions
**Techniques:** appliqué, painting, stamping or printing **Size Range:** 6" x 6" and up **Price Range:** $200 to $400/sq. ft.

## RUTH MANNING
177 ROGERS PKY
ROCHESTER, NY 14617-4205
TEL 716-467-6250
Established: 1980
**Products:** tapestries **Techniques:** dyeing, weaving **Size Range:** 1' x 1' to 4' x 6' **Price Range:** $100 to $200/sq. ft.

## CAMILLE MANSFIELD
MANSFIELD STUDIOS
507 MODOC AVE
RENO, NV 89509-3339
TEL 702-333-5282
Established: 1994
**Products:** art quilts **Techniques:** appliqué, embroidery, quilting, piecing, hand dyeing **Size Range:** 40" x 40" to 120" x 120" **Price Range:** $1,000 to $10,000/piece

## SHARON MARCUS
TAPESTRY
4145 SW CORBETT AVE
PORTLAND, OR 97201-4201
TEL 503-796-1234
FAX 503-796-1234
Established: 1975
**Products:** tapestries **Techniques:** weaving **Size Range:** 3' x 3' to 9'6" x 15' **Price Range:** $350/sq. ft.

## JANE GOLDING MARIE
620 CHICAGO AVE
HASTINGS, NE 68901-5831
TEL 402-463-2669
Established: 1973
**Products:** fabric constructions **Techniques:** painting, embroidery, wrapping
**Size Range:** 12" x 12" to 8' x 12'
**Price Range:** $100 to $150/sq. ft.

## MARY KAY COLLING CONTEMPORARY PAPER ART
MARY KAY COLLING
VILLAGE GATE SQ
274 N GOODMAN ST
ROCHESTER, NY 14607
TEL 716-442-8946
Established: 1988
**Products:** paper **Techniques:** appliqué, casting, painting **Size Range:** no size limit **Price Range:** $100 to $300/sq. ft.

## MARTHA MATTHEWS
7200 TERRACE DR
CHARLOTTE, NC 28211-6143
TEL 704-364-3435
Established: 1973
**Products:** tapestries **Techniques:** weaving **Size Range:** 2' x 3' to 8' x 20' **Price Range:** $1,200 to $48,000/piece; $240 to $300/sq. ft.

## ★ THERESE MAY
**651 N 4TH ST**
**SAN JOSE, CA 95112-5143**
**TEL 408-292-3247**
**Established: 1965**
**Products:** art quilts
**Techniques:** appliqué, embroidery, painting **Size Range:** 1' x 1' to 14' x 14'
**Price Range:** $500 to $41,000/piece

**See page 159 for photographs and additional information.**

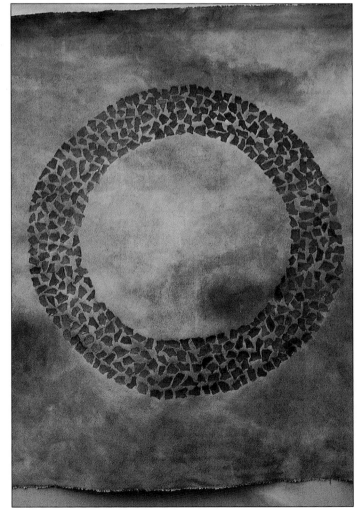

Patricia MacGillis, *Intergral*, 1996, unstretched canvas, acrylic paints, torn papers, 60" x 60"

# FIBER ART FOR THE WALL

## PHOEBE MCAFEE

6 MONTEZUMA ST
SAN FRANCISCO, CA 94110-5109
TEL 415-282-3448
Established: 1967
**Products:** tapestries
**Techniques:** weaving, appliqué, embroidery **Size Range:** 1' × 2' to 8' × 24'
**Price Range:** $200 to $50,000/piece

## JANE MCDOLE

ARTISTIC CREATIONS
10,000 DRYDEN
RENO, NV 89511
TEL 702-851-1115
Established: 1972
**Products:** mixed media installations
**Techniques:** weaving painting clay **Size Range:** 1' × 1½' to 4' × 36' **Price Range:** $300 to $20,000/piece

## ★ SUSAN MCGEHEE

**METALLIC STRANDS**
**540 23RD ST**
**MANHATTAN BEACH, CA 90266**
**TEL 310-545-4112**
**Established: 1989**
**Products:** woven-metal sculptures
**Techniques:** weaving **Size Range:** 2" × 24" to 5' × 38' **Price Range:** $140 to $180/sq. ft.

**See page 109 for photographs and additional information.**

## JULIE MCGINNIS

515 E ROCK ST
FAYETTEVILLE, AR 72701-4323
TEL 501-582-3707
Established: 1988
**Products:** art quilts
**Techniques:** dyeing, quilting, piecing
**Size Range:** 30" × 40" to 120" × 120"
**Price Range:** $300 to $4,000/piece

## SALLY MCKENNA

SALLY MCKENNA SCULPTURE
7050 E DIXILETA DR
CAVE CREEK, AZ 85331
TEL 602-585-7034
FAX 602-585-5290
Established: 1978
**Products:** mixed media installations
**Techniques:** weaving, painting **Size Range:** 2'6" × 1'6" to 20' × 12' **Price Range:** $1,200 to $95,000/piece

## DIANNE MCKENZIE

COMET STUDIOS
PO BOX 337
THE SEA RANCH, CA 95497-0337
TEL 707-785-2567
FAX 707-785-2567
E-Mail: comet@mcn.org
Established: 1974
**Products:** tapestries **Techniques:** dyeing, weaving **Size Range:** 6' × 8' to 12' × 20' and up **Price Range:** $250 to $500/sq. ft.

## BARBARA BARRICK MCKIE

GRAPHIC MEMORIES BY MCKIE
40 BILL HILL RD
LYME, CT 06371-3501
TEL 860-434-5222
FAX 860-434-5222
E-Mail: genebarb@aol.com
Established: 1974
**Products:** art quilts
**Techniques:** dyeing, appliqué, quilting
**Price Range:** $350 to $10,000/piece

## JOAN MICHAELS-PAQUE

JMP ATELIER
4455 N FREDERICK AVE
MILWAUKEE, WI 53211
TEL 414-962-2748
Established: 1961
**Products:** mixed media bas-reliefs
**Techniques:** fiber constructions **Size Range:** 12" × 24" to 6' × 18' **Price Range:** $350 to $30,000/piece

## SUSAN MILL

MILLAY RD
BOWDOINHAM, ME 04008
TEL 207-666-3029
FAX 207-666-3555
Established: 1982
**Products:** mixed media installations
**Techniques:** felting, sculpting **Size Range:** 9" × 7" to 7' × 5' **Price Range:** $300 to $2,000/piece

## BETH MINEAR

171 MONUMENT RD
ORLEANS, MA 02653-3507
TEL 508-255-3430
Established: 1978
**Products:** rugs, floor or wall **Techniques:** weaving **Size Range:** 3' × 5' and up **Price Range:** $70 to $80/sq. ft.

## NORMA MINKOWITZ

25 BROADVIEW RD
WESTPORT, CT 06880-2303
TEL 203-227-4497
Established: 1960
**Products:** mixed media installations
**Techniques:** painting, fiber construction **Size Range:** 12" × 23" to 50" × 63" **Price Range:** $3,000 to $10,000/piece

## MISSION VISTA STUDIOS

LIZ HUNNICUTT
812 GIN RD
ENNIS, TX 75119
TEL 972-878-0548
Established: 1987
**Products:** paper **Techniques:** weaving, painting, dyeing **Size Range:** 3' × 3' and up **Price Range:** $460 to $10,000/piece

## MISSION WEAVER

ELLEN SULLIVAN-BERNHARDY
10 COSTA DEL SOL
MONARCH BEACH, CA 92629
TEL 714-443-5275
FAX 714-443-5278
Established: 1995
**Products:** tapestries **Techniques:** weaving **Size Range:** 18" × 12" to 72" × 48" **Price Range:** $10 to $50/sq. ft.

## PATTI MITCHEM

28 WITCHTROT RD
SOUTH BERWICK, ME 03908-2170
TEL 207-384-2195
FAX 207-384-1938
Established: 1976
**Products:** fiber installations **Techniques:** weaving **Size Range:** 2' × 3' to unlimited **Price Range:** $90 to $180/sq. ft.

## KATHLEEN MOLLOHAN

524 S ROBERTS ST
HELENA, MT 59601-5435
TEL 406-442-9028
Established: 1983
**Products:** tapestries
**Techniques:** beading, painting, weaving
**Size Range:** 4' × 5' to 6' × 9' **Price Range:** $130 to $150/sq. ft.

## ★ DOTTIE MOORE

**1134 CHARLOTTE AVE**
**ROCK HILL, SC 29732-2452**
**TEL 803-327-5088**
**Established: 1975**
**Products:** art quilts
**Techniques:** painting, embroidery, appliqué **Size Range:** 2' × 2' to 6' × 8' **Price Range:** $100 to $300/sq. ft.

**See page 160 for photographs and additional information.**

## EDWARD MORDAK

801 SUTTER ST #305
SAN FRANCISCO, CA 94109-6108
TEL 415-673-8046
Established: 1985
**Products:** mixed media installations, paper **Techniques:** beading, painting, weaving, knotting **Size Range:** 30" × 20" to 5' × 10' **Price Range:** $600 to $12,000/piece

## ROSLYN MORESH

PO BOX 294
HOOLEHUA, HI 96729
TEL 806-567-6766
Established: 1979
**Products:** paper **Techniques:** dyeing, painting, casting **Size Range:** 2" × 3" to 38" × 48" **Price Range:** $40 to $6,000/piece

## LORETTA MOSSMAN

LM TAPESTRIES
2524 BROWN ST
PHILADELPHIA, PA 19130
TEL 215-763-4060
FAX 215-483-4864
Established: 1980
**Products:** tapestries **Techniques:** painting, appliqué, embroidery **Size Range:** unlimited **Price Range:** $900 to $10,000/piece; $200 to $300/sq. ft.

## STEPHANIE NADOLSKI

NADOLSKI FINE ART & DESIGN
25287 BARSUMIAN DR
BARRINGTON, IL 60010-1118
TEL 847-526-5208
FAX 847-526-5208
Established: 1975
**Products:** mixed media installations, handmade paper **Techniques:** painting, casting, stamping or printing **Size Range:** 20" × 20" to 60" × 84" **Price Range:** $250 to $6,000/piece

## ★ NAN GOSS INC.

**NAN GOSS-BILODEAU**
18801 SE 263RD ST
KENT, WA 98042
TEL 206-639-9138
FAX 206-639-4898
Established: 1984
**Products:** mixed media assemblages
**Techniques:** painting, embroidery, beading **Size Range:** 5" × 7" to 36" × 96" **Price Range:** $.75 to $3.00/sq. ft.

See page 173 for photographs and additional information.

## DOMINIE NASH

8612 RAYBURN RD
BETHESDA, MD 20817-3630
TEL 202-722-1407
Established: 1972
**Products:** art quilts **Techniques:** dyeing, quilting, silkscreen **Size Range:** 18" × 14" to 84" × 72" **Price Range:** $400 to $4,000/piece; $150 to $200/sq. ft.

## MIRIAM NATHAN-ROBERTS

1351 ACTON ST
BERKELEY, CA 94706-2501
TEL 510-525-5432
Established: 1982
**Products:** art quilts
**Techniques:** airbush, appliqué, quilting
**Size Range:** 30" × 30" to 96" × 108"
**Price Range:** $100 to $200/sq. ft.

## JEAN NEBLETT

628 RHODE ISLAND ST
SAN FRANCISCO, CA 94107-2628
TEL 415-550-2613
FAX 415-821-2772
Established: 1977
**Products:** art quilts **Techniques:** appliqué, painting, quilting **Size Range:** 4" × 5" to 5' × 6' **Price Range:** $200 to $9,600/piece

## DANA H. NELSON

155 FAIRVIEW RD
STOCKBRIDGE, GA 30281-1045
TEL 770-389-8562
FAX 770-507-6583
Established: 1980
**Products:** tapestries
**Techniques:** dyeing, embroidery, weaving **Size Range:** 18" × 18" to 12'6" × 14' **Price Range:** $50 to $10,000/piece

## KEIKO NELSON

KEIKO NELSON ART STUDIO
2604 3RD ST
SAN FRANCISCO, CA 94107
TEL 415-824-1545
FAX 510-527-4822
Established: 1976
**Products:** mixed media installations. paper **Techniques:** painting, screen printing, casting **Size Range:** 5" × 5" to 200" × 200" **Price Range:** $500 to $50,000/piece

## ANNA NESBITT

ROSE CREATIONS
3310 PIPER'S GLEN DR
LAFAYETTE, IN 47905
TEL 317-474-5229
Established: 1985
**Products:** 'home portraits' on canvas panels **Techniques:** painting **Size Range:** 11" × 14" to customer request **Price Range:** $200 to $3,000/piece

## ROCHELLE NEWMAN

PYTHAGOREAN PRESS
PO BOX 5162
BRADFORD, MA 01835-0162
TEL 508-372-3129
Established: 1963
**Products:** tapestries
**Techniques:** weaving, wrapping, crocheting **Size Range:** 2' × 3' to 8' × 8' **Price Range:** $100 to $150/sq. ft.

## ANNE MCKENZIE NICKOLSON

5020 N ILLINOIS ST
INDIANAPOLIS, IN 46208-2612
TEL 317-257-8929
FAX 317-257-8929
Established: 1978
**Products:** fabric constructions **Techniques:** embroidery, airbrush, appliqué **Size Range:** 10" × 10" to 14' × 14' **Price Range:** $200 to $250/sq. ft.

## NITIA

NITIA COLLINS
2901 DYER ST
DALLAS, TX 75205-1907
TEL 214-361-8808
Established: 1992
**Products:** wool installations
**Techniques:** hand tufted **Size Range:** 1' × 1' to 6' × 9' **Price Range:** $40 to $100/sq. ft.

## CYNTHIA NIXON

CYNTHIA NIXON STUDIO
427 S NIXON RD
STATE COLLEGE, PA 16801-2318
TEL 814-238-4811
Established: 1978
**Products:** art quilts
**Techniques:** painting, appliqué, quilting **Size Range:** 1' × 1' to 10' × 20' **Price Range:** $200 to $15,000/piece

## ELIZABETH NORDGREN

6 RYAN WAY
DURHAM, NH 03824-2916
TEL 603-868-2873
Established: 1973
**Products:** fiber installations
**Techniques:** dyeing, painting, weaving **Size Range:** 3" × 5" to 6' × 12' **Price Range:** $100 to $5,000/piece

## INGE NØRGAARD

907 PIERCE ST
PORT TOWNSEND, WA 98368-8046
TEL 360-385-0637
Established: 1972
**Products:** tapestries **Techniques:** weaving **Size Range:** 3" × 3" to 10' × 15' **Price Range:** $100 to $50,000/piece

## SUSAN M. OAKS

6581 FOX RUN
SAN ANTONIO, TX 78233-4706
TEL 210-656-8440
Established: 1979
**Products:** framed fiber collage **Techniques:** dyeing, painting, stamping/printing **Size Range:** 8" × 10" to 3'6" × 4'6" **Price Range:** $200 to $850/piece

## VIRGINIA O'DONNELL

4031 SE 149TH AVE
PORTLAND, OR 97236-2421
TEL 503-761-8596
Established: 1989
**Products:** art quilts
**Techniques:** dyeing, appliqué, wrapping **Size Range:** 40" × 40" to 10' × 10' **Price Range:** $350 to $3,000/piece

## SHEILA O'HARA

7101 THORNDALE DR
OAKLAND, CA 94611-1031
TEL 510-339-3014
Established: 1977
**Products:** tapestries **Techniques:** weaving **Size Range:** 12" × 20" to 20' × 30' **Price Range:** Trade discount available/piece; $250 to $1,000/sq. ft.

## IRA ONO

IRA ONO DESIGNS
PO BOX 112
VOLCANO, HI 96785-0112
TEL 808-967-7261
Established: 1968
**Products:** mixed media installations. paper **Techniques:** Japanese-paste paper **Size Range:** 8" × 10" to 9' × 14' **Price Range:** $140 to $4,000/piece

Sybil Shane, *Abundance*, mohair, rayon, marbled paper, hand-painted silk, handmade paper, 27" × 37", photo: Michelle Oldland Photography

# FIBER ART FOR THE WALL

**LISTED ARTISTS** work at a professional level in the area of fiber art for the wall.

| | |
|---|---|
| ESTABLISHED | The year the artist began working as a professional. |
| PRODUCTS | Types of fiber art created by the artist for display on walls. |
| TECHNIQUES | Techniques typically used by the artist to create the work. |
| SIZE RANGE | Range of sizes for the artist's typical art for the wall. |
| PRICE RANGE | From lowest to highest, typical retail prices for the artist's fiber art for the wall. Prices are reported per piece and/or per square foot. |

CAN'T FIND A CERTAIN ARTIST?

Check the Index of Artists and Companies for a comprehensive listing of every artist in *The Designer's Sourcebook 12.*

NEED AN ARTIST FOR YOUR PROJECT?

See the Commissions Clearinghouse on THE GUILD's Web site. List project specs. Artists respond directly.

Try it! *http://www.guild.com*

## ELLEN OPPENHEIMER

448 CLIFTON ST
OAKLAND, CA 94618-1163
TEL 510-658-9877
Established: 1970
**Products:** art quilts
**Techniques:** dyeing, quilting, printing
**Size Range:** 34" × 34" to 82" × 82"
**Price Range:** $100 to $150/sq. ft.

## ★ ORIGINALS BY WIN

**WIN PETERMAN
PO BOX 1866,
161 WINDCLIFF RD
PRINCE FREDERICK, MD 20678
TEL 410-535-3419
FAX 410-535-4976
Established: 1992
Products:** fabric constructions **Techniques:** painting, dyeing, airbrush **Size Range:** 12" × 10" and up **Price Range:** $50 to $200/sq. ft.

See page 38 for photographs and additional information.

## LEAH ORR

LEAH ORR STUDIO
926 N ALABAMA
INDIANAPOLIS, IN 46202-3319
TEL 317-637-4532
FAX 317-637-9235
Established: 1977
**Products:** wire works: copper, PVC, telephone **Techniques:** weaving, wrapping, knotting **Size Range:** 20" × 20" to 20' × 10' **Price Range:** $1,000 to $10,000/piece

## BARBARA OTTO

8940 15TH ST N
LAKE ELMO, MN 55042
TEL 612-739-3798
Established: 1988
**Products:** art quilts **Techniques:** painting, stamping, printing, resist, discharge **Size Range:** 2' × 3' to 8' × 8' **Price Range:** $300 to $2,500/piece

## CAROL OWEN

54 FEARRINGTON POST
PITTSBORO, NC 27312-8549
TEL 919-542-0616
Established: 1970
**Products:** paper **Techniques:** laminating, painting, assemblage **Size Range:** 16" × 16" to 4' × 8' **Price Range:** $100 to $150/sq. ft.

## PAPER PEOPLE

DAVID LECLERC AND PAMELA HUR
PO BOX 213
CUMMAQUID, MA 02637
TEL 508-362-2414
Established: 1975
**Products:** paper **Techniques:** painting, casting **Size Range:** 12" × 18" to 16' × 50' **Price Range:** $200 to $20,000/piece

## PAPERS OF DISTINCTION BY WENDY

WENDY WHITNEY HARBATH
121 GALENA RD PO BOX 509
FOOTVILLE, WI 53537
TEL 608-876-4139
**Products:** handmade paper **Techniques:** laminating, embossing, stitching **Size Range:** 6" × 6" to 30' × 40' **Price Range:** $70 to $1,000/piece

## OYOO HYUNJOO PARK

SOYOO ART STUDIO
193 CLOSTER DOCK RD
CLOSTER, NJ 07624-1907
TEL 201-767-8766
FAX 201-767-0497
Established: 1978
**Products:** tapestries **Techniques:** painting, Gobelin tapestry weaving **Size Range:** 7" × 7" to 10' × 10' **Price Range:** $250 to $50,000/piece

Kathleen Sharp, *Coming Home*, 1996, quilt commission, 4'x 8', photo: Richard Johns, Superior Color

## SHARRON PARKER

ARTSPACE STUDIO 217
201 E DAVIE ST
RALEIGH, NC 27601-1869
TEL 919-828-4533
TEL 919-872-2227
**Products:** wall hangings **Techniques:** felting, stitching **Size Range:** 10" × 12" to 5' × 10' **Price Range:** $200 to $8,000/piece

## DIANN PARROTT

DIANN PARROTT - YARDAGE ART
875 ST CLAIR AVE #4
ST PAUL, MN 55105-3278
TEL 612-222-4149
FAX 612-222-4149
Established: 1984
**Products:** pieced installations **Techniques:** yardage printing, sewing, hand fringing **Size Range:** 3' × 3' to 25' × 25' **Price Range:** $150 to $250/sq. ft.

## JACQUE PARSLEY

2005 INDIAN CHUTE
LOUISVILLE, KY 40207-1184
TEL 502-893-2092
Established: 1976
**Products:** fabric constructions **Techniques:** appliqué, embroidery, collage/assemblage **Size Range:** 12" × 12" to 4' × 6' **Price Range:** $800 to $2,000/piece

## PAM PATRIE

PATRIE STUDIO
314 SW 9TH AVE #5
PORTLAND, OR 97205-2803
TEL 503-284-2963
Established: 1974
**Products:** tapestries
**Techniques:** weaving, painting, needlepoint **Size Range:** 2' × 5' to 10' × 100' **Price Range:** $200 to $500/sq. ft.

## EVE S. PEARCE

RR 1 BOX 3880
BENNINGTON, VT 05201-9604
TEL 802-823-5580
Established: 1980
**Products:** tapestries **Techniques:** weaving **Size Range:** 2' × 2' to 4' × 8' **Price Range:** $200 to $250/sq. ft.

## KATHRYN ALISON PELLMAN

734 S DETROIT ST #3
LOS ANGELES, CA 90036
TEL 213-936-9692
Established: 1987
**Products:** art quilts **Techniques:** appliqué, quilting **Size Range:** 1' × 1' to 12' × 12' **Price Range:** $200 to $10,000/piece

## KAREN PERRINE

512 N K ST
TACOMA, WA 98403-1621
TEL 206-627-0449
Established: 1977
**Products:** fiber installations
**Techniques:** dyeing, painting, quilting
**Size Range:** 8" × 8" to 8' × 16' **Price Range:** $100 to $300/sq. ft.

## JUDITH H. PERRY

JUDITH H. PERRY DESIGNS
1916 WASHINGTON
WILMETTE, IL 60091
TEL 847-251-9056
Established: 1978
**Products:** art quilts
**Techniques:** painting, dyeing, quilting
**Size Range:** 16" × 20" to 60" × 90"
**Price Range:** $150 to $7,000/piece

## LINDA S. PERRY

ART QUILTS
96 BURLINGTON ST
LEXINGTON, MA 02173-1708
TEL 617-863-1107
Established: 1972
**Products:** art quilts
**Techniques:** dyeing, printing, metallic leaf **Size Range:** 2' × 3' to 5' × 8'
**Price Range:** $125/sq. ft.

## SUE PIERCE

PIERCEWORKS
14414 WOODCREST DR
ROCKVILLE, MD 20853-2335
TEL 301-460-8111
Established: 1978
**Products:** art quilts
**Techniques:** appliqué, painting, quilting
**Size Range:** 15" × 15" to 6' × 12'
**Price Range:** $200 to $10,000/piece

## RAY PIEROTTI

PO BOX 54385
ATLANTA, GA 30308
TEL 404-874-6672
FAX 404-874-6672
Established: 1966
**Products:** fabric and wood screens
**Techniques:** painting, dyeing, drawing
**Size Range:** 12" × 14" to 96" × 144"
**Price Range:** $300 to $15,000/piece; $75 to $250/sq. ft.

## PIPSISSEWA

FRANCES PUSCH
HC 68 BOX 46F
CUSHING, ME 04563-9505
TEL 207-354-0148
Established: 1992
**Products:** pieced-fabric pictures
**Techniques:** sewing **Size Range:** 2½" × 3½" (8" × 10" framed) **Price Range:** $42/piece

## PLASTIC BUCKET COMMUNICATIONS/DAES STUDIO

DAVID A. ELIZONDO
PO BOX 28528
SAN ANTONIO, TX 78228-0528
TEL 210-616-0735
FAX 210-616-0735
Established: 1975
**Products:** mixed media installations
**Techniques:** painting, wrapping, tying
**Size Range:** 1' × 1' to 5' × 3' **Price Range:** $100 to $600/piece

## JUDITH PLOTNER

JUDITH PLOTNER ART
QUILTS/L'ATELIER PLOTNER
214 GOAT FARM RD
GLOVERSVILLE, NY 12078-7315
TEL 518-725-3222
Established: 1962
**Products:** art quilts
**Techniques:** painting, quilting, piecing
**Size Range:** 15" × 15" to 6' × 7' **Price Range:** $400 to $6,000/piece

## BEVERLY PLUMMER

2720 WHITE OAK LEFT
BURNSVILLE, NC 28714
TEL 704-675-5208
Established: 1978
**Products:** paper **Techniques:** painting **Size Range:** 20" × 22" to 8' × 40'
**Price Range:** $120 to $800/piece; $100 to $150/sq. ft.

## JASON POLLEN

4348 LOCUST ST
KANSAS CITY, MO 64110-1531
TEL 816-561-6261
FAX 816-561-6404
**Products:** fused-silk works **Techniques:** painting, dyeing, screen printing fusing **Size Range:** 15" × 20" to 4' × 7'
**Price Range:** $4,000 to $10,000/piece

## DEE FORD POTTER

DEE FORD POTTER ART STUDIO
45 NW GREELEY AVE
BEND, OR 97701-2911
TEL 541-382-4797
Established: 1972
**Products:** woven sculpture **Techniques:** weaving, painting, resin forming, assemblage **Size Range:** 1' × 1' to full wall **Price Range:** $100 to $14,000/piece

Sheila Satow Fiber & Metal Art, *Enlightenment*, 1996, leather wall piece, acrylic paint, airbrush, pyrography, 42" × 40", photo: George Post Photography

# FIBER ART FOR THE WALL

## SUZANNE PRETTY

SUZANNE PRETTY TAPESTRY
 STUDIO
4 ELM ST
FARMINGTON, NH 03835-1508
TEL 603-755-3964
Established: 1969
**Products:** tapestries **Techniques:** weaving **Size Range:** 30" × 30" to 5' × 15' **Price Range:** $250 to $450/sq. ft.

## MARILYN PRICE

MARILYN PRICE STUDIO
6181 RIVERVIEW DR
INDIANAPOLIS, IN 46208
TEL 317-251-4732
Established: 1966
**Products:** textile murals
**Techniques:** screen printing, quilting, stamping **Size Range:** 4' × 3' to 8' × 30' **Price Range:** $2,000 to $19,000/piece; $150 to $225/sq. ft.

## NANCY PRICHARD

2604 W CHUBB LAKE AVE
VIRGINIA BEACH, VA 23455-1322
TEL 804-363-9272
Established: 1980
**Products:** paper **Techniques:** collage
**Size Range:** 16" × 18" to 36" × 36"
**Price Range:** $275 to $450/piece

## GAYLE PRITCHARD

31001 CARLTON DR
BAY VILLAGE, OH 44140-1428
TEL 216-871-1419
Established: 1985
**Products:** art quilts
**Techniques:** painting, quilting, collage
**Size Range:** 24" × 24" to 100" × 80"
**Price Range:** $150 to $3,500/piece

## QUILTS BY DONNA

DONNA SHARP
4214 N PRESTON HWY
SHEPHERDSVILLE, KY 40165-9408
TEL 502-955-8673
FAX 502-955-6779
Established: 1981
**Products:** art quilts **Techniques:** quilting **Size Range:** 4' × 4' to 9' × 10'
**Price Range:** $160 to $4,000/piece; $16 to $17/sq. ft.

## BILL RAFNEL

THE LOOMINARY
1326 GRANDVIEW RD
VISTA, CA 92084
TEL 619-726-8178
Established: 1985
**Products:** damask wall hangings **Techniques:** weaving **Size Range:** 45" × 32" to 8' × 20' **Price Range:** $80 to $260/sq. ft.

## MARY CURTIS RATCLIFF

630 NEILSON ST
BERKELEY, CA 94707
TEL 510-526-8472
Established: 1972
**Products:** mixed media installations
**Techniques:** painting, weaving, knotting
**Size Range:** 31" × 38" to 45" × 90"
**Price Range:** $750 to $3,500/piece

## COLLINS REDMAN

PO BOX 5287
WOODLAND PARK, CO 80135
TEL 303-647-2250
Established: 1988
**Products:** tapestries wall or floor
**Techniques:** weaving, dyeing **Size Range:** 20" × 20" to 80" × 60" **Price Range:** $75 to $150/sq. ft.

## FRAN REED

F. REED FIBERS
2424 SPRUCEWOOD ST
ANCHORAGE, AK 99508-3975
TEL 907-276-7717
Established: 1975
**Products:** fiber installations, fish skin and gut forms **Techniques:** weaving, airbrush, stitching **Size Range:** 40" × 40" to 5' × 20' **Price Range:** $1,000 to $25,000/piece; $100 to $1,000/sq. ft.

## WENDY REGIER

QUARRY ROAD STUDIOS
QUARRY RD RR1 BOX 10
PROCTORSVILLE, VT 05153-9701
TEL 802-226-7331
E-Mail: awregier@sover.net
Established: 1980
**Products:** fiber installations **Techniques:** weaving, dyeing, double faced pick-up **Size Range:** 24" × 15" to 80" × 45" **Price Range:** $48 to $80/sq. ft.

## MYRA REICHEL

121 E SIXTH ST
MEDIA, PA 19063-2503
TEL 610-565-5028
Established: 1973
**Products:** tapestries
**Techniques:** weaving, inlaid weaving, tapestry **Size Range:** 6" × 6" to 30' × 40' **Price Range:** $50 to $500/sq. ft.

## ROBIN REIDER

WEAVINGS BY ROBIN
PO BOX 687
CHIMAYO, NM 87522-0687
TEL 505-351-4474
Established: 1980
**Products:** tapestries **Techniques:** dyeing, weaving **Size Range:** 45" × 16" to 75" × 50" **Price Range:** $180 to $3,000/piece

## PAULA RENEE

RIVERCREST, 103 GEDNEY ST #1H
NYACK, NY 10960
TEL 914-358-3059
Established: 1978
**Products:** fiber installations **Techniques:** weaving, painting, woven paintings **Size Range:** 1' × 1' and up **Price Range:** $100 to $300/sq. ft.

Denise M. Snyder, *Raffia*, 1995, raffia, leather, wood, 50" × 58"

## SISTER REMY REVOR

MARIAN STUDIO
2900 N MENOMONEE RIVER PKY
MILWAUKEE, WI 53222-4545
TEL 414-258-4810
**Products:** screen printed panels **Techniques:** dyeing, screen printing, stamping
**Size Range:** 36" × 24" to 48" × 96"
**Price Range:** $200 to $400/piece

## ★ AMANDA RICHARDSON

**RICHARDSON KIRBY
AN VELLAN
CREAN BOTTOMS
ST. BURYAN
PENZANCE
CORNWALL TR19 6HD
U.K.
TEL 011-44-1736-810-485
FAX 011-44-1736-810-485
Established: 1978**
**Products:** fiber installations **Techniques:** dyeing, laminating, Richardson Tapestry **Size Range:** 3' × 4' to unlimited **Price Range:** $500/sq. ft.

**See page 195 for photographs and additional information.**

## KIM H. RITTER

18727 POINT LOOKOUT
NASSAU BAY, TX 77058
TEL 281-333-3224
FAX 281-333-8581
E-Mail: kritquilt@msn.com
Established: 1994
**Products:** art quilts
**Techniques:** painting, dyeing, quilting
**Size Range:** 24" × 24" to 90" × 90"
**Price Range:** $300 to $3,000/piece;
$50 to $100/sq. ft.

## RIVER WEAVING AND BATIK COMPANY

MARY TYLER
326 W KALAMAZOO AVE #401
KALAMAZOO, MI 49007
TEL 616-345-3120
Established: 1980
**Products:** fabric constructions
**Techniques:** painting, dyeing, hot wax batik **Size Range:** 3' × 2' to 8' × 6'
**Price Range:** $100 to $200/sq. ft.

## NANILEE S. ROBARGE

1260 HAIGHT ST #4
SAN FRANCISCO, CA 94117-3040
TEL 415-241-9182
Established: 1991
**Products:** weavings
**Techniques:** dyeing, silkscreen, weaving
**Size Range:** 12" × 15" to 6' × 6' **Price Range:** $100 to $7,000/piece

## ROCOCO STUDIO OF FIBER, COLOR & DESIGN

CAROL ANN MCCOLLUM
18 HORSESHOE RIDGE
BARNARDSVILLE, NC 28709
TEL 704-626-3777
Established: 1993
**Products:** fiber installations, kimono floats **Techniques:** weaving, dyeing, original designs **Size Range:** 10" × 4" to 5' × 5' **Price Range:** $145 to $3,000/piece

## GRETCHEN ROMEY-TANZER

TANZER'S FIBERWORK
33 MONUMENT RD
ORLEANS, MA 02653-3511
TEL 508-255-9022
Established: 1987
**Products:** tapestries **Techniques:** dyeing, silkscreen, weaving **Size Range:** any size **Price Range:** $30 to $50/piece

## SIROTA ROSENTHAL

70 BROOKSIDE DR
HAMDEN, CT 06517
TEL 203-281-5854
E-Mail: rosepjesa@aol.com
Established: 1975
**Products:** mixed media installations
**Techniques:** painting, dyeing, wrapping
**Price Range:** $90 to $10,000/piece

## GLORIA F. ROSS

GLORIA F. ROSS TAPESTRIES
21 E 87 ST
NEW YORK, NY 10128-0506
TEL 212-369-3337
Established: 1965
**Products:** tapestries **Techniques:** weaving **Size Range:** 5' × 2½' to 18' × 45' **Price Range:** $2,000 to $200,000/piece; $55 to $500/sq. ft.

## BILLI R. S. ROTHOVE

CELEBRATION STUDIOS
135 MONEYMAKER CIRCLE
GATLINBURG, TN 37738
TEL 423-436-0451
FAX 423-430-4101
Established: 1974
**Products:** art quilts
**Techniques:** dyeing, embroidery, beading **Size Range:** 20" × 30" to 36" × 48"
**Price Range:** $800 to $1,800/piece

## REBECCA ROUSH

901 N FOREST #108
BELLINGHAM, WA 98225
TEL 360-650-9127
E-Mail: rebroush@aol.com
Established: 1988
**Products:** beaded wall pieces **Techniques:** beading **Size Range:** 6" × 6" to 3' × 3' **Price Range:** $100 to $10,000/piece

## BERNIE ROWELL

BERNIE ROWELL STUDIO
1525 BRANSON AVE
KNOXVILLE, TN 37917-3843
TEL 423-523-5244
Established: 1975
**Products:** fiber installations **Techniques:** appliqué, embroidery, painting
**Size Range:** 30" × 40" to 6' × 24'
**Price Range:** $80 to $95/sq. ft.

## ZUZANA RUDAVSKÁ

GOLDEN SPIRAL PRODUCTIONS
254 WYTHE AVE
BROOKLYN, NY 11211
TEL 718-486-6520
FAX 718-486-6420
Established: 1986
**Products:** mixed media installations fiber wall hangings **Techniques:** dyeing, appique, laminating, "own techniques" **Size Range:** unlimited **Price Range:** $2,000 to $20,000/piece

## JUDE RUSSELL

733 NW EVERETT ST #17
PORTLAND, OR 97209-3517
TEL 503-295-0417
Established: 1979
**Products:** art quilts
**Techniques:** airbush, appliqué, painting
**Size Range:** 2' × 3' to 7' × 24' **Price Range:** $1,850 to $24,000/piece

## KAREN JENSON RUTHERFORD

KAREN JENSON RUTHERFORD
  STUDIO
513 S 21ST ST
TERRE HAUTE, IN 47803-2531
TEL 812-234-2928
Established: 1978
**Products:** fiber installations
**Techniques:** weaving, painting, paper making **Size Range:** 11" × 8" to 5' × 9'
**Price Range:** $500 to $5,000/piece

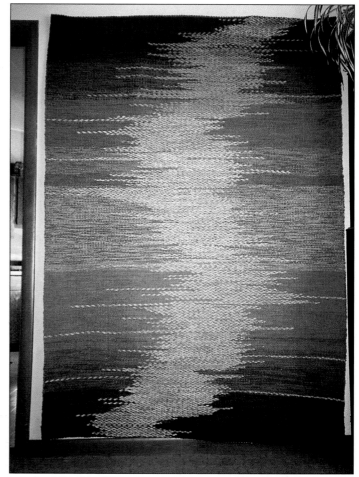

Jessica Speer, *Moonlight*, 1995, handwoven wool, compensated inlay, 60" × 100"

## ARTURO ALONZO SANDOVAL

HIGH-TECH ART FORMS
PO BOX 237
LEXINGTON, KY 40584-0237
TEL 606-273-8898
Established: 1969
**Products:** fabric constructions **Techniques:** weaving, machine stitching, interlacing collage **Size Range:** 8" × 8" to 30' × 40' **Price Range:** $250 to $75,000/piece; $150 to $500/sq. ft.

## STEPHANIE SANTMYERS

QUILT ART
7 PIPERS GLEN CT
GREENSBORO, NC 27406-5500
TEL 910-852-6439
Established: 1985
**Products:** art quilts
**Techniques:** quilting watercolor quilts
**Size Range:** 36" × 36" to 72" × 72"
**Price Range:** $225 to $2,200/piece

## SHIRLEY SARRACH

703 VICTORY DR
COLLINSVILLE, IL 62234
TEL 618-345-9664
Established: 1992
**Products:** silk painting and prints **Techniques:** painting, dyeing, electrostatic prints **Size Range:** 14" × 11" and up **Price Range:** $85 and up/piece

## JOY SAVILLE

244 DODDS LN
PRINCETON, NJ 08540-4108
TEL 609-924-6824
Established: 1976
**Products:** fabric constructions **Techniques:** piecing **Size Range:** 28" × 28" to unlimited **Price Range:** $2,000 to $30,000/piece

## SUSAN SAWYER

RR 1 BOX 107
EAST CALAIS, VT 05650-9506
TEL 802-456-8836
Established: 1971
**Products:** art quilts
**Techniques:** piecing quilting appliqué
**Size Range:** 8" × 8" to 84" × 84"
**Price Range:** $100 to $7,000/piece; $125 to $150/sq. ft.

## TOMMYE MCCLURE SCANLIN

403 S PARK ST
DAHLONEGA, GA 30533
TEL 706-864-7288
Established: 1972
**Products:** tapestries **Techniques:** weaving **Size Range:** 3" × 3" to 90" × 60" **Price Range:** $200 to $400/sq. ft.

## DEIDRE SCHERER

PO BOX 156
WILLIAMSVILLE, VT 05362-0156
TEL 802-348-7807
FAX 802-348-7136
Established: 1970
**Products:** fabric constructions **Techniques:** appliqué, machine-stitching, piecing, layering **Size Range:** 8" × 6" to 6' × 15' **Price Range:** $500 to $25,000/piece

## JULIA SCHLOSS

HANDWOVEN ORIGINALS
RR 1 BOX 5053
BAR HARBOR, ME 04609-9748
TEL 207-288-9882
Established: 1976
**Products:** tapestries **Techniques:** weaving **Size Range:** 2' × 2' and up **Price Range:** $600 to $10,000/piece; $100 to $150/sq. ft.

## MARY C. SCHNIBBEN

THE CRYSTAL BIRD
8224 LEAWOOD LN
WOODRIDGE, IL 60517
TEL 630-985-0897
Established: 1990
**Products:** mixed media installations
**Techniques:** weaving, painting, beading
**Size Range:** 18" × 12" to 10' × 6' **Price Range:** $250 to $8,000/piece

## LAURA SCHOONOVER

2640 SANDERS DR
ST LOUIS, MO 63129-4241
TEL 314-846-0048
Established: 1990
**Products:** mixed media installations
**Techniques:** weaving, casting, quilting
**Size Range:** 6" × 11" to 65" × 75" **Price Range:** $100 to $500/piece

## ★ JOAN SCHULZE

808 PIPER AVE
SUNNYVALE, CA 94087-1245
TEL 408-736-7833
FAX 408-736-7833
Established: 1970
**Products:** art quilts
**Techniques:** laminating, painting, quilting
**Size Range:** 16" × 20" to 10' × 20'
**Price Range:** $800 to $30,000/piece

See page 163 for photographs and additional information.

## ★ ANN SCHUMACHER

3743 EATON GATE LN
AUBURN HILLS, MI 48320
TEL 810-449-9240
FAX 810-844-9240
E-Mail: shillon@oakland.edu
Established: 1975
**Products:** tapestries
**Techniques:** weaving, dyeing, embroidery **Size Range:** 10" × 10" to 5' × 7'
**Price Range:** $225 to $450/sq. ft.

See page 182 for photographs and additional information.

## APRIL SCOTT

PO BOX 576
EL DORADO, KS 67042
TEL 316-321-6694
Established: 1982
**Products:** tapestries **Techniques:** weaving, embroidery, weft-face brocade **Size Range:** 18" × 24" to 8' × 10' **Price Range:** $400 to $24,000/piece

## LIBBY SEABERG

667 10TH ST
BROOKLYN, NY 11215-4501
TEL 718-768-7280
TEL 212-431-5321
FAX 718-768-7280
Established: 1968
**Products:** mixed media installations
**Techniques:** painting, laminating, drawing **Size Range:** 12" × 13¹/₂" to 90" × 200" **Price Range:** $300 to $3,000/piece

## AMANDA SEARS

PO BOX 244
SANTA CRUZ, CA 95061-0244
TEL 408-457-1630
Established: 1983
**Products:** raffia rugs **Techniques:** dyeing, tufting **Size Range:** 2' × 3' to 9' × 12' **Price Range:** $85 to $100/sq. ft.

## WARREN SEELIG
## SHERRIE GIBSON

328 MAIN ST STUDIO 300
ROCKLAND, ME 04841
TEL 207-594-0138
FAX 207-594-0138
Established: 1976
**Products:** fabric constructions, mixed media installations **Techniques:** assemblage **Size Range:** 16" × 24" to 14' × 32' **Price Range:** $1,200 to $6,000/piece

## SALLY A. SELLERS

3919 WAUNA VISTA DR
VANCOUVER, WA 98661-6031
TEL 360-693-4160
Established: 1989
**Products:** art quilts
**Techniques:** appliqué, painting, quilting
**Size Range:** 2' × 2' to 6' × 6' **Price Range:** $450 to $4,000/piece

## DIANNA SHAFFER

3011 NE HANCOCK ST
PORTLAND, OR 97212
TEL 503-281-5405
Established: 1976
**Products:** fiber installations **Techniques:** screen printing, appliqué, laminating **Size Range:** 12" × 12" to 8' × 15' **Price Range:** $100 to $4,000/piece; $95 to $200/sq. ft.

## ★ SYBIL SHANE

PO BOX 478
NEVADA CITY, CA 95959
TEL 916-265-9086
FAX 916-265-9086
Established: 1994
**Products:** silk and paper assemblages **Techniques:** painting, dyeing, wrapping, 3D construction **Size Range:** 7" × 14" to 3¹/₂' × 2¹/₂' **Price Range:** $200 to $2,000/piece

See photograph page 221.

## VERLA SHANER

4036 N 116TH CIR
OMAHA, NE 68164
TEL 402-492-9366
Established: 1990
**Products:** art quilts **Techniques:** dyeing, screen printing piecing **Size Range:** 12" × 12" to 8' × 8' **Price Range:** $400 to $1,200/piece

## ★ KATHLEEN SHARP

17360 VALLEY OAK DR
MONTE SERENO, CA 95030-2218
TEL 408-395-3014
Established: 1978
**Products:** art quilts **Techniques:** embroidery, appliqué, quilting **Size Range:** 14" × 14" to 6' × 10' **Price Range:** $300 to $15,000/piece

See photograph page 222.

## BARBARA SHAWCROFT

4 ANCHOR DR #243
EMERYVILLE, CA 94608-1564
TEL 510-658-6694
FAX 510-658-8264
**Products:** mixed media installations, 3D-sculptural wall installations **Techniques:** hand constructed, 3D **Size Range:** 2" × 2" to 50' × 20' **Price Range:** $1,500 to $50,000/piece

## ★ SHEILA SATOW FIBER & METAL ART

SHEILA SATOW
PO BOX 3085
SOUTH PASADENA, CA 91031
TEL 213-257-1023
FAX 213-255-8288
E-Mail: aqek65a@prodigy.com
Established: 1988
**Products:** leather **Techniques:** painting, airbrush, appliqué **Size Range:** 2' × 2' and up **Price Range:** $225 and up/piece

See photograph page 223.

## SUSAN SHIE
## JAMES ACORD

TURTLE MOON STUDIOS
2612 ARMSTRONG DR
WOOSTER, OH 44691-1806
TEL 216-345-5778
Established: 1977
**Products:** art quilts **Techniques:** appliqué, embroidery, painting, airbrush, beading, leather, clay **Size Range:** 6" × 8" to 100" × 100" **Price Range:** $200 to $25,000/piece

## SALLY SHORE

SALLY SHORE/WEAVER
LUDLAM LANE
LOCUST VALLEY, NY 11560
TEL 516-671-7276
Established: 1971
**Products:** fiber installations **Techniques:** weaving **Size Range:** 9" × 9" to 7' × 15' **Price Range:** $150 to $10,000/piece

## DIANE SHULLENBERGER

RR 1 BOX 259
JERICHO, VT 05465
TEL 802-899-4993
Established: 1978
**Products:** fabric constructions **Techniques:** layering, stitching **Size Range:** 21" × 23" to 32" × 36" **Price Range:** $1,000 to $2,000/piece

## ANE SHUSTA

PO BOX 18
SNOQUALMIE PASS, WA 98068
TEL 206-434-6115
Established: 1983
**Products:** tapestries **Techniques:** weaving **Size Range:** 3' × 5' to 5' × 8' **Price Range:** $1,000 to $10,000/piece

## ELANA SIEGAL

1825 W 14TH AVE
VANCOUVER, BC V6J 2J3
CANADA
TEL 604-736-2774
Established: 1990
**Products:** fiber installations **Techniques:** felting **Size Range:** 10" × 8" to 8' × 6' **Price Range:** $150 to $5,000/piece

## LAURA LAZAR SIEGEL

10 CROSSWAY
SCARSDALE, NY 10583-7118
TEL 914-723-9392
FAX 212-808-0406
Established: 1960
**Products:** fiber installations **Techniques:** painting, dyeing **Size Range:** 22" × 28" to 5' × 7' **Price Range:** $800 to $2,500/piece

## LOUISE SILK

CITY QUILT
210 CONOVER RD
PITTSBURGH, PA 15208-2604
TEL 412-361-1158
Established: 1978
**Products:** art quilts **Techniques:** appliqué, quilting, stamping/printing **Size Range:** 8" × 8" to 18' × 18' **Price Range:** $50 to $5,500/piece

## ELLY SIMMONS

ELLY SIMMONS FINE ART
BOX 463-36 SPRING AVE
LAGUNITAS, CA 94938
TEL 415-488-4177
Established: 1981
**Products:** tapestries **Techniques:** weaving **Size Range:** 18" × 27" to 80" × 60" **Price Range:** $850 to $5,000/sq. ft.

## MARY JO SINCLAIR

SINCLAIR STUDIO
10 MILTON ST
SAINT AUGUSTINE, FL 32095-2114
TEL 904-824-1441
FAX 904-824-1441
Established: 1978
**Products:** mixed media installations **Techniques:** weaving, painting, laminating **Size Range:** 3' × 4' to unlimited **Price Range:** $2,000 to $25,000/piece

## ★ SUSAN SINGLETON

AZO INC.
1101 E PIKE ST
SEATTLE, WA 98122-3915
TEL 206-322-0390
FAX 206-322-5062
Established: 1971
**Products:** paper **Techniques:** painting, dyeing, gold leafing **Size Range:** 15 × 15" to 12' × 12' **Price Range:** $100 to $150/sq. ft.

See page 175 for photographs and additional information.

Vangrodworks – Art by Design, *Eastern Garden Series I*, silk painting, 15" × 30"

# FIBER ART FOR THE WALL

## DELDA SKINNER

8111 DOE MEADOW DR
AUSTIN, TX 78749
TEL 512-288-1116
Established: 1979
**Products:** mixed media paper **Techniques:** painting, stamping, handmade paper **Size Range:** 12" x 12" to 48" x 72" **Price Range:** $300 to $2,000/piece

## LOUISE SLOBODAN

COASTAL TEXTURES STUDIO
135 HOLLAND RD
NANAIMO, BC V9R 6V9
CANADA
TEL 604-753-7359
Established: 1980
**Products:** art quilts **Techniques:** quilting, screen printing, laser printing, photo screen **Size Range:** 2' x 2' to 8' x 7' **Price Range:** $50 to $100/sq. ft.

## MARY E. SLY

SAN JUAN SILK
PO BOX 1925
FRIDAY HARBOR, WA 98250-1925
TEL 206-378-7110
Established: 1980
**Products:** silk, floral wall hangings **Techniques:** resist, hand painted with dyes **Size Range:** 15" x 65" to 60" x 60" **Price Range:** $95 to $2,500/piece

## C. ELIZABETH SMATHERS

3002 SIMMONS AVE
NASHVILLE, TN 37211-2425
TEL 615-331-4619
Established: 1985
**Products:** tapestries **Techniques:** weaving **Size Range:** 18" x 18" to unlimited **Price Range:** $100 to $225/sq. ft.

## ELLY SMITH

PO BOX 523
MEDINA, WA 98039-0523
TEL 206-720-1247
Established: 1974
**Products:** framed stitcheries, family samplers **Techniques:** embroidery **Size Range:** 9" x 8" to 74" x 74" **Price Range:** $300 to $4,000/piece; $250 to $300/sq. ft.

## ★ GLORIA ZMOLEK SMITH

ZPAPERSMITH
PO BOX 1294
CEDAR RAPIDS, IA 52406-1294
TEL 319-365-9611
FAX 319-365-9611
Established: 1983
**Products:** handmade paper quilts **Techniques:** embroidery, wrapping, origami **Size Range:** unlimited **Price Range:** $100 to $200/sq. ft.

See page 176 for photographs and additional information.

## PATTY CARMODY SMITH

4309 TONKAWOOD RD
MINNETONKA, MN 55345
TEL 612-933-7230
Established: 1995
**Products:** hand-hooked fiber art **Techniques:** hand hooking **Size Range:** 26" x 24" to 72' x 96" **Price Range:** $80 to $110/sq. ft.

## ★ DENISE M. SNYDER

DENISE M. SNYDER HAND-WOVEN
3018 ALDERWOOD
BELLINGHAM, WA 98225
TEL 360-647-1152
Established: 1987
**Products:** fiber installations **Techniques:** weaving, wrapping, knotting **Size Range:** 1' x 1' to 8' x 10' **Price Range:** $100 to $1,200/piece

See photograph page 224.

## STINA SODERSTROM

STINA WEAVINGS
29 LANG RD W
STIUYVESANT, NY 12173
TEL 518-758-1388
Established: 1989
**Products:** tapestries **Techniques:** weaving **Size Range:** 2' x 2' to 6' x 6' **Price Range:** $100 to $3,000/piece

## KAREN N. SOMA

1134 N 81ST ST
SEATTLE, WA 98103
TEL 206-522-8541
Established: 1975
**Products:** art quilts **Techniques:** dyeing, quilting, screen printing **Size Range:** 24" x 24" to 60" x 72" **Price Range:** $800 to $2,000/piece

## LYN SOUTHWORTH

821 14TH ST #4
SANTA MONICA, CA 90403
TEL 310-395-2537
FAX 310-395-2537
E-Mail: lyn@todaro.com
Established: 1985
**Products:** mixed media installations **Techniques:** painting, dyeing, giclée **Size Range:** 12" x 12" to 60" x 48" **Price Range:** $200 to $4,000/piece; $150 to $250/sq. ft.

## HOLLY M. SOWLES

HOLLY SOWLES FINE ARTS
1230 MANITOU
BOISE, ID 83706
TEL 208-345-9458
Established: 1991
**Products:** mixed media installations, paper **Techniques:** painting, dyeing, wrapping, stamping **Size Range:** 17" x 12" to 60" x 48" **Price Range:** $8 to $2,000/piece

## ★ JESSICA SPEER

ONE OF A KIND RUG WEAVER
PO BOX 362
ROCKLAND, MI 49960-9999
TEL 906-886-2672
Established: 1987
**Products:** wall and floor rugs **Techniques:** weaving, dyeing, embroidery **Size Range:** 3' x 5' and up **Price Range:** $30 to $100/piece

See photograph page 225.

## KATHY SPOERING

KATHY SPOERING, TAPESTRIES
2306 DOGWOOD CT
GRAND JUNCTION, CO 81506-8473
TEL 970-242-9081
Established: 1989
**Products:** tapestries **Techniques:** weaving **Size Range:** 18" x 18" to 48" x 48" **Price Range:** $1,100 to $6,000/piece

## SPRINGFLOWER

PO BOX 54
GAYS MILLS, WI 54631-0054
TEL 608-735-4941
Established: 1986
**Products:** belts to hang on wall **Techniques:** embroidery, weaving **Size Range:** 4" x 1" to 6' x 2" **Price Range:** $10 to $30/piece

## KAREN STAHLECKER

PO BOX 201566
ANCHORAGE, AK 99520-1566
TEL 907-566-0039
Established: 1976
**Products:** paper **Techniques:** handmade papers **Size Range:** 12" x 12" to 8' x 8' **Price Range:** $300 to $8,000/piece

## CARE STANDLEY

1040 TALBOT AVE
ALBANY, CA 94706-2332
TEL 510-525-8609
Established: 1982
**Products:** tapestries **Techniques:** weaving **Size Range:** 1' x 1' to 4' x 6' **Price Range:** $650 to $10,000/piece

## ★ SUSAN E. STARR

SUSAN STARR & CO.
1580 JONES RD
ROSWELL, GA 30075-2726
TEL 770-993-3980
FAX 770-993-5683
Established: 1975
**Products:** mixed media installations **Techniques:** weaving, casting, wrapping **Size Range:** any size **Price Range:** $400 to $20,000/piece; $100 to $175/sq. ft.

See page 101 for photographs and additional information.

## STARSINGER STUDIOS

FIBER ALCHEMY
209 S SHERWOOD VILLAGE DR
TUCSON, AZ 85710
TEL 520-721-0649
Established: 1982
**Products:** fiber installations **Techniques:** dyeing, felting, stitching **Size Range:** open **Price Range:** $150 to $7,000/piece

## HILLARY STEEL

HILLARY L. STEEL - HANDWEAVER
1502 SHARON DR
SILVER SPRING, MD 20901
TEL 301-587-8373
Established: 1981
**Products:** resist dyed, woven wall pieces **Techniques:** weaving, dyeing, resist dyeing **Size Range:** 14" x 14" to 10' x 10' **Price Range:** $250 to $15,000/piece

## ELINOR STEELE
61 WEYBRIDGE ST
MIDDLEBURY, VT 05753-1024
TEL 802-388-6546
Established: 1974
**Products:** tapestries **Techniques:** weaving **Size Range:** 2' x 3' to 8' x 12' **Price Range:** $200 to $400/sq. ft.

## LEORA KLAYMER STEWART
LLAMA STUDIOS
203 PARK PL #2F
BROOKLYN, NY 11238-4375
TEL 718-783-0379
Established: 1970
**Products:** textile restoration **Techniques:** weaving, embroidery, wrapping **Size Range:** 6" x 6" to 20' x 24' **Price Range:** $100 to $2,000/piece; $50 to $100/sq. ft.

## JOY STOCKSDALE
919 MIDPINE WAY
SEBASTOPOL, CA 95472
TEL 707-829-1756
FAX 707-829-3285
Established: 1981
**Products:** fiber installations **Techniques:** painting, quilting, silkscreen **Size Range:** 3' x 4' to 8' x 10' **Price Range:** $250 to $1,000/piece

## GLENNE STOLL
900 S GENEVA
AURORA, CO 80231
TEL 303-364-3927
FAX 303-355-2401
Established: 1970
**Products:** art quilts **Techniques:** quilting, piecing **Size Range:** 2' x 2' to 12' x 12' **Price Range:** $200 to $10,000/piece; $50 to $150/sq. ft.

## NANCY TAYLOR STONINGTON
N. TAYLOR STONINGTON, INC.
PO BOX 2269
VASHON, WA 98070-6809
TEL 206-463-2860
FAX 206-463-6598
E-Mail: cbnts@stoningtongallery.com
Established: 1971
**Products:** fiber murals **Techniques:** painting, laminating **Size Range:** 3' x 6' to 18' x 20' **Price Range:** $10,000 to $45,000/piece

## SUSAN STOVER
1080 23RD AVE #301
OAKLAND, CA 94606
TEL 510-533-8404
Established: 1991
**Products:** mixed media installations **Techniques:** weaving, painting, mixed media **Size Range:** 12" x 12" to 96" x 60" **Price Range:** $500 to $7,500/piece; $100 to $500/sq. ft.

## MEREDITH STRAUSS
2621 KENNINGTON DR
GLENDALE, CA 91206-1826
TEL 818-246-2600
Established: 1983
**Products:** cotton cord **Techniques:** dyeing, painting, interlacing **Size Range:** 2' x 2' to unlimited **Price Range:** $1,000 to $50,000/piece; $150 to $180/sq. ft.

## JOAN STUBBINS
2616 S MAHONING AVE
ALLIANCE, OH 44601-8212
TEL 216-823-7328
Established: 1988
**Products:** tapestries **Techniques:** dyeing, embroidery, weaving **Size Range:** 20" x 30" x 40" x 55" **Price Range:** $100/sq. ft.

## ★ STUDIO 5 FIBER DESIGN
**VICKI B. SCHOENWALD**
**408 N CHESTNUT**
**NORTH PLATTE, NE 69101**
**TEL 308-534-6483**
**FAX 308-534-1289**
**E-Mail: studio5@nque.com**
**Established: 1990**
**Products:** fiber installations **Techniques:** weaving, embroidery, hooking **Size Range:** 14" x 14" to 5' x 5' **Price Range:** $200 to $50,000/piece

**See page 197 for photographs and additional information.**

## JANICE M. SULLIVAN
4166A 20TH ST
SAN FRANCISCO, CA 94114-2850
TEL 415-431-6835
Established: 1984
**Products:** fabric constructions **Techniques:** weaving, painting, airbrush **Size Range:** 20" x 20" to 96" x 108" **Price Range:** $200 to $300/sq. ft.

## LYNNE SWARD
625 BISHOP DR
VIRGINIA BEACH, VA 23455-6543
TEL 804-497-7917
Established: 1974
**Products:** art quilts **Techniques:** appliqué, beading, embellishment **Size Range:** 8" x 8" to 36" x 80" **Price Range:** $200 to $4,000/piece

## SUZANNE TAHENY
SUZANNE TAHENY SILKS
30932 SHERWOOD RD
FORT BRAGG, CA 95437
TEL 707-964-0054
Established: 1985
**Products:** art quilts **Techniques:** painting, dyeing, quilting **Size Range:** 30" x 26" to 45" x 64" **Price Range:** $450 to $1,400/piece

## TERRY TAUBE
73-1100 ALIHILANI DR
KAILUA-KONA, HI 96740
TEL 808-325-5496
Established: 1985
**Products:** paper **Techniques:** casting, dyeing, weaving **Size Range:** all sizes **Price Range:** $100 to $200/sq. ft.

## CAMERON TAYLOR-BROWN
418 S MANSFIELD AVE
LOS ANGELES, CA 90036-3516
TEL 213-938-0088
FAX 213-938-0088
Established: 1982
**Products:** mixed media installations **Techniques:** weaving, embroidery, painting **Size Range:** 24" x 24" and up **Price Range:** $100 to $175/sq. ft.

## RENA THOMPSON
705 ALMSHOUSE RD
CHALFONT, PA 18914-3803
TEL 215-345-8185
Established: 1980
**Products:** tapestries **Techniques:** weaving, double-weave pickup **Size Range:** 50" x 50" to 50" x 100" **Price Range:** $1,500 to $3,800/piece; $85 to $140/sq. ft.

## LYNN THOR
CONTEMPORARY FIBER DESIGNS
PO BOX 70 632 TUNNEL RD
TUNNEL, NY 13848-0070
TEL 607-693-1572
Established: 1975
**Products:** fiber installations **Techniques:** weaving, inlay, painted warp **Size Range:** 12" x 14" to 30" x 45" **Price Range:** $125 to $850/piece

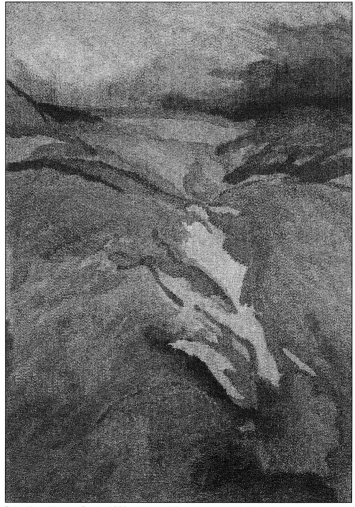

Betty Vera, *Memory Garden*, 1995, cotton and linen tapestry, mixed techniques, Hotel Kitano collection, New York, NY, photo: Adam Reich

# FIBER ART FOR THE WALL

## KAREN THURMAN
353 41ST ST
OAKLAND, CA 94609
TEL 510-655-6406
**Products:** felt wall hangings **Techniques:** felting **Size Range:** 3' × 4' to 5' × 7' **Price Range:** $350 to $700/piece

## DANIELE TODARO
TODARO & ASSOCIATES
4920 W 63RD ST
LOS ANGELES, CA 90056
TEL 213-299-9393
FAX 213-299-9394
Established: 1974
**Products:** textile collage **Techniques:** appliqué, quilting, stamping, printing, collage **Size Range:** 1' × 1' to 6' × 9' **Price Range:** $100 to $150/sq. ft.

## CAROLYN AND VINCENT TOLPO
PO BOX 134
SHAWNEE, CO 80475-0134
TEL 303-670-1733
Established: 1979
**Products:** fiber installations **Techniques:** painting, wrapping **Size Range:** 30" × 36" to 10' × 30' **Price Range:** $600 to $12,000/piece

## RAYMOND D. TOMASSO
INTER-OCEAN CURIOSITY STUDIO
2998 S BANNOCK ST
ENGLEWOOD, CO 80110-1519
TEL 303-789-0282
Established: 1978
**Products:** paper **Techniques:** airbush, casting, painting **Size Range:** 9" × 11" to 8' × 8' **Price Range:** $500 to $10,000/piece; $160 to $300/sq. ft.

## MARJORIE TOMCHUK
44 HORTON LN
NEW CANAAN, CT 06840-6824
TEL 203-972-0137
FAX 203-972-3182
Established: 1965
**Products:** paper **Techniques:** airbush, casting, painting, embossings **Size Range:** 10" × 13" to 4' × 6' **Price Range:** $175 to $3,000/piece

## PAMELA TOPHAM
LANDSCAPE TAPESTRIES
PO BOX 1057
WAINSCOTT, NY 11975-1057
TEL 516-537-2871
Established: 1976
**Products:** tapestries, landscape tapestries **Techniques:** weaving **Size Range:** 12" × 14" to 9' × 18' and up **Price Range:** $1,200 and up/piece; $450/sq. ft.

## JUDITH TOMLINSON TRAGER
TRAGER STUDIO QUILTS
2132 KINCAID PL
BOULDER, CO 80304-1900
TEL 303-443-5976
FAX 303-492-0969
Established: 1973
**Products:** art quilts **Techniques:** embroidery appliqué quilting **Size Range:** 20" × 30" to 96" × 96" **Price Range:** $800 to $3,000/piece

## ANNE TRIGUBA
HOUSE OF TRIGUBA, INC.
1463 RAINBOW DR NE
LANCASTER, OH 43130
TEL 614-687-1338
Established: 1986
**Products:** art quilts **Techniques:** painting, appliqué, quilting **Size Range:** 24" × 20" to 70" × 70" **Price Range:** $800 to $5,000/piece

## MICHELE TUEGEL
MICHELE TUEGEL PAPERWORKS
433 MONTE CRISTO BLVD
TIERRA VERDE, FL 33715-1840
TEL 813-821-7391
Established: 1977
**Products:** paper **Techniques:** casting, laminating **Size Range:** 8" × 10" to 40" × 60" **Price Range:** $75 to $1,500/piece

## TUMBLEWEED FABRIC & DESIGNS
ANNE WINTON
260 NORTHWOOD WAY #3
PO BOX 777
KETCHUM, ID 83340
TEL 208-726-2580
FAX 208-788-9098
Established: 1991
**Products:** baby quilts **Techniques:** painting, quilting **Size Range:** 16" × 16" to 76" × 82" **Price Range:** $50 to $550/piece

## JUDITH UEHLING
152 WOOSTER ST
NEW YORK, NY 10012-5331
TEL 212-254-2075
FAX 212-254-2075
Established: 1970
**Products:** paper **Techniques:** painting, casting, bronze **Size Range:** 23" × 28" to 8'4" × 44" **Price Range:** $750 to $5,000/piece

## CONNIE UTTERBACK
3641 MIDVALE AVE #204
LOS ANGELES, CA 90034-6600
TEL 310-841-6675
Established: 1981
**Products:** fabric constructions **Techniques:** construction technique **Size Range:** 2' × 3' to 7' × 12' **Price Range:** $700 to $9,500/piece

## FRANCES VALESCO
135 JERSEY ST
SAN FRANCISCO, CA 94114
TEL 415-648-3814
Established: 1969
**Products:** mixed media installations **Techniques:** dyeing, painting, printing **Size Range:** 11" × 14" to mural size **Price Range:** $150 to $10,000/piece

## LYDIA VAN GELDER
FIBER ARTS
758 SUCHER LN
SANTA ROSA, CA 95401-3623
TEL 707-546-4139
Established: 1950
**Products:** fiber installations **Techniques:** weaving, dyeing, shifu **Size Range:** 72" × 30" to 6' × 9' **Price Range:** $750 to $3,000/piece

## ★ VANGRODWORKS — ART BY DESIGN
JOHN AND PHYLLIS VANGROD
8420 ULMERTON RD STE 477
LARGO, FL 33771-3882
TEL 813-530-0864
FAX 813-530-0864
http://www.gate.net/~vangrod
Established: 1970
**Products:** silk wall works **Techniques:** painting quilting resist dyeing **Size Range:** 12" × 12" to 4' × 8' **Price Range:** $60 to $120/sq. ft.

See photograph page 227.

## ALICE VAN LEUNEN
PO BOX 408
LAKE OSWEGO, OR 97034-0408
TEL 503-636-0787
FAX 503-636-0787
Established: 1968
**Products:** mixed media installations **Techniques:** painting, weaving, metallic foil work **Size Range:** 24" × 30" to 10' × 12' **Price Range:** $500 to $30,000/piece

## ★ SUSAN VENABLE
VENABLE STUDIO
214 S VENICE BLVD
VENICE, CA 90291-4537
TEL 310-827-7233
FAX 310-822-0050
Established: 1975
**Products:** mixed media installations **Techniques:** painting, copper wire constructions **Size Range:** 24" minimum, no upper limit **Price Range:** $2,000 to $75,000/piece

See page 102 for photographs and additional information.

## ★ BETTY VERA
41 UNION SQUARE W #521
NEW YORK, NY 10003-3208
TEL 212-924-2478
FAX 212-924-2478
Established: 1984
**Products:** tapestries **Techniques:** weaving, dyeing, warp painting **Size Range:** 1' × 1' to 8' × 10' **Price Range:** $500 to $30,000/piece

See photograph page 229.

## PAULINE VERBEEK-COWART
3924 STETSON DR
LAWRENCE, KS 66049-4160
TEL 913-865-5805
Established: 1992
**Products:** tapestries **Techniques:** weaving, dyeing, screen printing **Size Range:** 30" × 40" to 8' × 12' **Price Range:** $125 to $175/sq. ft.

## ★ MEINY VERMAAS-VAN DER HEIDE

**MEINY VERMAAS-VAN DER HEIDE: STUDIO ART QUILTS**
1219 E LA JOLLA DR
TEMPE, AZ 85282-5513
TEL 602-838-5262
FAX 602-838-5262
E-Mail: meiny@aol.com
Established: 1989
**Products:** art quilts **Techniques:** quilting, patchwork **Size Range:** 24" × 24" to 6' × 9' **Price Range:** $500 to $6,000/piece; $90 to $125/sq. ft.

See photograph this page.

## JUDITH VEROSTKA-PETREE

JUDITH VEROSTKA-PETREE, TAPESTRIES
2903 PARKWOOD AVE
RICHMOND, VA 23221
TEL 804-358-7659
Established: 1987
**Products:** tapestries **Techniques:** weaving **Size Range:** 1' × 2' to 4' × 8' **Price Range:** $50 to $200/sq. ft.

## JANE CASE VICKERS

THE ART CENTER
1015 ADAMS
EVANSVILLE, IN 47714
TEL 812-424-2735
FAX 812-424-2735
Established: 1990
**Products:** mixed media installations **Techniques:** painting, casting, collage **Size Range:** 11" × 9" to 6' × 4' **Price Range:** $75 to $600/piece

## JUDITH VIEROW

803 GILBERT ST
COLUMBUS, OH 43206-1518
TEL 614-444-4568
Established: 1974
**Products:** art quilts **Techniques:** appliqué, painting, quilting, piecing, stitching **Size Range:** 16" × 20" to 96" × 96" **Price Range:** $500 to $10,000/piece

## VERA VLASOVA

C/O PATRIARCHI DOM
3059 PORTER ST NW
WASHINGTON, DC 20008
TEL 202-363-9610
FAX 202-363-9610
Established: 1990
**Products:** silk batik scarves & wall hangings **Techniques:** painting, dyeing, batik **Size Range:** 2' × 2' to 6' × 3' **Price Range:** $50 to $300/piece

## BETSY WADSWORTH-MANDELL

7405 E KERR CREEK RD
BLOOMINGTON, IN 47408
TEL 812-334-0567
Established: 1985
**Products:** art quilts **Techniques:** dyeing, stamping, beading **Size Range:** 24" × 36" to 60" × 48" **Price Range:** $500 to $5,000/piece

## BARBARA ALLEN WAGNER

THE CROW'S NEST
7 SKYLINE PL
ASTORIA, OR 97103-6439
TEL 503-325-5548
Established: 1955
**Products:** tapestries **Techniques:** embroidery, weaving, needlepoint **Size Range:** 1'6" × 3' to 5' × 8' **Price Range:** $200 to $400/sq. ft.

## DAVID WALKER

2905 PROBASCO CT
CINCINNATI, OH 45220-2712
TEL 513-961-9065
Established: 1987
**Products:** art quilts **Techniques:** appliqué, quilting, embellishment **Size Range:** 12" × 12" to 8' × 8' **Price Range:** $300 to $5,000/piece

## ALISON WAMPLER

CONTEMPORARY HANDHOOKED RUGS
RT 1 BOX 1850 MORGAN BAY RD
SURRY, ME 04684
TEL 207-667-6031
Established: 1992
**Products:** tapetas (wall rugs) **Techniques:** hooked fabrics **Size Range:** 24" × 24" to 56" × 10' **Price Range:** $100 to $200/sq. ft.

## LAURA WASILOWSKI

324 VINCENT PL
ELGIN, IL 60123
TEL 708-931-7684
Established: 1986
**Products:** art quilts **Techniques:** dyeing, quilting, stamping or printing **Size Range:** 1' × 1' to 5' × 6' **Price Range:** $100 to $200/sq. ft.

## MONA WATERHOUSE

102 DELBANK PT
PEACHTREE CITY, GA 30269-1184
TEL 770-487-2881
Established: 1978
**Products:** mixed media installations **Techniques:** painting, printing, paper and encaustic **Size Range:** 37" × 37" to 6' × 10' **Price Range:** $1,200 to $2,700/piece

## WEAVING/SOUTHWEST

RACHEL BROWN
216 B PUEBLO NORTE
TAOS, NM 87571
TEL 505-758-0433
Established: 1962
**Products:** tapestries **Techniques:** weaving **Size Range:** 24" × 24" to 96" × 60" **Price Range:** $21 to $300/sq. ft.

## HELEN WEBBER

HELEN WEBBER DESIGNS
555 PACIFIC AVE
SAN FRANCISCO, CA 94133-4609
TEL 415-989-5521
FAX 415-989-5746
Established: 1973
**Products:** tapestries **Techniques:** painting, casting, collage **Size Range:** 3' × 4' to 10' × 65' **Price Range:** $150 to $300/sq. ft.

## LEANNE WEISSLER

28 LINCOLN CIR
CRESTWOOD, NY 10707
TEL 914-337-6952
Established: 1975
**Products:** mixed media installations **Techniques:** painting, airbrush, drawing **Size Range:** 12" × 12" to 40" × 50" **Price Range:** $150 to $1,500/piece

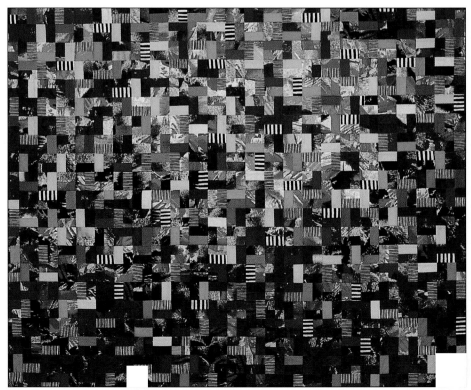

Meiny Vermaas-van der Heide, *Earth Quilt #64: Full Circle II*, 1996, studio art quilt, machine-pieced and machine-quilted cottons, 49"H × 59"W

# FIBER ART FOR THE WALL

## JOAN WEISSMAN

JOAN WEISSMAN CUSTOM RUGS AND TAPESTRIES
3710 SILVER SE
ALBUQUERQUE, NM 87108
TEL 505-265-0144
FAX 505-268-9665
Established: 1071
**Products:** tapestries
**Techniques:** weaving hand-tufted wool
**Size Range:** 4' × 4' to 30' × any length
**Price Range:** $65 to $95/sq. ft.

## CAROL D. WESTFALL

162 WHITFORD AVE
NUTLEY, NJ 07110
TEL 201-235-0813
FAX 201-235-0218
Established: 1972
**Products:** fiber art
**Techniques:** weaving, quilting, computer collage
**Size Range:** 2" × 2" to 3' × 2'
**Price Range:** $350 to $3,000/piece

## JUDI MAUREEN WHITE

RENAISSANCE FIBRES
2062 E MALIBU DR
TEMPE, AZ 85282-5966
TEL 602-320-7557
TEL 602-838-0416
Established: 1970
**Products:** mixed media installations
**Techniques:** painting, weaving, sculpting
**Size Range:** 12" × 24" to 96" × 240"
**Price Range:** $200 to $500/sq. ft.

## ★ MARGE WHITE

NEEDLING IN THE PINES
PO BOX 4, 3055 FAIRWAY DR
ARNOLO, CA 95223
TEL 209-795-4240
FAX 209-795-0654
E-Mail: marjon@cdepot.net
Established: 1979
**Products:** art quilts
**Techniques:** appliqué, quilting, trapunto
**Size Range:** 16" × 21" and up
**Price Range:** $110/sq. ft.

See page 164 for photographs and additional information.

## NANCY WHITTINGTON

105 WATTERS RD
CARRBORO, NC 27510
TEL 919-933-0624
FAX 919-933-0631
Established: 1975
**Products:** art quilts
**Techniques:** appliqué, dyeing, painting
**Size Range:** 32" × 22" to 56" × 60"
**Price Range:** $600 to $3,500/piece; $150/sq. ft.

## ELIZABETH WILEY

EW WEAVES
1481 BUCKHORN RD PO BOX 1181
WILLITS, CA 95490-1181
TEL 707-459-9293
Established: 1982
**Products:** woven wall pieces
**Techniques:** weaving, dyeing, embroidery
**Size Range:** 18" × 18" to 108" × 108"
**Price Range:** $100 to $4,000/piece; $20 to $200/sq. ft.

## JODY WILLIAMS

FLYING PAPER
3953 16TH AVE S
MINNEAPOLIS, MN 55407-2828
TEL 612-721-2891
Established: 1982
**Products:** handmade paper
**Techniques:** casting, stamping/printing, collage
**Size Range:** 6" × 8" to 36" × 60"
**Price Range:** $250 to $3,000/piece

## JEANNE WILLIAMSON

18 ERLANDSON RD
NATICK, MA 01760-2333
TEL 508-655-4560
FAX 508-651-1696
Established: 1985
**Products:** art quilts
**Techniques:** appliqué, quilting, stamping
**Size Range:** 24" × 24" to 45" × 45"
**Price Range:** $80/sq. ft.

## JAY WILSON

WILSON & YAMADA ART STUDIO
3155 NAHENAHE PL
KIHEI, HI 96753-9314
TEL 808-874-3597
Established: 1976
**Products:** tapestries
**Techniques:** dyeing, weaving
**Size Range:** 6' × 4'. to 8' × 12'
**Price Range:** $15,000 to $75,000/piece

## NANCY WINES-DEWAN

CONTEMPORARY MAINE TEXTILES
PO BOX 861
YARMOUTH, ME 04096-0861
TEL 207-846-6058
Established: 1970
**Products:** tapestries
**Techniques:** weaving
**Size Range:** 10" × 10" to 120" × 144"
**Price Range:** $200 to $250/sq. ft.

## LAURIE WOHL

1030 E 50TH ST
CHICAGO, IL 60615
TEL 773-924-5597
Established: 1976
**Products:** unweavings
**Techniques:** painting, beading, unweaving
**Size Range:** 11" × 7" to 8'6" × 6'
**Price Range:** $200 to $400/sq. ft.

## YARDSTICKS

ROSEMARIE HOHOL AND ROGER HAUGE
1129 MAPLE AVE
EVANSTON, IL 60202
TEL 847-864-8131
Established: 1992
**Products:** woven twig frame baskets
**Techniques:** weaving, dyeing, beading
**Size Range:** 5" × 7" to 40" × 40"
**Price Range:** $70 to $500/piece

## YARDSTICKS

ROGER HAUGE
ROSEMARIE HOHOL
847 CHICAGO AVE 1C
EVANSTON, IL 60202-1287
TEL 847-864-8131
Established: 1992
**Products:** woven wall pieces
**Techniques:** weaving, dyeing, wrapping
**Size Range:** 5" × 7" to 40" × 40"
**Price Range:** $75 to $1,000/piece

## ELLEN ZAHOREC

ISLAND FORD STUDIO
396 AMAZON AVE
CINCINNATI, OH 45220-1139
TEL 513-861-7419
FAX 513-861-4419
**Products:** mixed media, collaged wall pieces
**Techniques:** painting
**Size Range:** 8" × 10" to unlimited
**Price Range:** $100 to $5,000/piece; $100/sq. ft.

## MAUREEN ZALE

PO BOX 117
UNION LAKE, MI 48387-0117
TEL 810-698-1748
Established: 1993
**Products:** mixed media installations
**Techniques:** painting, wrapping, fabric manipulation
**Size Range:** 20" × 16" to 40" × 60"
**Price Range:** $175 to $1,000/piece

## ★ HARRIET ZEITLIN

HARRIET ZEITLIN STUDIO
202 S SALTAIR AVE
LOS ANGELES, CA 90049-4127
TEL 310-472-0534
Established: 1950
**Products:** fabric constructions
**Techniques:** painting, appliqué, quilting
**Size Range:** 2' × 2' to 10' × 7'
**Price Range:** $800 to $10,000/piece

See page 198 for photographs and additional information.

## ★ MARY ZICAFOOSE

3323 S 104TH AVE
OMAHA, NE 68124-2512
TEL 402-343-1589
Established: 1979
**Products:** tapestries
**Techniques:** dyeing, weaving, weft-faced ikat
**Size Range:** 2' × 2' to 20' × 15'
**Price Range:** $85 to $300/sq. ft.

See page 45 for photographs and additional information.

## BHAKTI ZIEK

5225 GREENE ST
PHILADELPHIA, PA 19144-2927
TEL 215-844-4402
Established: 1980
**Products:** tapestries
**Techniques:** dyeing, painting, weaving
**Size Range:** 4" × 8" to 9' × 20'
**Price Range:** $100 to $300/sq. ft.

## ORGANIZATIONS

### AMERICAN ASSOCIATION OF WOOD TURNERS

3200 LEXINGTON AVE
SHOREVIEW, MN 55126-8118
FAX 612-484-1724
TEL 612-484-9094

Mary Redig, Administrator

The American Association of Woodturners (AAW) is a non-profit organization dedicated to the advancement of woodturning. Over 80 chapters throughout the United States provide education and information for those interested in woodturning. Members include hobbyists, professionals, gallery owners, collectors, and wood and equipment suppliers.

### AMERICAN CRAFT COUNCIL

72 SPRING ST
NEW YORK, NY 10019-4019
FAX 212-274-0650
TEL 212-274-0630

Michael W. Monroe, Executive Director

The American Craft Council is a national, non-profit educational organization founded in 1943. The council presents nine national juried craft fairs annually; offers occasional workshops and seminars, as well as services, to professional craftspeople; maintains a special library on 20th-century craft; and publishes the bimonthly magazine *American Craft*. Membership is open to all.

### AMERICAN SOCIETY OF FURNITURE ARTISTS

PO BOX 7491
HOUSTON, TX 77248-7491
FAX 713-721-7600
TEL 713-556-5444

Adam St. John, President

The American Society of Furniture Artists (ASOFA) is a non-profit organization dedicated to the field of 'art furniture' and to the artists who create it. The society's nationwide scope promotes the highest professional standards and provides its members with significant avenues for continued artistic and professional development.

### AMERICAN TAPESTRY ALLIANCE

3616 EDMUND BLVD
MINNEAPOLIS, MN 55406
FAX 612-729-3966
TEL 612-729-3966
E-Mail: 71574.1224@Compuserve.com

Jean Smelker-Hugi, President

The American Tapestry Alliance was founded in 1982 to: (1) promote an awareness of and an appreciation for tapestries designed and woven in America; (2) establish, perpetuate and recognize superior quality tapestries by American artists; (3) encourage greater use of tapestries by corporate and private collectors; (4) educate the public about tapestry; and (5) coordinate national and international juried tapestry exhibitions.

### CREATIVE GLASS CENTER OF AMERICA

1501 GLASSTOWN ROAD
PO BOX 646
MILLVILLE, NJ 08332-1566
FAX 609-825-2410
TEL 609-825-6800

The Creative Glass Center is a public attraction devoted to increasing know-how of glass works. The center offers insight to glass arts through the Museum of American Glass, an informational resource center providing fellowships; demonstrations in the T.C. Wheaton Glass Factory; and various tours throughout Wheaton Village.

### THE EMBROIDERERS' GUILD OF AMERICA, INC.

335 W. BROADWAY #100
LOUISVILLE, KY 40202
FAX 502-584-7900
TEL 502-589-6956

Karulynn Koelliker, President

The Embroiderer's Guild of America, Inc. (EGA) has more than 20,000 members and over 350 chapters across North America. EGA is a non-profit, educational organization founded in 1958 to foster high standards of design, color and workmanship in embroidery; to teach the embroidery arts; and to preserve our needle arts heritage. *Needle Arts* is the magazine of the organization.

### THE FURNITURE SOCIETY

BOX 18
FREE UNION, VA 22940
TEL 804-973-1488

Sarah McCollum, Contact

The purpose of The Furniture Society is to advance the art of furniture making by inspiring creativity, promoting excellence, and fostering understanding of this art and its place in society. The Furniture Society is open not only to professional furniture makers, but to all who have an interest in the art of furniture making, including galleries, arts professionals, collectors, and amateur furniture makers in all media.

### GLASS ART SOCIETY

1305 FOURTH AVE #711
SEATTLE, WA 98101-2401
FAX 206-382-2630
TEL 206-382-1305

Alice Rooney, Executive Director

The Glass Art Society (GAS), an international non-profit organization, was founded in 1971 to encourage excellence and advance appreciation, understanding and development of the glass arts worldwide. GAS promotes communication among artists, educators, students, collectors, gallery and museum personnel, art critics, manufacturers and others through an annual conference and through the *Glass Art Society Journal* and newsletters.

### HANDWEAVERS GUILD OF AMERICA

3327 DULUTH HIGHWAY #201
DULUTH, GA 30136-3373
FAX 770-495-7703
TEL 770-495-7702
E-Mail: Compuserve 73744.202

Sandra Bowles, Executive Director

The Handweavers Guild of America, Inc. (HGA) is an international non-profit organization dedicated to upholding excellence, promoting the textile arts, and preserving our textile heritage. HGA provides a forum for education, opportunities for networking, and inspiration and encouragement for handweavers, handspinners and related fiber artists. HGA publishes a quarterly journal for members, *Shuttle Spindle & Dyepot*.

### INTERNATIONAL SCULPTURE CENTER

1050 17TH ST NW #250
WASHINGTON, DC 20036
FAX 202-785-0810
TEL 202-785-1144

Jeanne C. Pond, Executive Director

The International Sculpture Center (ISC) is a non-profit membership organization devoted to the advancement of contemporary sculpture. Members receive listings of job and commission opportunities; access to conferences and workshops; a slide registry service; insurance; discounts on services and tools used by sculptors; and much more. The ISC also seeks to educate the public at large about contemporary sculpture and publishes *Sculpture* magazine.

# SELECTED ORGANIZATIONS & PUBLICATIONS

## INTERNATIONAL TAPESTRY NETWORK

PO BOX 112229
ANCHORAGE, AK 99511-2229
FAX 907-346-2216
TEL 907-346-2392
E-Mail: itnet@alaska.net
http://www.alaska.net/~itnet

International Tapestry Network (ITNET) is a not-for-profit organization in support of contemporary tapestry worldwide. ITNET displays tapestries of individual artists on the Internet, creating a resource for curators, collectors, architects, art professors, museums, gallery owners and anyone else interested in contemporary tapestry.

## NATIONAL COUNCIL ON EDUCATION FOR THE CERAMIC ARTS

PO BOX 158
BANDON, OR 97411
FAX 541-347-7076
TEL 800-99N-CECA

Regina Brown, Executive Secretary

The National Council on Education for the Ceramic Arts (NCECA) is a professional organization of individuals whose interests, talents, or careers are focused on the ceramic arts. NCECA strives to stimulate and improve education in the ceramic arts, and to gather and disseminate information and ideas that are vital and stimulating to teachers, studio artists and others throughout the creative studies community. NCECA hosts a national conference each spring.

## NATIONAL WOODCARVERS ASSN.

PO BOX 43218
CINCINNATI, OH 45243
TEL 513-561-0627

Edward F. Gallenstein, President

The National Woodcarvers Association (NWCA) promotes woodcarving and fellowship among its members; encourages exhibitions and area get-togethers; publishes *Chip Chats*, a bi-monthly magazine; and assists members in finding tool and wood suppliers, as well as markets for their work.

## SOCIETY OF AMERICAN SILVERSMITHS

PO BOX 3599
CRANSTON, RI 02910-0599
FAX 401-461-3196
TEL 401-461-3156
TEL 800-584-2352
E-Mail: slvrsmth@ids.net
http://www.ids.net/~slvrsmth/sashome.htm

Jeffrey Herman, Executive Director

The Society of American Silversmiths (SAS) was founded in 1989 to preserve the art and history of contemporary handcrafted hollowware, flatware and sculpture. SAS also provides its juried artisan members with support, networking and greater access to the market, partly through its annual traveling exhibitions. A unique referral service commissions work from artisan members for collectors, corporations and museums.

## SURFACE DESIGN ASSOCIATION

PO BOX 20799
OAKLAND, CA 94620
FAX 707-829-3285
TEL 707-829-1756

Joy Stocksdale, Administrator

The Surface Design Association promotes surface design through education; encouragement of individual artists; communication of technical information and information concerning professional opportunities; and the exchange of ideas through conferences and publications.

## TILE HERITAGE FOUNDATION

PO BOX 1850
HEALDSBURG, CA 95448
FAX 707-431-8455
TEL 707-431-8453

Joseph A. Taylor, President

The Tile Heritage Foundation is a national non-profit organization dedicated to promoting awareness and appreciation of ceramic surfaces in the United States. In addition to maintaining a reference and research library, Tile Heritage publishes a biannual magazine and a quarterly newsletter, conducts annual symposiums, and supports research in the field of ceramic history and conservation.

## WOODWORKING ASSOCIATION OF NORTH AMERICA

PO BOX 478
TAMWORTH, NH 03886
FAX 603-323-7500
TEL 603-323-7500

Laura Bonica, Managing Editor

The Woodworking Association of North America (WANA) serves as a networking agency for both hobbyists and professionals who engage in woodworking as an industry, as a hobby or as an art. WANA publishes a quarterly newsletter which includes special purchases, project plans, and numerous opportunities for contacting fellow woodworkers, including an annual retreat.

## PUBLICATIONS

## AMERICAN CERAMICS

9 E 45 ST #603
NEW YORK, NY 10017
FAX 212-661-2389
TEL 212-661-4397

$28/year

*American Ceramics*, an art quarterly, was founded to enhance the preservation of ceramics' rich heritage and to document contemporary developments in the field. Articles feature the best and brightest ceramists: rising stars and established luminaries, as well as those early pioneers who transformed ceramics into a genuine art form.

## AMERICAN CRAFT

AMERICAN CRAFT COUNCIL
72 SPRING ST
NEW YORK, NY 10012-4019
FAX 212-274-0650
TEL 212-274-0630

$40/year

*American Craft*, a bimonthly magazine, focuses on contemporary craft through artist profiles, reviews of major shows, a portfolio of emerging artists, a national calendar and news section, and book reviews, as well as illustrated columns reporting on commissions, acquisitions and exhibitions.

## ART CALENDAR

PO BOX 199
UPPER FAIRMOUNT, MD 21867-0199
FAX 410-651-5313
TEL 410-651-9150

$32/YEAR

*Art Calendar*, a monthly magazine, publishes extensive listings of exhibition and income opportunities for artists. Listings are enhanced by interviews with artists, dealers and curators; organizational profiles; special reports on art world scams and rip-offs; and practical articles on topics like self-promotion and exhibition strategies, the psychology of creativity, and art law.

## CERAMICS MONTHLY

PROFESSIONAL PUBLICATIONS, INC.
735 CERAMIC PL
PO BOX 6102
WESTERVILLE, OH 43086-6102
FAX 614-891-8960
TEL 614-523-1660

$22/year

*Ceramics Monthly* offers a broad range of articles—including artist profiles, reviews of exhibitions, historical features, and business and technical information—for potters, ceramic sculptors, collectors, gallery and museum personnel, and interested observers.

## FIBERARTS

50 COLLEGE ST
ASHEVILLE, NC 28801
FAX 704-253-7952
TEL 704-253-0467
TEL ORDERS 800-284-3388

$22/year

Five annual issues of *Fiberarts* focus on contemporary textile art, including clothing, quilts, baskets, paper, tapestry, needlework and surface design. Features include artist profiles, critical essays, book reviews, and extensive listings of opportunities, events and resources.

## FINE WOODWORKING

THE TAUNTON PRESS, INC.
PO BOX 5506
NEWTOWN, CT 06470-5506
FAX 203-426-3434
TEL 203-426-8171

$29/year

*Fine Woodworking* is a bimonthly magazine for all those who strive for and appreciate excellence in woodworking—veteran professional and weekend hobbyist alike. Articles by skilled woodworkers focus on basics of tool use, stock preparation and joinery, as well as specialized techniques and finishing.

## GLASS CRAFTSMAN

64 WOODSTOCK DRIVE
NEWTOWN, PA 18940
FAX 215-860-1812
TEL 215-860-9947

$25/year

*Glass Craftsman* is a full-color bimonthly publication featuring articles on the creative use of the glass arts and crafts. In addition to how-to information and artist and studio profiles, each issue contains book reviews, career tips, a home-studio section, and a complete calendar of glass-related events.

## GLASS: THE URBANGLASS ART QUARTERLY

URBANGLASS
647 FULTON ST
BROOKLYN, NY 11217
FAX 718-625-3889
TEL 718-625-3685

$28/year

*Glass Magazine*, a full-color quarterly for design professionals, artists and collectors, features profiles of contemporary artists, an educational directory, and critical reviews of national and international exhibitions.

## GLASS ART

TRAVIN INC.
PO BOX 260377
HIGHLANDS RANCH, CO 80163-0377
FAX 303-791-7739
TEL 303-791-8998

$24/year U.S.

*Glass Art*, published bimonthly, includes business articles geared towards glass retailers and professional studios, as well as features on hot and cold glass techniques and artist profiles.

## HOME FURNITURE

THE TAUNTON PRESS, INC.
63 S MAIN ST
NEWTOWN, CT 06470-5506
FAX 203-426-3434
TEL 203-426-8171
TEL 800-888-8286

$20/year

*Home Furniture*, a full-color bi-monthly magazine, is both a portfolio of top contemporary furniture makers and a review of furniture design. Articles include artist profiles and discussions of furniture history and design.

## METALSMITH

5009 LONDONDERRY DR
TAMPA, FL 33647
FAX 813-977-8462
TEL 813-977-5326

$26/year

*Metalsmith* is the premier full-color publication of the metal arts in the United States. It is published five times per year by the Society of North American Goldsmiths. Award-winning articles offer critical analysis, historical insight and observations on the changing terrain of professional crafts. The late summer issue is a special venue that allows for guest jurors or curators to add a unique voice to the field.

## SCULPTURE

INTERNATIONAL SCULPTURE CENTER
1050 17TH ST NW #250
WASHINGTON, DC 20036
FAX 202-785-0810
TEL 202-785-1144
E-Mail: sculpt@dgsys.com

$45/year

*Sculpture*, published ten times a year, focuses on established and emerging sculptors and contemporary sculpture. Each issue includes profiles, feature articles, interviews, reviews, and technical information. *Sculpture* also includes listings of opportunities for sculptors, including competitions, residencies, workshops and other information.

## SHUTTLE SPINDLE & DYEPOT

HANDWEAVERS GUILD OF AMERICA,
INC. (HGA)
3327 DULUTH HIGHWAY #201
DULUTH, GA 30136-3373
FAX 770-495-7703
TEL 770-495-7702
E-Mail; Compuserve 73744.202

$30/year

*Shuttle Spindle & Dyepot*, a quarterly four-color journal, includes features of historical and technical interest; artists profiles; book reviews; a "Gallery" section featuring the work of contemporary fiber artists; and a calendar of events and opportunities.

## SURFACE DESIGN JOURNAL

SURFACE DESIGN ASSOCIATION
PO BOX 20799
OAKLAND, CA 94620
FAX 707-829-3285
TEL 707-829-1756

$45/year

*Surface Design Journal*, a full-color quarterly magazine, is published by the Surface Design Association (SDA), a nonprofit organization of artists, educators, designers, and collectors. Subscription to the *Surface Design Journal* is provided as a benefit of membership in the SDA.

## TILE HERITAGE

TILE HERITAGE FOUNDATION
PO BOX 1850
HEALDSBURG, CA 95448
FAX 707-431-8455
TEL 707-431-8453

$20/year

*Tile Heritage: A Review of American Tile History*, a biannual publication, features articles on both historic and contemporary ceramic tiles. From the time of the earliest cave paintings and molded clay forms, people have sought to conceptualize themselves and inspire others through this decorative art form.

## WOODSHOP NEWS

SOUNDINGS PUBLICATIONS, INC.
35 PRATT ST
ESSEX, CT 06426
FAX 203-767-1048
TEL 203-767-8227

$15.97/year

*Woodshop News*, published monthly, includes features and descriptions about new technology, artists and their techniques, trade news and source information.

# Home Furniture magazine...

## ...inspiration and information for furniture design.

Whether you need fresh design inspiration for yourself or your clients, or you are seeking to expand your furniture sales, Home Furniture is for you. It presents some of the best work being done today. And, it reaches affluent furniture and accessory buyers.

Home Furniture is the new bi-monthly magazine from The Taunton Press, publishers of Fine Woodworking, Fine Gardening, Fine Cooking and Fine Homebuilding.

### Each Issue:

- Provides a full-color showcase of finely-crafted, thoughtfully designed furniture.
- Helps you understand the design challenges faced by furniture makers and designers.
- Shows you options and choices that make furniture design better.
- Discusses furniture styles, both well-known and some not so well-known, to help expand readers' knowledge and tastes.

**ATTENTION FURNITURE MAKERS and GALLERIES:** We offer a special *craftsman's corner* advertising section designed to make it easy and economical for you to reach this important new part of your market. Call us for more details and a free media kit including a sample issue.

Home Furniture, 191 South Main St., Newtown, CT 06470-5506   1-800-283-7252

---

# The ABC Directory of Arts & Crafts Events

## *"Your BEST Source For Arts & Crafts Event Information!"*

**Dates • Locations • Descriptions • Fees • Attendance**

Since its introduction in 1993, the Southeast Edition of the **ABC Directory** has become known among arts & crafts event exhibitors as *"Your BEST Source For Arts & Crafts Event Information!"* Because this reputation has generated significant interest among exhibitors across the country, **ABC will be expanding in 1997 to offer a total of five regional publications.** These new publications will provide detailed coverage of arts & crafts events for the *entire continental United States!*

Each edition covers over 1500 events and includes vital information such as show locations, dates, booth fees, estimated attendance, show descriptions, and contact information.

The July 1997 - June 1998 Mid-Year Edition for the Southeast is available now. It covers events in AL, FL, GA, KY, MS, NC, SC, TN, VA & WV. **1998 Annual Editions will be available for all regions in early December 1997.**

**Single Editions are $14.95 each.**
*Discount offered on orders of 2 or more editions.*

**Exhibitor Info • Phone & Fax • Contacts • Maps**

*For credit card orders, please call* **(800)678-3566** *or send check or money order to:*
**ABC • PO Box 5388 • Maryville, TN 37802-5388** ✒ Fax: (423)681-4733 • DrArtCraft@aol.com

# INDEX OF ADVERTISERS BY STATE

# INDEX OF ARTISTS AND COMPANIES

# INDEX OF ARTISTS AND COMPANIES

# ::: THE GUILD®

*The industry standard in artist sourcebooks.*

# INTERNATIONAL FIELD GUIDE TO ARTISTS

FOR OVER 13 YEARS, GUILD SOURCEBOOKS HAVE LINKED DESIGN PROFESSIONALS AND COLLECTORS WITH TOP NORTH AMERICAN ARTISTS PRODUCING UNIQUE WORKS FOR PURCHASE OR COMMISSION. NOW . . . THREE ANNUAL SOURCEBOOKS FROM **THE GUILD**

---

THE ARCHITECT'S SOURCEBOOK

## ARCHITECTURAL ARTS & SCULPTURE

architectural glass

architectural metal

architectural elements

liturgical art

sculpture

murals and tromp l'oeil

architectural ceramics, mosaics and wall reliefs

atrium sculpture

restoration

public art

---

THE DESIGNER'S SOURCEBOOK

## ART FOR THE WALL, FURNITURE & ACCESSORIES

tapestries & art quilts

painted finishes

art for the wall in paper, ceramics and mixed media

two-dimensional

the finest handmade furniture

one-of-a-kind lighting

accessories for homes and businesses

textiles and floor coverings

---

THE WHOLESALE BUYER'S GUIDE TO CRAFT ARTISTS

## THE HAND BOOK

**ARTIST DIRECTORY**
2700 artists and companies

**PRODUCT DIRECTORY**
100 categories to help buyers select inventory

**RESOURCE DIRECTORY**
schools
suppliers
conferences
publications
organizations
wholesale shows

---

**CALL 1-800-969-1556 FOR ORDER INFORMATION.**